T0349987

Praise for *The Airbnb Way*

The Airbnb Way explores the "how" of hospitality. It offers actionable examples of hospitality principles as shared through the stories of Airbnb leaders, guests, and hosts alike. This book is relevant for anyone who seeks to drive a welcoming and differentiated brand experience. It is for those who choose "to be a host"—in the sharing economy, their service business, or personal life.

—**Chip Conley**, hospitality entrepreneur and
strategic advisor of Airbnb

Joseph Michelli shares his insights in yet another great book, this time about Airbnb. He's a master of understanding what makes successful companies tick and then sharing his discoveries with the reader. While the principles in this book are straightforward, you'll learn both the basics and the graduate-level skills of creating a great organization. You'll enjoy learning about an iconic brand from an iconic author.

—**Mark Sanborn**, "Top 5 Leadership Gurus," globalgurus.net,
Wall Street Journal and *New York Times* bestselling author

The Airbnb Way is a book about belonging, empowerment, trust, hospitality, and community. Joseph shares practical tips on differentiating your corporate or personal brand, elevating your service level, and innovating solutions to meet employee and customer needs. Michelli's new book can help you drive culture and create outstanding experiences for those you serve.

—**Tony Hsieh**, CEO of Zappos and *New York Times*
bestselling author of *Delivering Happiness*

Airbnb is a company that has changed the way many people travel, and it has given many individuals a path to entrepreneurship. With a commitment to building a company culture that promotes belonging, trust, empowerment, and community, Airbnb leaders inspire hosts to create magical and memorable travel. In this book Joseph Michelli takes you into the world of Airbnb leaders, employees, and hosts. He offers insights on how you can differentiate your personal or corporate brand—fueled by stories told *The Airbnb Way*.

—**Michael E. Gerber**, *New York Times* bestselling author
of *The E-Myth* books

The Airbnb Way provides insights on how Airbnb leaders create a culture of hospitality. More important, it shows how the Airbnb host community welcomes and fosters belonging for guests across the globe. In *The Airbnb Way*, Joseph Michelli provides a road map for delivering engaging and differentiating branded interactions. The book's practical tools apply broadly. Whether you are engaged in the sharing economy or are a global leader seeking to drive memorable experiences across your organization, you will want to spend some time learning from this book.

        —**Alfred Lin**, partner at Sequoia Capital

The Airbnb Way, Michelli's latest masterpiece, describes leadership and business lessons that every leader and organization must take in. Belonging, trust, hospitality, empowerment, and community are key tenets for all people-oriented businesses, and this book is a must-read for those who serve others.

        —**David Feinberg**, VP Google Health

I've spent my career helping companies transform their customer experiences. Many of the lessons I share with my clients are echoed in the pages of *The Airbnb Way*. In it, Joseph Michelli helps you understand what it means to "host" and deliver hospitality—no matter where or what you seek to offer customers. Through *The Airbnb Way*, you will learn from Airbnb leaders and hosts as they drive magical end-to-end experiences.

        —**Jeanne Bliss**, chief customer officer for Lands' End,
                    Allstate, Coldwell Banker, Mazda, and Microsoft;
                    customer experience pioneer; and author of bestselling
                    books, including *Would You Do That to Your Mother?* and
                    Chief Customer Officer

I know the importance of convenience and emotionally engaging experiences. *The Airbnb Way* captures stories and insights to help you make it easier for your customers to work with you. It also shares the leadership genius that fueled a transformative travel brand. This is not just a book for hospitality professionals. It is written for anyone who wants to make the lives of those they serve better and more convenient.

        —**Shep Hyken**, customer service and experience
                  expert and *New York Times* bestselling author of
                  The Amazement Revolution

the
airbnb
way

5 Leadership Lessons
for Igniting Growth Through Loyalty,
Community, and Belonging

Joseph A. Michelli

NEW YORK   CHICAGO   SAN FRANCISCO   ATHENS
LONDON   MADRID   MEXICO CITY   MILAN
NEW DELHI   SINGAPORE   SYDNEY   TORONTO

1 2 3 4 5 6 7 8 9   LCR   24 23 22 21 20 19

ISBN   978-1-260-45544-1
MHID   1-260-45544-0

e-ISBN 978-1-260-45545-8
e-MHID   1-260-45545-9

Book design by Mauna Eichner and Lee Fukui

Library of Congress Cataloging-in-Publication Data

Names: Michelli, Joseph A., author.
Title: The Airbnb way : 5 leadership lessons for igniting growth through
    loyalty, community, and belonging / Joseph A. Michelli.
Description: New York : McGraw-Hill, [2020] | Includes bibliographical
    references and index.
Identifiers: LCCN 2019028357 (print) | LCCN 2019028356 (ebook) |
ISBN
    9781260455441 (hardcover) | ISBN 9781260455458 (ebook)
Subjects: LCSH: Airbnb (Firm)—Influence. | Hospitality industry. |
    Disruptive technologies. | Success in business. | Peer-to-peer travel.
Classification: LCC TX941.A594 M53 2020 (ebook) | LCC TX941.A594
(print) |
    DDC 338.4/791—dc23
LC record available at https://lccn.loc.gov/2019028357

McGraw-Hill Education books are available at special quantity discounts to use as premiums and sales promotions or for use in corporate training programs. To contact a representative, please visit the Contact Us pages at www.mhprofessional.com.

This book is an independent project of Joseph Michelli and McGraw-Hill Publishing. Airbnb provided assistance to source the host stories featured in the book.

Penelope Leigh
Michael
Emma
Daniel
Robert
Gracie
Brigham

Vi amerò per sempre, e anche di più

Contents

PART I
belonging

PART II
trust

PART III
hospitality

PART IV
empowerment

PART V
community

Foreword

A decade ago, during Airbnb's first year, 21,000 guests arrived at our Homes listed on Airbnb. In 2019, we're celebrating our 500 millionth guest arrival. Airbnb hosts have welcomed half a billion guests across 191 countries in over 81,000 cities around the world.

We've spent much of the past decade helping people welcome travelers into their homes, make connections, and even discover lasting friendships. As I write this, somewhere in the world, more than 350 people per minute are checking into an Airbnb.

A funny thing happened along the way: We realized that our hosts were helping us reimagine travel for the better. At the same time so many other brands began to commoditize tourism, Airbnb was empowering experiences that are local, authentic, and unique—what we call magical travel.

On Airbnb, every home is different, meaning guests are guaranteed a completely unique experience with every trip. Every experience we offer is handcrafted by local residents sharing their passions and hobbies with a few guests at a time. Often Hosts are also welcoming you into neighborhoods and places that tourists don't normally visit, providing a trip that is truly local and keeps more of the benefits of tourism within the community you visit.

Many companies focus on their customers. I was lucky enough to spend almost 19 years at Amazon, which famously takes its focus on the customer to the level of obsession. As attuned as Amazon is to its customers, Airbnb is likewise focused on our community. We're a genuinely community-driven company, one of the first in the world at our scale. We don't just elevate our guests—we enable our hosts to connect in meaningful ways while providing spectacular hospitality as well as earning income, and that is the core of Airbnb.

In his conversations with hosts from around the world, Joseph does an extraordinary job of capturing their powerful stories of community and connection. For many hosts, opening their doors to guests has helped them learn more about different cultures, values, and worldviews—an invaluable education—while earning important supplemental income along the way.

At a time of debate about the benefits of the peer-to-peer economy for those who rely on it to earn income, Airbnb's economic empowerment is powerful and indisputable: Our hosts set their own prices, and the vast majority of the economics stay with them and their local communities. Not only does travel on Airbnb directly boost the communities we serve, hosting is geographically diverse, inclusive, and in a sustainable way.

Today, Airbnb is dedicated to building an end-to-end travel platform that champions hosts of all kinds who want to offer the unique, memorable hospitality we stand for, and connecting them with our growing community of guests who enjoy personalized hospitality instead of commoditized tourism. We are laser-focused on helping all hosts succeed, making it as easy as possible for them to work with us and providing tools to earn their trust and support their growth.

At Airbnb, with our strong foundation of our community, we aspire to be a new kind of company: a 21st Century Company that balances the needs of all our stakeholders, including hosts, guests, and the places in which we operate. As you'll learn further in the following pages, magical travel on Airbnb is truly a group effort on a global scale.

Greg Greeley
President of Homes, Airbnb

Acknowledgments

Andrew Carnegie once wrote, "Teamwork is the ability *to work together toward a common vision*, the ability to *direct individual accomplishments toward organizational objectives*. It is the *fuel that allows common people to attain uncommon results*."

Publishing a book is a team accomplishment. I am a very common person fueled by a very uncommon team!

While my name appears on the cover of this book, the unsung heroes can be classified into five groups. Those who:

1. Take time to read, learn, and grow

2. Stewarded this project through Airbnb

3. Nurtured this book through the acquisition and editing process

4. Work closely with me on a daily basis

5. Extend their inspiration, insights, support, and unconditional love

YOU THE READER

Scholars in the area of reading behavior suggest fewer people are spending time with noses in books (they are also spending less time actively engaged in outdoor play, face-to-face interaction, and other core activities of my youth). To the degree that those scholars are correct, your commitment to lifelong learning is bucking a trend. Your behavior signals your specialness. Personally, I've known that "readers are leaders" long before those reading experts weighed in.

Thank you for your readership. There is no reason to write unless people like you are ready to learn and grow.

AIRBNB

This book exists because of Charlie Urbancic in Public Affairs at Airbnb. Charlie embodies Airbnb's core value to "be a host" in all that he does. He creates belonging, fosters trust, empowers, and partners with Airbnb leaders, employees, and the host community to avail critical access to Airbnb.

Product counsel Mariam Cline played an essential role in facilitating progress at all critical transitions in the book writing process. She was available, engaged, constructive, and unflinchingly supportive.

I am deeply grateful to Brian Chesky for saying yes to the project and to Greg Greeley for his support of my career and his most kind Foreword.

ACQUISITION AND EDITING

Donya Dickerson, editorial director at McGraw-Hill, is one of my favorite people on the planet. I credit my writing career to her. As is the case with each of our prior projects, Donya set visionary stretch goals, removed obstacles, pushed for excellence, provided pep talks, and fully invested her intellect, skill, and compassion.

Donya is an inspiration, a trusted advisor, a gifted editor, and a transforming force.

Stephanie Stott, thanks for interning with us. You did more than carry your own in both the research and review process. May your writing career change lives.

Heidi Newman, your professional eye and copyediting abilities infused energy into the manuscript. Thank you for the extra effort and quick turnarounds.

Lloyd Rich, you are a rock, and I am grateful for your expertise in guiding the contracting process. I've been blessed to have your sage and effective counsel throughout my career.

THE MICHELLI EXPERIENCE

Jessica, you are joy, energy, and balance. You take on everything that is asked of you and reach beyond to fill in gaps that are often unseen by others. You have blessed our team and my life.

Kelly, you are extraordinarily responsive, bright, analytic, and calming. Your insights, instincts, social consciousness, and congeniality are inspiring to our team and to me. Thanks for guiding *The Airbnb Way.*

INSPIRATION, INSIGHTS, SUPPORT, AND LOVE

Patti, you fit into more than one category. You manage the business while filling our home with light, love, kindness, and support. You are bright, tender, and the "ultimate Gigi." Thank you for picking me up in the aftermath of sorrow and lifting me to a place beyond my imagination. No words will suffice!

My life is filled with friends, whom I will thank individually and privately for the ways they have inspired and supported me. However, I can't close this section without acknowledging my children and grandchildren who are a source of purest joy. You will never know how deeply you are loved, but at least I can recognize you here. Thank you Fiona, Neven, Andrew, Leah, Penelope, Jessica, Patt, Daniel, Emma, Michael, Matt, Megan, Brigham, Gracie, and Robert.

There is a Malayan proverb that says, "One can pay back the loan of gold, but one dies forever in debt to those who are kind." I am forever in debt to all those listed above . . . and so many more!

Airbnb's Magical
End-to-End Journey

A few years ago, a photo made the rounds on the Internet. It was a snapshot of words written by Alberto Brea, blogger, speaker, and chief growth strategist at DiMassimo Goldstein, that were scrawled on a whiteboard in some corporate office. Those words read:

> Amazon did not kill the retail industry.
> They did it to themselves with bad customer service.
> Netflix did not kill Blockbuster.
> They did it to themselves with ridiculous late fees.
> Uber did not kill the taxi business.
> They did it to themselves by limiting the number of taxis
>   and fare control.
> Apple did not kill the music industry.
> They did it to themselves by forcing people to buy full-
>   length albums.

Airbnb did not kill the hotel industry.
They did it to themselves with limited availability and
    pricing options.
Technology by itself is not the real disruptor.
Being non–customer centric is the biggest threat to any
    business.

This book highlights Airbnb—one of the disruptors referred to by Mr. Brea. In the span of a decade, Airbnb has deservedly earned its reputation and success by creating a global customer-focused movement that leverages effort-reducing technology to enable inspired human interactions.

While some will gravitate to this book to learn how to be a successful Airbnb host, this is also a book for anyone who wants to create meaningful and profitable human experiences—whether they are delivered in the context of employment, entrepreneurship, or personal life.

The Airbnb Way was designed to serve you if you are (or plan to be) a part of one of the following:

- A business that delivers outstanding technology-aided, human-powered experiences to other businesses (business to businesses—B2Bs) or to consumers (business to consumers—B2Cs)

- A company positioned to disrupt an established industry

- An organization seeking to retain a strong or dominant market position

- The *sharing economy*—which I broadly define as any sale transacted through an online market, whether business to business (B2B) or peer to peer (P2P)

- An improved sales or service experience

Since customer experience excellence involves a journey as opposed to a finite destination, who better to study than a company dedicated to journey creation? In fact, leaders at Airbnb have broadly described their company as:

> A global travel community that offers magical end-to-end trips, including where you stay, what you do, and the people you meet. Airbnb uniquely leverages technology to economically empower millions of people around the world to unlock and monetize their spaces, passions, and talents to become hospitality entrepreneurs.

Let's begin our "magical end-to-end trip" into the world of Airbnb and its host community by first defining some of the territories we will and won't be exploring.

Our adventure is set for you to:

- Learn an inclusive form of hospitality that produces meaningful and lasting connections

- Acquire tools needed to build trust and community

- Examine the value of technology-aided and human-powered service experiences

- Understand how to "do good" for those you serve while also doing well in business

As for territory outside the bounds of this book, we will stay away from well-worn paths. For example, we *won't* embark on detailed stories of Airbnb's humble beginnings, nor will we venture into the many controversies faced by this market disruptor. Those topics are well chronicled elsewhere and are eloquently shared in Leigh Gallagher's book, *The Airbnb Story: How Three Ordinary Guys Disrupted an Industry, Made Billions . . . and Created Plenty of Controversy.*

Instead, we will study Airbnb's leadership and explore how the team at Airbnb encourages hosts to provide a universally welcoming experience. One cautionary note before we dive into Airbnb's leadership and team impact: Airbnb is in hypergrowth! All numbers reported in this book were accurate as of the time of this writing, but they have likely surged by the time of your reading. Throughout the book, we will be examining how Airbnb's 3,000-plus current employees, located in approximately 40 global offices, partner with hosts to source over 6 million Airbnb listings. Those listings span more than 100,000 cities in nearly 200 countries. Together, Airbnb employees along with the host community have accommodated more than 500 million guest arrivals.

Since they are the experts on the topic, most of our journey will be guided by Airbnb hosts. You may be a part of the host community or have relatives, neighbors, or colleagues who are hosts. This globally diverse entrepreneur community includes anyone who lists on the Airbnb platform seeking to craft consistent and emotionally engaging hospitality.

Before we start our journey, let's take the remainder of this chapter to:

- Highlight the disruptive success of Airbnb

- Look broadly at how technology has changed service expectations and behavior

- Examine Airbnb's technology and human service delivery in the context of commerce and travel

- Offer a preview of the themes of the book

WHAT CAN BE DONE IN A DECADE?

It's hard to fathom just how much Airbnb has accomplished in 10 years.

The need that fueled the creation of Airbnb began in 2007 when two roommates (Brian Chesky and Joe Gebbia) were looking for a way to pay rent on their San Francisco apartment. The pair, who met at the Rhode Island School of Design, saw an income opportunity associated with a major design conference coming to San Francisco. In advance of the conference, Chesky and Gebbia purchased three air mattresses and crafted a simple website so conference attendees could reserve their makeshift accommodations. During the conference, two men and one woman paid $80 each per night to stay on Chesky and Gebbia's air mattresses. Shortly thereafter, Chesky and Gebbia partnered with a former roommate and computer scientist, Nathan Blecharczyk, to develop the online marketplace we know today as Airbnb. Over an approximately 10-year span, Airbnb has grown to these heights:

- It has listed over 5 million properties worldwide (approximately 2 million of which are instantly bookable).

- It has processed over 400 million guest arrivals.

- It has earned high corporate valuations (at least $38 billion as of May 2018).

- It has generated substantial wealth for hosts (in 2018, Airbnb announced that female hosts—55 percent of the overall community—made $10 billion in revenue in the prior year).

To fully comprehend Airbnb's growth, one need only consider Airbnb's guest bookings in 2008 compared to 2018. According to Internet Online Property (IOLproperty.co.za), Airbnb had approximately 400 total guest bookings for the entire year in 2008, and it had approximately 400 guest bookings every two minutes in 2018. By 2018, approximately 2 million guests were staying in Airbnb-listed property on any given night.

Early on, Airbnb was US centric, with approximately 59 percent of bookings coming from the United States in 2009. As of 2017, the global nature of the brand was reflected in the fact that only 29 percent of guest bookings were coming from the United States.

Not only have listings become more global, but the options available on Airbnb have also increased in variety. When it comes to homes, accomodations can go from a $10-per-night stay in a Backpackers Hostel in Jakarta, Indonesia's Old Town, to a $10,075-per-night stay in an exclusive villa in Austin, Texas. Of course, for $10,075, you and 15 of your closest friends can luxuriate in two homes and a guest house.

In addition to more traditional accommodations, as of August 2018, the breadth of Airbnb listings included the following:

- 10,449 RVs

- 2,194 yurts

- 1,403 islands

- 8,951 tiny houses

- 9,000 boats

- 2,194 treehouses

- 183 igloos

- 918 tipis

- 155 windmills

- 758 caves

The demographics of guests have also shifted over time. In the beginning, Airbnb customers were overwhelmingly leisure travelers. They skewed toward budget-conscious and experience-minded millennials (it's estimated that 60 percent of early adopters were millennials).

As of 2017, the age distribution of Airbnb guests appears to have widened. While Airbnb does not report this data and the accuracy of third-party sources can't be validated, Statista suggests that 36 percent of US and European Airbnb users were between the ages of 25 and 34, and 23 percent were between 35 and 44. The percentage of 45- to 55-year-old guests (14 percent) was roughly the same as 18- to 24-year-old guests (15 percent). Statista also suggested 12 percent of guests were over 55.

Even though age and global demographics expanded, the sheer number of millennial guests continues to grow (jumping 120 percent from 2016 to 2017). During that same period, Airbnb reported that seniors were the fastest-growing host demographic and that "senior women consistently are the best-rated hosts on Airbnb."

Along with shifts in listings, hosts, and guests, Airbnb has seen an expansion of business travelers. In 2014, the company launched Airbnb for Business—now called Airbnb for Work—a platform that business travelers can use in planning for their specific needs.

Appreciating that approximately 25 percent of employees travel for work and that many more entrepreneurs and small business owners make a living on the road, Airbnb for Work began listing accommodations optimized for business travelers. It also focused on longer-term relocation needs of families. To access Airbnb for Work, people sign up as an individual business traveler or have their HR or travel manager create a free business account.

Due to business travel innovations, bookings through Airbnb for Work tripled from 2015 to 2016 and tripled again from 2016 to 2017. According to Ryan Pierce, a senior travel manager for Salesforce, "Airbnb for Work allows our business travelers the flexibility to find different types of accommodations and provides them an individual experience while traveling. This also helps the business maximize budgets while giving travel managers access to insights and visibility to ensure traveler safety."

By September of 2018, employees from 700,000 companies arranged travel with Airbnb for Work. Of those bookings, 40 percent came from large enterprise businesses (5,000-plus employees), another 40 percent from small businesses (fewer than 250 employees), and the remaining 20 percent from midsized companies (between 250 and 5,000 employees).

In February 2018, Airbnb added four new property types on its platform: *vacation home*, *unique space*, *B&B*, and *boutique*. With that announcement, Airbnb provided greater ease in locating the range of offerings on the platform (from unique spaces like igloos to accommodations in a boutique hotel). This improvement was intended to "give a choice of accommodation options to guests, provide greater transparency over the types of accommodations available, and help hosts better showcase what's unique about them to better match with guests' preferences."

Leaders have also strategically expanded the company beyond the short-term housing market. In November 2016, CEO Brian Chesky announced how Airbnb would leverage its global travel community to deliver end-to-end travel experiences. Chesky shared, "Airbnb has been about homes. Today, Airbnb is launching 'Trips,' bringing together where you stay, what you do, and the people you meet all in one place. We want to make travel magical again by putting people back at the heart of every trip."

Trips includes Homes (their existing business) and Experiences, and they may include flights and services in the future. Airbnb's Experiences product refers to bookable host-led activities. These Experiences are carefully selected so hosts can share their passions and interests in a broadening number of cities. For example, you might participate in a perfume creation workshop in Paris, learn how to make paella in Barcelona, or be a gaucho for a day in Buenos Aires.

In keeping with the evolution of Airbnb's Trips expansion, Airbnb for Work also added Experiences in 2018. The Experiences section of Airbnb for Work features team building activities led by local experts. These Experiences afford an array of team opportunities to include social impact excursions. An example of a Social Impact Experience includes paddling with penguins in Cape Town, South Africa, where 100 percent of the proceeds go to the AfriOceans Conservation Alliance.

In 2017, citing that 66 percent of American travelers "make restaurant reservations while away from home," Airbnb forged a partnership with Resy, a restaurant reservation technology company, to create a dedicated Restaurant tab on the Airbnb app and website. As a result, travelers can search for restaurants near them, explore various cuisines, or look for a dining option by the time of day (breakfast, lunch, dinner). In New York City, for example, the choice can range from $15 per person for Yucatan tacos to $200 per person to dine at an exclusive eight-seat Japanese tasting bar.

The growth and success of Airbnb's Trips services have been swift. For example, the Experiences component began in 2016 with offerings in 12 cities (Detroit, London, Paris, Nairobi, Havana, San Francisco, Cape Town, Florence, Miami, Seoul, Tokyo, and Los Angeles). By 2018 Airbnb was facilitating Experiences in more than 1,000 cities and had enabled well over a million bookings.

Airbnb's service extensions are constantly evolving. Greg Greeley, president of Homes at Airbnb, shared that service innovation on the homes side of the business is evidenced by Airbnb Plus—a select group of highly rated homes offered by hosts particularly focused on detail. Airbnb Plus listings undergo an in-person verification process assessing quality, style, and cleanliness via a 100-point checklist that includes fast Wi-Fi with download speeds of at least 5 Mbps and a kitchen stocked with "essentials like a frying pan, salt, pepper, and cooking oil." Greg told me, "We are listening to the community in all that we do and continue to expand to add richness that supports local authentic travel. The platform will continually evolve to develop people-powered homes and experiences."

Given that leaders at Airbnb seek to transform travel experiences from the beginning to the end of a traveler's journey, it's reasonable to expect a tireless cadence of innovations and expanded service offerings throughout the decades ahead.

Airbnb's growth is truly meteoric and extraordinary, but growth doesn't necessarily translate into profitability. Writing in a May 2018 article for *Forbes*, the contributor group Great Speculations noted, "A key factor that separates Airbnb from a bulk of the multi-billion dollar startups ('unicorns') is that it is now cash flow positive.... While ride-hailing pioneer Uber has yet to turn a profit despite its impressive growth worldwide, Airbnb ... also has a sizable cash balance—putting it in an enviable financial position among the unicorns." From three air mattresses to status as a rare cash-flow-positive, multi-billion-dollar business, let's look at how Airbnb leaders leveraged technology and people to create customer-centric solutions that addressed previously unmet customer and travel service provider needs and fueled the company's success.

HOW TECHNOLOGY IS CHANGING BEHAVIOR AND SERVICE EXPECTATIONS

We all know that the Internet and mobile technology have fundamentally changed our behavior and how we expect to be served. The impact of digital technology is present in every aspect of our lives and is having an effect at a level greater than many of us may fully appreciate.

Research conducted by LivePerson, an online messaging and marketing company, shows that human interaction, social behavior, and even sleep habits are being altered by our mobile devices. In a study of millennials and generation Z consumers, LivePerson found the following:

- 65 percent now communicate digitally more than they do in person, on any given day.

- 42 percent consider it acceptable to text at a family dinner.

- 40 percent believe it is appropriate to text in a movie theater.

- 29 percent bring their phone into a shower or bath.

- 70 percent sleep with their phone within arm's reach.

- 52 percent check their phone in the middle of the night if they wake up briefly.

Years ago, people attended activities and later talked about those events either in person or by phone. Today, we simultaneously attend and share those experiences. This is particularly evident with the omnipresent cell phone use at concerts or by the sheer number of food pictures shared on social media.

Some of the greatest impacts of technology involve the way we shop and purchase—especially when it comes to increased expectations for service speed, ease, enriched information, and immediate communication. At our fingertips or through voice query, we can now explore and dream about a world of products and services enhanced by the following:

- Websites

- Digital ads

- Online communities

- Apps and application programming interfaces (APIs)

- Social networking

- Social media

- Wearables

- Augmented reality (AR) programs and applications

- Virtual reality (VR) programs and applications

- Bots

Airbnb leaders were acutely aware of the emerging digital consumer as they launched their company in the late 2000s. They believed that technology should be a tool that serves a broader customer experience strategy and that technology alone could not be the strategy. Consistently, Airbnb leaders focused on using innovative technology to empower the host community to deliver warm, human experiences to guests.

PEOPLE *AND* TECHNOLOGY

As you will see later in the chapter, Airbnb leaders built their company to capitalize on the best features of technology in order to enable personal human care. With a rise in technology use (and possibly because of it), many of us are wanting more personalized and human interactions. For example, PricewaterhouseCoopers (PwC) surveyed a wide swath of consumers ranging from baby boomers (born as early as 1946) to generation Z (born as late as 2012).

The 2018 PwC study titled *The Future of Customer Experience* was conducted in 12 countries (Argentina, Australia, Brazil, Canada, China, Colombia, Germany, Japan, Mexico, Singapore, the United Kingdom, and the United States), and it found the following:

1. Great customer experiences drive loyalty and enable premium pricing.

2. Bad customer experiences result in customer churn.

3. Convenience, speed, and helpful people are of the utmost importance to consumers.

4. Quality interactions between employees and customers are essential.

5. There is considerable agreement across generations on the key elements of good service. The differences that do exist are a function of *how* certain segments want those elements delivered.

6. Customer experience excellence is a considerable opportunity and a strategic imperative.

The wisdom of Airbnb leaders concerning the importance of deploying technology to enable human service is supported by a number of PwC findings:

- An average of 48 percent of US consumers believe friendly, welcoming service differentiates a business and produces success; only 32 percent believe the same about cutting-edge technology.

- While people embrace technology, people want to immediately interact with another person if they encounter a technical problem. Only 3 percent of US consumers want "their experiences to be as automated as possible."

- 64 percent of US consumers and 59 percent of all consumers feel "companies have lost touch with the human element of customer experience. 71 percent of Americans would rather interact with a human than a chatbot or some other automated process."

The importance of crafting customer-centric service solutions that blend people and technology (like those developed by Airbnb) are further validated by a variety of other sources, including a comprehensive study by Salesforce (a cloud-computing customer experience management software provider), titled *State of the Connected Customer*, second edition, in which 84 percent of customers said, "Being treated like a person, not a number, is very important to winning their business." The relevance of this research does more than support Airbnb's business model. It emphasizes the importance of building customer loyalty through technological convenience and human connection.

Visionary thinkers and market leaders, like those at Airbnb, have and will continue to invest in a holistic approach to customer experience excellence. They will advance automated solutions to handle routine tasks and position people to listen, understand, empathize, help others, appreciate, and celebrate those they serve.

Above all else, the findings from the PwC study, as shown in the figure that follows, suggest respondents across the globe expect that quality human contact will be increasingly required as technology improves.

Human Versus Automated Interaction: Percent Who Indicate "I'll Want to Interact with a Real Person More as Technology Improves"

The World Economic Forum (WEF) has a similar view on the importance of human service skills. From the standpoint of future employability, the WEF has noted that jobs in the digital age will require more human problem-solving skills, communication effectiveness, adaptability, persistence, empathy, and overall social intelligence. In essence, the ability to deliver "human" and "personal" care will be a critical counterbalance to technology.

Later in this chapter, you will see how Airbnb has effectively taken a people *and* technology approach toward personal care. You will also explore how the mission of Airbnb supports social intelligence and "hosting" ability.

A NEW WORLD OF TRAVEL

Up to now, I've highlighted dramatic changes in technology and service expectations, and I've suggested that Airbnb leaders have positioned the company to address ease and convenience through technology while also helping hosts nurture warm and personal interactions. Let's take a moment to look at changing expectations in the estimated $8.27 trillion global travel industry and provide context for how Airbnb has leveraged technology and people to exceed expectations in the sector.

A recent interchange on a travel forum speaks to the "dark ages" of travel planning. At the beginning of the thread, a young person posted a question after watching a 1970s sitcom: "It dawned on me that people in those days didn't have the luxury of booking a hotel via the Internet, much less to read reviews about the lodging.... I'm curious how did would-be tourists find out that a particular hotel actually existed in the city they intended to visit? Guidebooks? Or did they just 'wing it' when they touched down?" Respondents to that post (people like me who lived "in those days") offered answers like travel agents, calls made to hotel chains using the technology of the day (a landline), and resources like customized travel guides created by the American Automobile Association (AAA). The exchange poignantly encapsulates just how much travel planning has changed from one generation to the next.

Business leadership Professor Mari Jansen van Rensburg describes travel planning in the digital age by noting: "The Internet and social media technologies have become entrenched in this industry and proved themselves to be perfect tools for serving clients. Not only does the Internet serve as a channel for travelers to search for information, but it also allows the visualization of travel products and services through video clips and graphical images.... Today travelers have more choices and are better informed."

In keeping with Professor van Rensburg's findings, I've observed dramatic changes in what consumers value when it comes to travel services and accommodations. In 2008, McGraw-Hill published my book titled *The New Gold Standard: 5 Leadership Principles for Creating a Legendary Customer Experience Courtesy of The Ritz-Carlton Hotel Company*. At that time, hotels like the Ritz-Carlton were the primary accommodation options for travel. To satisfy and retain customers, hotel owners and chain operators looked for ways to deliver desirable guest experiences optimized to achieve the following:

1. Create stays with no unpleasant surprises.

2. Assure predictable branded environments (for example, the same room layout and a common "look" and "feel").

Writing in *Mashable*, MJ Franklin noted that the hotel industry's pursuit of "predictability" was at odds with emerging customer desires. According to MJ, "Sometimes when you're traveling or booking a vacation, the last thing you want to do is stay in a hotel. Sure, they're convenient—but hotels can also be booooooorrrring.

(It's the persistent sameness of hotels. Such repetition and ubiquity tend to trigger an existential crisis spiral where you begin to question how everything can be so different and yet all the same ...)."

Much like MJ, travelers today are expressing a diverse set of needs and interests that are far beyond "predictable" encounters. Increasingly they seek "personal," "memorable," "soulful," and "transparent" experiences. Many guests want to venture beyond the confines of a resort hotel to "travel local" and experience a "sense of place." Let's pick up the Airbnb story in the context of these emerging, travel-specific trends.

AIRBNB'S TECHNOLOGY-AIDED AND HUMAN-POWERED EXPERIENCE

Early in Airbnb's evolution, leaders envisioned a new way to travel. They essentially asked, "What if people could go online and find their desired travel accommodation within three clicks?" "What if people could discover emotionally engaging alternatives to an average 325-square-foot hotel room located in a high-traffic area?" "What if travelers could explore more humanized accommodations and readily select from choices curated to their price, location, and personality preference?" "What if travel were welcoming, inclusive, and personal?"

The answer to those what-ifs is Airbnb!

With backgrounds in design thinking and software engineering, the founders of Airbnb (Brian Chesky, Joe Gebbia, and Nathan Blecharczyk) leveraged technology to develop a web-based user interface that made finding, selecting, and booking travel easier. In the process, they also made it easy for homeowners to earn extra income, whether that be through renting a second home or simply listing a spare bedroom. Despite technological benefits, Airbnb entered the online booking industry, seemingly at a disadvantage, by having to go up against established players like Vacation Rental by Owner (Vrbo, now part of Expedia's HomeAway) or Bedand Breakfast.com.

In her book *The Airbnb Story: How Three Ordinary Guys Disrupted an Industry, Made Billions . . . and Created Plenty of Controversy*, author Leigh Gallagher offers her view on how Airbnb gained market dominance despite the odds. "What Airbnb specifically has done, is to toss aside the barriers and build an easy, friendly, accessible platform inviting anyone to do it. Unlike on previous websites, Airbnb listings were designed to showcase home renters' personalities; the company invested in professional photography to make sure the spaces look lush and inviting; and searching, messaging, and payment were all self-contained, seamless, and friction-free. . . . And one of the biggest but least discussed reasons it was so different is that Airbnb was urban."

In support of Leigh's last point, most listings on other platforms were for vacation rentals of second homes only. By contrast Airbnb attracted hosts with a far more diverse set of options to address broader traveler needs and circumstances. Moreover, leaders at Airbnb readily created, tested, and deployed advanced technologies and intuitive design to foster service speed, ease of use, reliability, personalization, and trust on their digital platform.

Since the Airbnb experience begins on the digital platform, let's walk through some of the key benefits afforded by Airbnb's technology—starting with page speed. When people visit a web platform like Airbnb.com, they expect rapid load times. Felix Gessert, CEO of Baqend, a cloud service company that uses unique algorithms to shorten web page load times, notes, "Page speed has become a defining factor in this race, as over 40 percent of users abandon a site if it has not loaded within the first three seconds." In comments captured in a *New York Times* article, waiting a little more than the blink of an eye (just over 400 milliseconds) can cause visitors to click to another page. According to Gessert. "We tested the 10 travel destination and accommodation sites with the highest market share in the United States for their performance. Tech companies in the travel industry seem to take the issue seriously. The site of market share leader Trip Advisor loads within 0.7 seconds. Only Airbnb is faster, loading in under 0.5 seconds, thus coming close to the famous blink of an eye." That blink-of-the-eye speed gives Airbnb the opportunity to win business, but it takes thoughtful service design to effectively steward technology throughout a customer's journey.

In addition to quick load times, the Airbnb website and app platform enable seamless customer flow. For example, new app users are onboarded with just a few questions, which are asked clearly and conversationally. Digital platforms immediately anticipate a user's most likely need (the desire to explore travel options) by providing a prominent search box. That search function enables prospective travelers to input the who, where, and when of their desired trip and click a large search button. On the app, the Explore tab personalizes each interaction by populating your name. For example, I am asked, "What can we help you find, Joseph?" Based on my answer, the search is customized to my needs.

Machine learning or artificial intelligence (AI) is deployed in every reservation made on the platform to ensure personalization and security. Those technologies help surface the best options for each user as that guest searches for listings. AI also helps prevent fraud and assists hosts to optimize pricing.

Picture recognition technology can use machine learning to scan, tag, categorize, and filter images on the Airbnb site. To understand the benefits of this technology, assume an image of a listing has a picture of a bunk bed but the bunk bed information failed to be included in the text description of the property. Also, assume that you have a history of choosing homes with bunk beds. Picture recognition technology could select that specific property as an option for your consideration in the context of your past behavior on the platform.

Natural language processing (NLP) enables text-based content (like guest reviews) to be scanned and filtered. If you are looking for feedback about a home, instead of seeing off-topic posts made about a listing (comments about the city but *not* the home or host), NLP can filter the unrelated information so the reviews you see are curated yet unbiased.

Technology tools at Airbnb are a result of people developing solutions to empower others (both guests and hosts). Every technology solution and all the guest and host interactions the technology supports are guided by the company's human and humane mission. That mission has evolved and is best described in a blog post written by cofounder Brian Chesky in 2014:

> What started as a way for a few friends to pay the rent has now transformed into something bigger and more meaningful than we ever imagined. And what we realized is that the Airbnb community has outgrown the original Airbnb brand. So Joe, Nate, and I did some soul-searching over the last year. We asked ourselves, "What is our mission? What is the big idea that truly defines Airbnb?" It turns out the answer was right in front of us. For so long, people thought Airbnb was about renting houses. But really, we're about home. You see, a house is just a space, but a home is where you belong. And what makes this global community so special is that for the very first time, you can belong anywhere. That is the idea at the core of our company: belonging.

Chesky suggested that belonging, trust, and community are less common than at prior times in history. He also believes that relationships give our lives the greatest meaning. Chesky added this:

That's why Airbnb is returning us to a place where everyone can feel they belong. Like us, you may have started out thinking you were just renting out a room to help pay the bills. Or maybe you were just booking a bed for a night on an unexpected layover. However we first entered this community, we all know that getting in isn't a transaction. It's a connection that can last a lifetime. That's because the rewards you get from Airbnb aren't just financial—they're personal—for hosts and guests alike. At a time when new technologies have made it easier to keep each other at a distance, you're using them to bring people together. And you're tapping into the universal human yearning to belong—the desire to feel welcomed, respected, and appreciated for who you are, no matter where you might be. Belonging is the idea that defines Airbnb.

In Chapters 2 and 3, we will fully unpack what it means to "belong anywhere," how Airbnb supports that mission, and what hosts do every day to make it a reality. For now, let's take a moment to see what it can look like when an Airbnb host meets a guest's "universal yearning . . . to feel welcomed, respected, and appreciated."

An Airbnb traveler booked a week-long stay in a private room at Host April Brenneman's family's home in Portland, Oregon. On the first day of the man's stay, April observed that he was experiencing abdominal pain. When April asked how she could help and if he needed to go to a nearby hospital, the guest suspected he was having a recurrence of kidney stones and indicated that he was going to rest and drink lots of fluids. By 8 p.m. that evening, the man was in excruciating pain. April transported him to a local emergency room.

April shared, "The hospital was jam-packed, and they put him on a gurney in the hallway as he writhed in pain. I kept asking the hospital staff to get him to a room or to provide medication. I also called his wife to give her regular updates on his status." April's husband joined her and her guest in the emergency room. As the night wore on, knowing her husband had an early morning meeting the next day, April said, "I'll stay with our guest tonight since I won't be able to sleep until I know he is OK." By 4 o'clock the next morning, April's guest had stabilized. He was provided the medication he needed, discharged from the hospital, and driven back to his Airbnb room by April.

April's story is representative of common experiences being delivered by the Airbnb community. It clearly shows why Chesky concludes that Airbnb "isn't a transaction. It's a connection that can last a lifetime."

LOOKING BACK AND MOVING FORWARD

Leaders at Airbnb have blended together an alluring mix of people *and* technology solutions that have revolutionized the travel industry in the short span of a decade. Those leaders have empowered hosts to generate revenue in the "sharing economy" and have assisted hosts to deliver easy and magical travel experiences for guests across the globe.

In the international marketplace, Airbnb and its host community have garnered attention and recognition for the business, economic, and social impact of their collective efforts. More important, Airbnb has attracted your interest in learning more about *The Airbnb Way*.

So, what will you encounter on this journey from the perspective of themes? *The Airbnb Way* is crafted to share five essential concepts that underpin outstanding Airbnb experiences:

- **Belonging:** Creating a world where everyone can feel they belong anywhere

- **Trust:** Challenging fears of "stranger danger" and enabling people to experience the basic trustworthiness of others

- **Hospitality:** Helping people deliver "service with heart"

- **Empowerment:** Activating people to achieve economic and interpersonal goals

- **Community:** Making a positive contribution to others

Each of the above themes centers on core customer experience needs and opportunities. Results from primary research and analysis of Airbnb's leadership strategy will be enhanced and made relatable through conversations with Airbnb hosts and guests. Chapters will position content and share stories that will provide actionable insights and tools to help you strengthen the way you serve others and drive loyalty.

Context has been provided.

Planning is complete.

It's time to venture forward in the direction of service, hospitality, customer experience, and community building *The Airbnb Way.*

A QUICK TOUR

Please allow me to provide you an overview of *The Airbnb Way*, just as an Airbnb host might orient guests to a new environment or experience. Each of the five foundational themes of this book (**belonging, trust, hospitality, empowerment,** and **community**) will be explored across two chapters.

The first chapter will look at the themes from the vantage point of Airbnb's leadership and staff. The second chapter will share stories, insights, and tools from international Airbnb hosts as they deliver experiences in keeping with the themes. Each chapter title is written as a prescriptive and actionable business principle. For example, the next two chapters are titled "Make It a People Business" and "Create Belonging."

Throughout the book, you'll find sections referred to as *Your Travel Planning Guide*, which are designed to help you reflect and plan relevant action steps to achieve your desired service experience. At the conclusion of each chapter, you will be offered a summary of key takeaways in a section referred to as *Points of Interest*.

PART I
belonging

Make It a
People Business

*The need for connection and community is primal,
as fundamental as the need for air, water, and food.*
—Dean Ornish,
physician and researcher

What business are you in? I'm not asking what sector of the economy you serve (for example, healthcare, retail, financial services). I'm asking if you are in a product-focused business, a service-centric business, or something else?

I've been fortunate to work with leaders at Starbucks and write two books about the company (*The Starbucks Experience: 5 Principles for Turning Ordinary into Extraordinary* and *Leading the Starbucks Way: 5 Principles for Connecting with Your Customers, Your Products, and Your People*). At the time of those writings, Starbucks CEO Howard Schultz shared a somewhat unexpected perspective on his company: "We are not in the coffee business serving people; we are in the people business serving coffee." By emphasizing the rich "human" experience at the core of Starbucks, Howard reinforced an enduring principle of success: "All business is personal."

Given that you picked up this book, I'll assume you already see yourself in the "people business" and appreciate that Airbnb can offer insights on interpersonal connection. You likely understand that sustainable success involves creating value for the people you call customers by providing value to the people you call colleagues, team members, or employees. To be effective in business as well as in life, we must develop skills to understand, meet, and even exceed the *needs* of those we serve.

Despite the importance of determining the motivations, wants, and needs of others, many business leaders only seek to offer practical benefits through the features and attributes of the products and services they provide. In the process, leaders often neglect the unconscious, emotional, psychological, and social needs of the customers and employees they serve.

In an Insights Association article titled "Why Business Doesn't Understand Consumers," Mark Ingwer, founder and managing partner of the Insight Consulting Group, cites studies that show 80 to 90 percent of new products or services fail to achieve sales projections despite "satisfaction" with those products. Mark adds, "The consumer may have appreciated the product, but if his or her unarticulated emotional needs went unmet, the appreciation means virtually nothing for a business trying to form a base of loyal buyers. This is a problem for businesses using a *logical*, traditional process to study the *emotional* . . . an approach that cannot readily deliver the accurate emotional insights required."

So how does a solopreneur, manager, or leader gain "accurate emotional insights" into "unarticulated emotional needs" of customers? How can you understand the needs of your customers more broadly and deeply? The short answer is to study brands like Airbnb who have earned a reputation for innovating solutions to address the unmet needs of their stakeholders.

Based on my experience as a customer experience consultant and my observation of the approach taken by Airbnb leadership, the process of human need assessment involves these three key steps:

1. Study human motivation and needs.

2. Seek partnerships with thought leaders and change agents.

3. Ask stakeholders to share their preferences, wants, and needs.

Let's explore how leaders at Airbnb followed these steps in pursuit of a deep emotional connection with team members, hosts, and guests.

STUDENTS OF HUMAN BEHAVIOR AND NEEDS

From early in the company's evolution, the leaders at Airbnb stewarded their organization, in the spirit of Howard Schultz, to also be a "people business" that fosters meaningful human connections enabled by technology. Since the beginning of Airbnb, Joe Gebbia, Nathan Blecharcyzk, and Brian Chesky actively sought guidance from books, case studies, and mentors to help them expand their thinking beyond technology or booking "homes."

Airbnb cofounder Joe Gebbia cites many people (including Apple's Jony Ive) who have inspired him in areas such as human-centric and frictionless design. Nathan Blecharcyzk acknowledges the importance of customer service insights gained from Tony Hsieh at Zappos (the focus of my book *The Zappos Experience: 5 Principles to Inspire, Engage, and WOW*), and cofounder Brian Chesky reports being mentored by leaders including Warren Buffett and hotelier Chip Conley.

Given Conley's future significance to Airbnb, let's take a moment to preview how he applied the "needs theory" of Abraham

Maslow to business. As you may recall, in 1943 Maslow theorized that human needs could be arranged in a hierarchy or pyramid. Basic needs shape the bottom of the pyramid and represent physiological (food, water, sleep) and safety needs. Above those needs on Maslow's hierarchy are psychological cravings for esteem, love, and belonging. Maslow identified our highest-level need as a quest for self-fulfillment.

Conley, founder and former CEO of Joie de Vivre Hospitality, used Maslow's hierarchy to conceptualize and successfully meet the needs of all stakeholders in his company's chain of boutique hotels. In his book *Peak: How Great Companies Get Their Mojo from Maslow*, Conley credited the application of Maslow's hierarchy with saving his business in the wake of the 9/11 terrorist attacks and the dot.com meltdown. Conley encouraged other leaders to develop a deeper understanding of the physical, psychological, and self-fulfillment needs of those they served—suggesting that every CEO should seek to be a "chief emotional officer." Brian Chesky, Airbnb's CEO, heeded Conley's guidance and sought him out.

PARTNERING FOR TRANSFORMATION

At the beginning of 2013, Brian Chesky asked Chip Conley to provide a fireside chat on hospitality innovation for the team at Airbnb. Even prior to that event, Chesky was strategizing ways to bring Conley (who was then semiretired) into Airbnb leadership on a full-time basis. Conley was initially hesitant to commit to a position at the company.

In a conversation with Chip Conley, he shared with me his recollection of the events following that fireside meeting: "I gave that talk on hospitality innovation and had no inkling that Brian was considering me to be a possible advisor at Airbnb. I think he wanted to see how I fit with his team and if my message would resonate." Chip continued, "Shortly after that, Brian asked me, 'If I would be a part-time advisor?' I suggested I wasn't sure if I would, and even if I did, the position would have to be very part-time— something on the order of 8 hours a week. Brian patiently negotiated me up to a 15-hour-a-week consulting role, and about six weeks later I started my first day at Airbnb. It was no 15-hour-a-week job, and it didn't take long before I was working full-time." Conley assumed the role of global head of hospitality and strategy for Airbnb in 2013, and he continues to function as a trusted advisor to Chesky.

Let's summarize what it took for Chesky to get Conley to assume a leadership role at Airbnb. Chesky actively looked for ways to grow as a leader and guide Airbnb's development, and he read Conley's work. He found value in what he read, so he asked Conley to partner with him. He then had to work with Conley's reticence to accept his initial offer. Chesky also had to remain patient and adapt to meet Conley's needs. Similar steps are essential for anyone committed to lead business transformation—particularly in the direction of serving others.

MORE PARTNERING

Around the time Conley was recruited, leaders throughout Airbnb were identifying additional partners and change agents who might help them form even more meaningful and lasting human connections. For example, Brian Chesky reached out to Douglas Atkin, an advertising and marketing executive and author of the book *The Culting of Brands*.

Atkin's unique professional journey and his areas of expertise were of particular interest to Airbnb. While working at a New York City ad agency, Atkin heard predictions that his profession was in peril. The reasons often given for the demise of advertising included the increasing similarity of products, the speed with which products could be replicated, and people's decreasing loyalty to brands.

In the midst of those predictions, Atkin attended a focus group involving young consumers who were discussing Converse shoes, the group's favorite brand of sneaker. That focus group's passion for the brand was so intense that Atkin concluded loyalty and brand zeal were far from dead. Instead, he believed that loyalty and zealotry simply needed to be better understood and harnessed to do "good" in the world.

Atkin began a study of what he called "best-in-class cult brands" which expanded into a multiyear odyssey involving hundreds of interviews with members and former members of actual cults. That work culminated in the book *The Culting of Brands*. In it, Atkin explored the reasons why people join cults, why they remain fervently engaged in them, and how cult behavior is a paradox. According to Atkin, people don't join cults or identify with cultlike brands because they want to conform. Instead, they join to fulfill their individuality. In essence, strong cultlike connections meet two of Maslow's higher-order needs—the need for belonging and the need for self-fulfillment.

In the context of these insights, Atkin left the world of advertising and took his knowledge of connections, belonging, and self-fulfillment to the world of social technology. Atkin became a partner and chief community officer at Meetup. Meetup describes itself as "the largest network of local communities that meet offline about their shared interests."

After working to help develop Meetup communities, Atkin's interests turned to "movements," which he describes as "communities on the move." As is Atkin's nature, he began researching and analyzing how movements activate large groups of people to do things to make the world better. Based on that study, Atkin cofounded a company called Purpose, which allowed him to consult on how to create movements and to incubate movements like All Out, whose mission is to mobilize "thousands of people to build a world where no person will have to sacrifice their family or freedom, safety or dignity, because of who they are or who they love." It was Atkin's research, writing, and consulting that led Airbnb to him.

In an interview for *Medium* with innovator and futurist David Passiak, Douglas Atkin shared how his path to Airbnb was similar to that of Chip Conley: "I first joined Airbnb as a consultant. I thought it was to help them with community because I'm a community guy. But Brian [Chesky] said, 'Hey, Douglas, you know a lot about brands from your past. Can you help us figure out what ours is?'" Atkin responded to Chesky's request for helping Airbnb find its brand by noting that Airbnb is its own community—one in which people may be called employees, hosts, or guests but also a community in which the distinctions between those labels rapidly become blurred:

> Employees are both hosts and guests; and guests are also hosts; and vice versa. We have this massive community. I think the question to ask is: What's the purpose of our community? Why does it exist? What is this community in the world to do, and what difference is it going to make? In other words, what is the vision, and how will this community make the world a better place?

Atkin believed any understanding of human motivation (such as insights he and Chip Conley brought to Airbnb) had to be linked to the "purpose of the Airbnb community."

From Atkin's perspective, a powerful human-centric vision occurs when leaders understand human needs and why their business exists in the context of exceeding those needs. Atkin clarified, "By establishing why the community exists, we'll know what the brand should become. But the brand is only one manifestation of the vision.

Vision will also be manifested in product design, our office space, and whom we hire."

Airbnb leaders like Gebbia, Blecharcyzk, and Chesky demonstrate a tireless curiosity and interest in people. They partner with those who will help them grow and evolve. In the case of Conley and Atkin, Airbnb leaders gravitated to similarly inquisitive and analytic agents of change. Before we explore how leaders at Airbnb solicited input from their community to refine Airbnb's purpose, vision, and brand, let's take a moment for you to reflect on your application of the information presented.

 YOUR TRAVEL PLANNING GUIDE

1. How consistently do you read, research, and study topics that might increase your awareness of human motivators?

2. How willingly do you explore ideas that may be at the edge of your thinking or comfort (for example, the factors that foster cult membership) in order to identify principles that can be constructively applied to business or life?

3. What global, national, or local thinkers or researchers inspire you? Have you reached out or will you reach out to them? If so, why? If not, why not?

4. What interests you on a par with Douglas Atkin's exploration of cults, communities, and movements or Chip Conley's application of needs theory? Where are you developing subject-matter expertise—particularly as it relates to the wants and needs of those you serve?

5. How could you apply Maslow's hierarchy of needs to the way you think about serving team members or customers?

6. How might the study of cultlike passion enhance the way you emotionally connect with your customers?

LISTENING FOR THE WHY

The philosopher Paul Tillich once said, "The first duty of love is to listen." I've modified Tillich's wisdom for leadership by suggesting that the first duty of leaders is to listen and the second is to listen more.

At Airbnb, listening involved asking team members, hosts, and guests (all facets of the Airbnb community) to share their thoughts on Airbnb's purpose, reason for existence, and the needs the brand can and does fulfill. Leaders were listening for Airbnb's "why."

In 2009, Simon Sinek's viral TED Talk titled *Start with Why*, and his book of the same name, sparked widespread interest among leaders who wanted to uncover the *why* of their brand. Unfortunately, as leaders sought to define the *why*, as opposed to the *what* or *how* of their business, many struggled to find a meaningful answer. As a consultant, I often see entrepreneurs craft a leader's rendition of the *why*. Frequently small business owners isolate themselves and contemplate the *why* of their businesses. Leaders in larger businesses often go away on retreats searching for their *why* by sifting through flipcharts filled with their own ideas and words. At Airbnb, however, the founders didn't seek a leader-generated *why*; instead, they wanted a *why* sourced by all facets of their community.

By reaching out to 485 employees, hosts, and guests, Airbnb garnered stories and data that clearly established Airbnb's *why*: "to create a world where anyone could belong anywhere." Ultimately, that *why* was shortened to read simply "Belong Anywhere."

In science, findings are accepted as truth when a consensus emerges from a convergence of results achieved across multiple research platforms. Using that same thinking, the truth of Belong Anywhere is reflected in a confluence of findings achieved through reading, partnership, and listening to their community. Airbnb's truth, or as I like to refer to it, *true north*, is to create a world where everyone can Belong Anywhere.

While many leaders never find their *true north*, *why*, or *brand essence*, even fewer leaders are able to share that *why* in ways that inspire, align, and drive action in the direction of a brand's true north. In a moment, we'll examine how leaders at Airbnb shared and sought to activate the Airbnb community to live a vision of global acceptance and belonging. Let's first consider your *why*.

 YOUR TRAVEL PLANNING GUIDE

1. How have you gone about exploring the *why* or *true north* of your business?

2. Does your *why* reflect a convergence of inputs (for example, the wants and needs of customers, the results of active listening to all stakeholders, research-based information, and the input of partners)?

3. Does your *true north* define your company's reason for being, or is it simply a description of *what* your business does or *how* it operates?

4. How aspirational, inspirational, and credible is your *true north* or *why*?

SHARING THE VISION AND BRAND

Chris Lehane, Airbnb's SVP of policy and communication, told me, "People face true global challenges—economic inequality, conflicts, climate. Given that these are global in nature, the only way we can successfully address these challenges is through a global response. However, today the question is being called as to whether we will have a closed world or an open world. We know a closed world leads to digital bubbles, walls, and travel bans. It is a world of isolationism, ultranationalism, and tribalism. An open world is a world where there is the freedom of movement of goods, ideas, and people. It is a world of trust, community, and belonging."

According to Chris, "Travel is fundamental to belonging. Confucius talked about traveling with an open heart. . . . And we know that since the first humans walked out of the Olduvai Gorge through the moment the first human walked on the moon, travel has always played an important role in advancing the human condition. Migration populated our planet."

Chris explained, "Immigration spread economic prosperity. Integration promoted diversity. Innovation expands our horizons. And exploration is about the future of our species. But what travel has done that is as important is support belonging. Pericles talked about *philoxenia*—the concept that Athens would welcome a stranger into their city-state—as a building block for a strong community. Not surprisingly, similar concepts exist around the world. In Afghanistan it is called *pashtunwali*. In South Africa it is *ubuntu*."

When speaking about how this connects to the mission at Airbnb, Chris reflects, "Brian has talked about how 99 percent of humans are alike and 99 percent of humans are good—and that humans from one culture spending time with humans from another place helps make that clear—especially when time is spent in someone's house. And because travel drives belonging that is needed for an open world, Airbnb's mission is that anyone can Belong Anywhere. But what this really spoke to was the fact that in 100,000 cities across 191 countries, a stranger knocked on a door and was welcomed into a home. In many cases, that guest and their host met, their families met, they spent time in their homes, they shared a meal, and after three or four days when the guest left, the guest and host were no longer strangers but friends." While researching this book, we routinely heard from guests and hosts who've maintained social contacts for years.

In keeping with Chris's comments, in 2014 when Brian Chesky announced Airbnb's vision to create a world where everyone can Belong Anywhere, Brian shared how those two words resonated with a universal yearning. He also announced a symbol of the vision, which would be incorporated into the Airbnb brand. That symbol, created in partnership with DesignStudio, a London-based design firm, was called the Bélo:

In announcing the Bélo, Brian Chesky shared:

We've created a symbol for us as a community. It's an iconic mark for our windows, our doors, and our shared values. It's a symbol that, like us, can belong wherever it happens to be. It's a symbol for people who want to try a new tea they've never heard of from a village they couldn't find on the map. It's a symbol for going where the locals go—the café that doesn't bother with a menu, the dance club hidden down a long alleyway, the art galleries that don't show up in the guidebooks. It's a symbol for people who want to welcome into their home new experiences, new cultures, and new conversations. We're proud to introduce the Bélo: the universal symbol of belonging.

It's noteworthy that the Bélo was designed to be a symbol—one inspired by a blend of images reflecting people, places, love, and Airbnb:

PEOPLE   PLACES   LOVE   AIRBNB

To create the Bélo, DesignStudio team members studied and immersed themselves in the Airbnb culture. This included visits to 13 cities across four continents. The DesignStudio team stayed with 18 hosts and noted all aspects of their hospitality experience. This group interviewed more than 120 Airbnb team members over three months. According to creatives at the DesignStudio, the Bélo project "set out to create a top-to-bottom transformation of the Airbnb brand to reflect the growing global audience." The Bélo was also created to be consistent with an approach espoused by German designer Kurt Weideman who said that a great symbol is "something you can draw in the sand with the toe."

The Bélo, which was incorporated into Airbnb's overall brand identity, represented a dramatic shift in Airbnb's overall brand imagery from this:

to this:

DesignStudio has suggested that the Bélo is "a community symbol that can be expressed differently by each community member and in every listing; it is not bound by language, culture or location. The end result is a symbol people feel compelled to share—one that accepts we are all different, one to wear with pride."

The Bélo and Belong Anywhere signified that Airbnb was *not* only in the people business, they were also in the belonging business. The launch of the Bélo and Airbnb's rebrand started a global conversation, one that had Airbnb trending for eight hours on Twitter. The next great challenge for leadership would be to move beyond the buzz of the launch and activate the potential of the Belong Anywhere vision.

ACTIVATING THE BRAND ACROSS ALL STAKEHOLDERS IN THE COMMUNITY

Airbnb leaders positioned their Belong Anywhere vision for success, but would that vision translate into action across the Airbnb host community? Leadership Professor John Kotter has been both a student of organizational change and a change effectiveness consultant for companies of all sizes. Writing for the *Harvard Business Review*, John observed, "The most general lesson to be learned from the more successful cases is that the change process goes through a series of phases that, in total, usually require a considerable length of time. Skipping steps creates only the illusion of speed and never produces a satisfying result. A second very general lesson is that critical mistakes in any of the phases can have a devastating impact, slowing momentum and negating hard-won gains." John outlines eight essential steps for transformational success that Airbnb's leaders essentially followed to ensure Belong Anywhere took hold:

1. Establish a sense of urgency.

2. Form a powerful coalition.

3. Create a vision.

4. Communicate the vision.

5. Empower others to act on the vision.

6. Plan for and create short-term wins.

7. Consolidate improvements to produce more change.

8. Institutionalize new approaches.

Up to now, we've reviewed how leaders at Airbnb acted with urgency to position the company as a people business. We've also discussed how they developed a coalition of thought leaders and stakeholders to guide the development of their vision. Brian Chesky's announcement in 2014 initiated the "communicate the vision" phase and provided context for the brand's symbol (the Bélo).

The remainder of this chapter will look at how Airbnb leaders facilitated movement from Kotter's "empower others" stage of change effectiveness to successfully "institutionalize new approaches" that make Belong Anywhere a priority in every Airbnb-related human interaction.

For Belong Anywhere and the Bélo to gain traction, Airbnb leaders needed to first drive awareness for the vision. They also needed to spark conversation about what it means to Belong Anywhere and help people associate belonging with the Bélo. As leaders, they needed to behave in accord with the vision and ultimately set expectations for the host community.

To help members of the Airbnb community understand Belong Anywhere and identify with the Bélo, Airbnb leaders deployed a wide array of tools. These included, but weren't limited to, the following:

- A one-minute, forty-five-second video (viewed well over a million times) introducing Belong Anywhere. (To view it yourself, please visit airbnbway.com/book-resources.)

- A platform called Create Airbnb, where people could create their own version of the Bélo (over 8,000 versions were crafted on the platform shortly after launch).

- A variety of marketing campaigns highlighting the vision and symbol (including merchandise, billboards, host meetups, and social media communications).

- A social challenge to create #onelessstranger. As Airbnb rang in 2015, Brian Chesky announced that Airbnb was sending $1 million to community members ($10 per person for 100,000 recipients). He asked those recipients to use the money to deliver a personal or creative act of kindness to fuel a global movement to help "rid the world of strangers." By sharing photos and stories of a kindness extended to someone who was once a stranger, the entire community was encouraged to take similar actions and translate those actions into the way they create belonging at Airbnb. The #onelessstranger actions were as varied as the hosts themselves, as exemplified by these social media posts:

Iona Macdonald @OniM... 19 Mar 2015
Kept meaning to do something with
@Airbnb's #OneLessStranger money;
now I have-The Island and the
Whales @kickstarter

Help finish The Island and the ...
kickstarter.com

Tools and initiatives in support of Belong Anywhere extended well beyond 2015. Airbnb leaders continually discuss, encourage, and celebrate actions that foster global belonging. (You will experience some of those stories and the lessons we can learn from them in Chapter 3.)

American psychologist Rollo May once said, "Communication leads to community . . . to understanding, intimacy, and mutual valuing." Airbnb leaders understand that they must view Belong Anywhere as a journey, not a destination. They must consistently commit time and resources to keep Airbnb's true north in the minds of those who deliver homes and experiences to guests. It is through the pursuit of this vision that the highest-level needs of travelers are met and a cultlike brand loyalty is achieved.

As you think about your own desired human experience, how consistently and continually are you sharing your vision? What diverse media resources do you deploy to enhance awareness, drive the conversation, and inspire action?

LEADERSHIP BEHAVIOR
AND BELONGING

The leaders at Airbnb are "all in" when it comes to sharing and living the Belong Anywhere vision. They also know they have the greatest control over how belonging is experienced by their employees.

If you are an employee of Airbnb, Belong Anywhere is reflected in leadership's encouragement of diversity, inclusion, and a "workplace where everyone feels welcome and all voices are heard." As such, Airbnb is transparent in posting the gender and ethnic diversity of its workforce on its website. Similarly, leaders encourage and support a wide array of employee groups (referred to as Airfinity groups) such as Airpride@, which has a mission of "keeping Airbnb an amazing place for LGBTQ people to work," or Veterans@, which "celebrates the contributions and sacrifices of Armed Forces veterans and supports veterans' causes internally and in the global community."

Leaders continue to examine and enhance the employee experience, always considering improvements through the lens of belonging. Areas of focus include everything from the way employees are recruited, selected, and developed, the design and layout of the physical work environment, and even the types of volunteer opportunities employees are afforded.

In writing about Airbnb's San Francisco headquarters for *Metropolis Magazine*, Eva Hagberg reflected on the welcoming nature of the physical environment and how it blends elements of work and home:

> Together, the parts are emblematic of . . . a new spatial blurring: one in which features that used to be considered part of home—a kitchen, a library, a nerd cave, a place to

nap—are now integrated into both the space and practice known as work. . . . Airbnb employees have the freedom to work wherever they want. The 72,000-square-foot facility contains few fixed work spaces. . . . Rather than a sense of individual ownership over corner offices or middle cubes, everyone's physical location feels random, ad hoc, and completely improvisational.

In addition to creating a physical environment that fosters belonging, founders and leaders have prioritized the development and growth of the Airbnb culture. Jenna Cushner, the director of Airbnb's Ground Control team told me, "My team was created very early in Airbnb's history, and it sprung from the deep commitment of our founders to drive our culture to ensure that we maintained success as we scaled. Our job is to help our employees build connections to our community, to our mission, and to our values. Through vigilance we must make sure that although we are a global community and company, everyone feels a part of Airbnb while also expressing important elements of their local cultures in offices around the world."

Dave O'Neil, the Ground Control team's values and culture senior manager, adds, "Through the years we have refined our values and the behaviors that support them. We've done this through a participatory process. We took a representative sample of our entire team across function, geography, gender, ethnicity, and so on, and we talked to more than 300 people. We also did a simple exercise to get them to describe the similarities between themselves and Airbnb. We used a Venn diagram to get a sense of which values are truly shared among stars on our teams. The process tightened the original values of our founders down to four." Those four values are the following:

1. **Champion the mission.** A value that highlights each employee's responsibility to live and advocate on behalf of the Belong Anywhere mission.

2. **Be a host.** More on this in Chapter 6.

3. **Embrace the adventure.** This encompasses being curious, asking for help, demonstrating an ability to grow, taking responsibility for and learning from mistakes, and bringing joy and optimism to work.

4. **Be a cereal entrepreneur.** The word "cereal" is a reference to the very early days of Airbnb when the founders creatively purchased inexpensive breakfast cereal and repackaged it in politically themed boxes—selling them for $40 per box during the 2008 Democratic Convention. That innovative approach garnered much-needed publicity and revenue for the fledgling enterprise. This value reflects the importance of creative scrappiness.

Dave notes that these four values, and the specific behaviors needed to live them, play an important role in selecting and onboarding new Airbnb employees. Dave says, "Candidates go through something we call our 'core values interview process.' It involves cross-functional interview teams and removes any sort of reporting line conflicts. During this interview, cross-functional teams spend a lot of time understanding a candidate's motivation to join Airbnb in relation to our mission. We are far less interested in how frequently candidates use Airbnb as hosts or guests and far more interested in how well they understand, fit with, and are motivated by our mission and values. We then spend a week during onboarding diving deeply into our mission and values. Fortunately, we have an experiential product so during that onboarding process new hires interact with an experienced Airbnb host and often go on Airbnb experiences."

Other belonging components of the employee experience include Airbnb's Global Citizenship program, where Airbnb employees are provided four hours a month to volunteer and give back to their communities. Frequently, these volunteer opportunities occur in partnership with the larger host community.

In support of a Belong Anywhere workplace, Airbnb leaders have made a number of public commitments, including these:

- **White House Equal Pay Pledge:** To identify and promote best practices for closing the national wage gap

- **White House Tech Inclusion Pledge:** To make the Airbnb workforce more representative of the demographics of the United States

Airbnb leaders are not only willing to make commitments to foster belonging. They also ask hosts to commit to inclusion and belonging.

SETTING EXPECTATIONS FOR THE HOST COMMUNITY

Creating Airbnb's inclusive and belonging culture has not been without challenges. In 2015 Harvard Business School researchers Benjamin Edelman, Michael Luca, and Dan Svirsky released a working paper that would later be published in *American Economic Journal: Applied Economics*. These researchers reported a disturbing finding regarding conscious and unconscious biases at play in the Airbnb booking relationship. Specifically, they found that "applications from guests with distinctively African-American names" were "16 percent less likely to be accepted relative to identical guests with distinctively White names."

In a 2016 email to all users of the platform, Airbnb's CEO Brian Chesky took responsibility for the company being "slow to address these problems." Through a series of communications, Airbnb leaders announced how they would go about educating hosts and guests about bias and about the "belonging" behaviors they expected from the Airbnb community. Seeking consultation from former US Attorney General Eric Holder and the former head of the American Civil Liberties Union, Laura Murphy, Airbnb took a series of actions in support of Belong Anywhere.

Starting in 2016, Airbnb began asking all hosts to sign a community commitment agreeing to behavior of equal treatment for all. It is a commitment every host must make today:

> Agreeing to this commitment will affect your use of Airbnb, so we wanted to give you a heads up about it.
>
> *What is the Community Commitment?* You commit to treat everyone—regardless of race, religion, national origin, ethnicity, disability, sex, gender identity, sexual orientation, or age—with respect, and without judgment or bias.
>
> *How do I accept the commitment?* On or after November 1, we'll show you the commitment when you log in to or open the Airbnb website, mobile or tablet app, and we'll automatically ask you to accept.
>
> *What if I decline the commitment?* If you decline the commitment, you won't be able to host or book using Airbnb, and you have the option to cancel your account. Once your account is canceled, future booked trips will be

canceled. You will still be able to browse Airbnb, but you won't be able to book any reservations or host any guests.

What if I have feedback about the commitment? We welcome your feedback about the Community Commitment and all of our nondiscrimination efforts. Feel free to read more about the commitment. You can also reach out to us at allbelong@airbnb.com.

The Airbnb Team

In a policy referred to as Open Doors, Airbnb announced, "If a Guest anywhere in the world feels like they have been discriminated against in violation of our policy—in trying to book a listing, having a booking canceled, or in any other interaction with a host—we will find that Guest a similar place to stay if one is available on Airbnb, or if not, we will find them an alternative accommodation elsewhere."

Having a signed agreement increases desired follow-up behavior, and the open-door policy gives guests redress when they have been harmed, but what happens when hosts violate their community agreement?

Author Bob Proctor once said, "Accountability is the glue that ties commitment to the result." In the case of Airbnb, leaders hold bad actors accountable in the rare but pernicious situations in which people have felt unwelcome. In March 2018, Alan McEwen, writing for the Scottish *Daily Record*, offered an example of one such action that prompted Airbnb's firm response: "A landlord has been banned for life from Airbnb after posting a sickening note barring Asian guests. Stephen Sheppard advertised a room in his two-bedroom Edinburgh flat with the message 'Please don't book if you are Asian' on the booking website. Sheppard, 31, later admitted making the posting—saying he'd had 'bad experiences' with Asian guests." Airbnb's response (banning the host for life) reflects a decisive action needed to curb behavior that is diametrically opposed to the Airbnb vision. In Chapter 4, you will see not only how Airbnb reacts to discrimination but how they are being proactive in preventing similar actions.

To be in the people business, leaders need to be visionary, inspire others, and drive accountability. They must also assess their own actions along the way.

How are you leading the vision for your organization and, in the process, considering the broad needs of your team members? What commitments have you made and sought on behalf of your desired experience? How do you hold colleagues accountable for acts that violate the needs and integrity of others?

In Chapter 3, you will hear from hosts and guests as they share what Belong Anywhere means to them. You will also explore how belonging is created in service experiences throughout the Airbnb community. Moreover, you will gain insights on the business and interpersonal impact that comes from fostering belonging and will understand the behaviors needed to "create belonging" in your business.

POINTS OF INTEREST
AS YOU MAKE IT A PEOPLE BUSINESS

➜ Airbnb's leaders studied human nature, sought partnerships with thought leaders and change agents, listened to stakeholders, and defined the *why* of their business (to create a world where everyone can Belong Anywhere).

➜ Those leaders also created a sense of purposeful urgency for the vision and shared the vision effectively using a multitude of communication and engagement methods.

→ Leaders held themselves accountable for making the vision come to life for those they served, including employees, hosts, and guests.

→ When faced with data that showed community behavior was inconsistent with the vision, Airbnb leaders sought consultation and developed policies (including seeking a written Community Commitment) in support of the vision.

→ When violations of the Community Commitment surface, leaders evaluate the situation and take necessary and swift actions to support the vision.

Create Belonging

*I long, as does every human being, to be
at home wherever I find myself.*
—Maya Angelou,
bestselling writer and poet

In a 1921 article for *Vanity Fair*, Robert Benchley observed that there are two classes of people: those who divide people into two classes and those who do not. Hosts who are aligned with Airbnb's vision—to create a world where anyone can belong anywhere—see no divisions when it comes to those they serve.

In this chapter, you will learn from Airbnb hosts who passionately embrace the concept of Belong Anywhere. They will share insights and lessons they've learned as they seek to foster guest perceptions of belonging. You will also hear from guests who feel Airbnb hosts treat them like friends or family—not like strangers seeking lodging. Moreover, you will see how fostering belonging creates customer engagement as well as how you and your team can develop inclusive service mindsets.

BELONGING AND A SERVICE MINDSET

In Chapter 2, you read Airbnb CEO Brian Chesky's perspective on what Belong Anywhere means to him, and you saw tools (for example, the Bélo, videos, and social media campaigns) designed to communicate that vision throughout the host community. You've seen accountability elements, such as Airbnb's Community Commitment, developed to encourage and assure hosts create belonging. What you haven't seen is the degree to which hosts embrace the vision and what it looks like when they do.

In this chapter, I will provide you with examples of hosts who are demonstrating outstanding guest experiences dedicated to creating belonging so you can constructively apply Airbnb host lessons in your business. Given that there are millions of hosted experiences and homes on the Airbnb platform, there is variability with regard to how much each host embraces the ethos of Airbnb. Fortunately, prospective travelers can evaluate the quality of past belonging experiences by looking at a host's reviews and ratings. (I will discuss the role of reviews and ratings extensively in Chapters 4 and 5 as we explore the theme of trust.)

To better understand how this sense of belonging can be created, my team and I spoke with countless guests and hosts and relied heavily on the input of a subset of Airbnb hosts known as Superhosts. The designation Superhost reflects a formal Airbnb title earned by individuals who maintain guest ratings of 4.8 or higher on a 1 to 5 scale. These Superhosts must respond to booking requests within 24 hours at least 90 percent of the time and book at least 10 stays a year. They also must honor every reservation request they receive—with the exception of a few well-defined extenuating circumstances. In essence, Superhosts must excel in delivering the highest-quality experiences and embrace the Belong Anywhere vision.

When I refer to hosts or Superhosts in the chapters ahead, I am talking about hundreds of people with whom we've interacted and not the entire universe of Airbnb hosts. The large community of hosts and Superhosts we met represent a wide range of ages (from 24 to 75). Some hosts offer experiences on the Airbnb platform like sourdough bread making; however, most of them list homes priced anywhere from $21 per night for a private (spare) room with a shared bath in Seville, Spain, to $342 a night for a private stay in an entire one-bedroom, one-bath apartment in Rome.

Despite their differences, these hosts and Superhosts have embraced Belong Anywhere in the context of a generally positive view of humankind. While some hosts have expressed their longstanding view that strangers were basically "good" and all people warranted respect, other hosts have said they were somewhat cynical, at least at first. Aroha Warburton, a Superhost who lists a private one-bedroom, one-bath in her apartment in South Brisbane Australia, noted, "I initially took an interest in hosting on Airbnb because of the economic benefits. I probably entered with some trepidation because of all the bad news you hear these days. However, hosting guests has given me a renewed faith in human nature. I have hosted hundreds of guests to date, and it has changed me for the better. I'm far more comfortable with people, and I have come to believe my life's purpose is to serve others."

Aroha's emerging perspective that life's purpose can be found through service reflects a common quality shared by outstanding Airbnb hosts. I refer to this shared phenomenon as an authentic "service mindset." This mindset is a learned or developed tendency to view belonging, caring, and compassion as essential to the wellbeing of both the service receiver and the service provider. Clearly not everyone who is in a service role possesses a service mindset.

Mindsets are shaped by an individual's personality as well as by life events. Some people are distrustful of customers or strangers and tolerate them as a necessary evil, while others take a very mercenary approach to service—to provide it as a means to an end. Fortunately, a mindset can be learned and adapted. If you view yourself as being in a service business, it's imperative that you either work to develop an authentic service mindset or consider a line of work better suited for you.

Efforts to consciously choose a service mindset usually reap self-sustaining rewards. For example, extending positive regard to others usually results in their acting favorably in return. Moreover, diverse research studies show that authentic service mindsets (and the actions that follow from them) produce business and interpersonal benefits. From a business perspective, the benefits of a service mindset include but are not limited to increases in:

- Revenue and profits

- Growth

- Customer retention

- Referrals

From an overall life perspective, positive effects include:

- Increased happiness

- Lower blood pressure

- A longer life

- An enriched sense of purpose

Hosts often report that they've developed or strengthened their service mindset in pursuit of Airbnb's Belong Anywhere vision. As such, they often define Belong Anywhere as part of their commitment to serve. For four years, Superhost Antonella Brugnola has listed a two-bedroom, 1½-bath apartment that sleeps five in Milan, Italy. Antonella describes what Belong Anywhere means to her: "It is how I want to serve others. Belong Anywhere means that guests look for a place to stay but find a place where they matter. It means helping a guest go from feeling the uneasiness of being in an unfamiliar place to feeling completely comfortable. For me, it means I must make sure my home is *their* home."

Peggy J. Sturdivant, a Superhost who accommodates up to seven guests in two bedrooms of her four-bedroom home near the University of Southern California in Los Angeles, describes Belong Anywhere as taking responsibility for her guests: "It means when anyone seeks a bed in my home, he or she will be treated with respect, care, and kindness."

Merrydith Callegari, an Airbnb Superhost from Hobart, Tasmania (an island state off Australia's southern coast), says, "Belong Anywhere is about connecting with guests based on our similarities and serving them with dignity and appreciation. It is about understanding that humans share similar hopes, fears, and aspirations, as well as realizing the things that divide us are relatively small when compared to the things that unite us."

Given these service mindsets regarding Belong Anywhere, it is not surprising that Airbnb hosts demonstrate commonalities in their "belonging" behaviors. This includes ways they seek to:

1. Actively listen

2. Practice empathy

3. Attentively welcome

4. Create inviting environments

5. Read the invisible signs

Throughout this chapter you'll experience examples of each of these belonging behaviors, and you'll be provided opportunities to explore ways to drive each of them in your business.

ACTIVELY LISTEN

Airbnb hosts and Superhosts understand that relationships must start with listening, so guests can know they are being heard. In his book *Caring Enough to Hear and Be Heard*, author David Augsburger stated, "Being heard is so close to being loved that for the average person they are almost indistinguishable." Once people feel they are heard, they can feel belonging. Once they feel belonging, a relationship can flourish. Airbnb guest Sophie Herbert explains:

> I was a medical student from the UK who had the opportunity to study abroad and work in Australian hospitals for five weeks. I decided to make the trip on my own, and I was a bit nervous. I'd stayed in Airbnbs before but never as a solo traveler and never for this long. I researched a number of seemingly excellent options but wanted to ask some questions to the hosts at the properties I was considering. I imagine my questions were a bit silly: some involved things like how easy it would be for me to get to my school and work locations, and others were about the prevalence of spiders, snakes, or sharks nearby their respective properties. One Superhost stood out in her kindness and speed of response. I took her listening skills and candor as signs that she would care about me when I was in her home. I felt a natural connection with her, even though all of our initial contacts had occurred online. As you might guess, my actual stay exceeded every expectation resulting

in an unparalleled belonging experience and a lasting connection and friendship.

Prearrival listening routinely involves asking open-ended questions to receive information that can be used to better serve customers when they arrive. For example, when I booked an Airbnb home in Westcliffe, Colorado, a small town nestled in the Sangre de Cristo Mountain range, my Airbnb host, Charley, immediately confirmed my booking and sent a message to me on the Airbnb platform asking open-ended questions (who, what, when, tell me about) to garner information about the purpose of my visit and my familiarity with the region. Based on my responses, Charley wrote:

> Welcome Joseph,
>
> This is a great house for a family gathering.... Sounds like you know the area. Let me know if I can help you in any way with your trip planning. You might want to search "visit Custer County." That website was developed by our local tourism board and lists upcoming events, activities, itineraries, and so on.
>
> We will follow up a few days before your arrival with check-in instructions.
>
> Charley

That initial discussion started a series of brief exchanges that significantly enhanced my ability to plan a memorable stay. Moreover, I felt that Charley genuinely wanted to understand me, my needs, and my desired experience outcomes. In short, I felt "heard" and eager to meet Charley.

Superhost Adrienne Penny, who lists a one-bedroom, one-bath rainforest beach studio in Noosa, Australia (southern Queensland's

Sunshine Coast), notes, "Conversations on the platform prior to a visit set the foundation for an ongoing and developing connection. As a host, I can ask a few select open-ended questions to better understand what my guests are looking for during their visit and can anticipate what I might do to address those needs. Thanks to these mostly text-based interactions, I'm not starting my relationship when my guests arrive. I am continuing a relationship we began online."

Adrienne, and other Superhosts like her, report that in addition to asking questions on the Airbnb communication platform, hosts also leverage additional previsit information to create relevant welcoming and belonging experiences. For example, host Emanuela Marino, who lists a one-bedroom, one-bath apartment in Rome, adds, "Airbnb guests are asked to provide profile information when they sign up on the platform. I always take the time to review guest profiles, and I find them helpful. For me, creating belonging involves taking an interest in the uniqueness of the person I am serving. Often when I am reviewing guest profiles, I start to think about ways I can customize their arrival experience or personalize some other element of their stay."

While service providers don't always have the benefit of having a customer profile available to them in advance of customer interactions, all too often they don't invest energy to find information that *is* available. Most of us can think of a time when we went to a service appointment only to meet with someone who hadn't looked at our file, our history in a customer relationship management database, or recent email exchanges. Alternatively, we likely remember times when we could have done additional preliminary research before engaging in a sales or service transaction (for example, we might have run a Google search or reviewed the person's LinkedIn profile). Unlike Emanuela, we missed an opportunity to extend the courtesy of showing our interest. Whether our queries are through questions directed at those we serve or through efforts to learn about them in other ways, the goal should be the same: to gain information that helps us understand our customers and their needs.

Understanding what people want and need is not an easy task, and it relies heavily on our communication effectiveness. Many Airbnb hosts report that serving international travelers has helped them make fewer assumptions about what they think they understand. Writing on the Airbnb Community Center, one host shared how a few seemingly common words were misconstrued. A prospective guest messaged a host stating she had some marked similarities in background with the host and she would be traveling on a limited budget. The guest ended the communication with a question about availability for a specific date. The host promptly responded, "Yes, the cottage is free then! I'll preapprove your trip. . . . We can firm up details closer to the time. For now, be assured your lodging is taken care of." Later the guest expressed displeasure when she found out she would be charged for the upcoming stay, noting that the host had said the cottage was "free" and the "lodging was taken care of."

To reduce the inevitable confusion that comes from concise communication and the complications of language differences, Airbnb hosts develop active communication skills such as paraphrasing and clarification seeking. Many of these skills are developed with the assistance of a web platform called the Airbnb Community Center. This platform serves as a place for hosts to seek advice, share stories, and learn best practices.

Laura Chambers, general manager of Airbnb's Homes Hosts, described the Airbnb Community Center by noting, "It's this special online place where hosts share credible information and advice with other hosts who are doing what they are doing every single day. We are excited to facilitate the forum and also use it for communication from and to our host community." Laura notes that she regularly posts on the Airbnb Community Center platform:

"Recently I celebrated Superhost week, discussed upcoming changes that will affect hosts, and congratulated people who've become Superhosts. My time in the Community Center involves creating blogs and responding to comments. It's not unusual for me to spend an hour and a half going through host comments from people who've reached out to me or asked questions."

Laura adds that she and many other Airbnb employees spend quite a lot of time online at the Community Center: "Often we are just chatting as people, not as representatives of the Airbnb brand. I am just Laura when I'm on the Community Center, not Laura Chambers the general manager of Homes Hosts. The Community Center is a place for celebrations and for addressing challenges. The other day I was online with an 85-year-old host who told me that hosting was his way of staying connected to the world. For us, the Community Center platform is an important way for Airbnb to stay connected with the host community and for them to connect with one another."

In the Community Center, the topic of communication effectiveness is often addressed. For example, hosts discuss topics like the need to restate what they've heard or read from guests so they can verify understanding. In the process of restating, they also give the guest an opportunity to identify any information that might not have been captured accurately. Hosts talk about the importance of asking follow-up questions to ensure that they are *not* making unwarranted assumptions. Superhost Antonella Brugnola suggests, "Communication is important, and it fuels belonging. For example, I host many Chinese guests, because I live near Chinatown in Milan. I only speak English and Italian, so I've asked a friend of mine to translate for me. That includes providing my house rules and other information in Chinese."

Superhost Majo Liendro, who lists a two-bed, one-bath property in Salta, Argentina, notes most of her guests speak either

Spanish or English, but she said that when she hosted guests who spoke only French, she used the Internet: "Google Translate helped us with the communication." Similarly, Superhosts Dave and Silke Monnie from Portland, Oregon, report: "We had a French family stay with us for six weeks this past summer. Neither of the parents spoke much English, so we spent a lot of time interacting through the Google Translate app. The couple would speak into their phone, and the app would listen to their voice and immediately translate French to English and vice a versa. It's remarkable how technology enabled us to transcend culture and language."

Effective communication during early service interactions predicts later relationship strength, ease of serving customers, and customer loyalty. Researchers Sharma Neeru and Paul Patterson found that "communication effectiveness directly impacts relationship commitment. . . . Further, regular communications can help develop a sense of closeness and ease in the relationship, and be instrumental in building emotional and social bonds, thus making the relationship more resistant to the occasional problems that inevitably develop from time to time. Social and emotional bonds have been shown in past research to present a psychological barrier to exiting the relationship." That same research specifically referenced the communication behaviors discussed in the chapter: active listening skills such as open-ended questions, paraphrasing, and clarifying. Neeru and Patterson's research also identified an additional skill necessary to produce strong customer-provider relationships. That skill is empathy.

PRACTICE EMPATHY

The word *empathy* has been in common use for about a century and likely derived from the German word *einfühlung*, which roughly translates to "feeling into." Empathy is essential for effective service delivery and is defined as a key component of emotional intelligence quotient (EQ).

In an article for *Medium* titled "The Ultimate Guide to Emotional Intelligence to Be Happy and Successful in a Brain-Dead World," Prakhar Verma highlights research showing strong links between EQ, career success, personal development, confidence, better relationships, and happiness. In its simplest form, empathy is an awareness of the emotional state of others. At an elevated level, empathy involves attempting to assume the frame of reference of other people so you can understand their feelings, thoughts, and attitudes. Cognitive neuroscientists have shown that when we feel pain, we activate the same neural pathways that are activated when we observe others who are suffering.

In the context of Airbnb, empathy requires hosts to think about what it would feel like if they were traveling to a city where they didn't know anyone or to imagine situations in which they were vulnerable, dependent on others, or were encountering language barriers. Host Emanuela Marino shares, "Since I have a Facebook group with 1,400 hosts from Rome, I hear a lot of stories about how hosts put themselves in the place of guests and do what the hosts would want to be done for them if they were traveling. In Rome, we've had many instances where a guest became ill while on vacation and where Airbnb hosts have served as translators. Who would want to be in a hospital where people don't understand you, or you can't understand them?"

Superhost Cynthia Mackey, who rents an upstairs bedroom in a home she owns in Oakland, California, describes how she specifically strives to place herself in the role of her guests: "I often have visitors coming to see grandchildren. Since many of them have adult children who can't take time off of work, I think about unique experiences those guests can have with their grandchildren during the workday. If I find out someone is visiting on vacation, I try to get a sense of what interests him or her so I can think about what regional activities would best fit someone like that person."

Airbnb hosts understand that empathy is not only the foundation for the host-guest relationship but also the foundation for all relationships. Far too often, service professionals fail to take the time to "feel into" the customer's vantage point and maintain a focus on what they might be thinking, feeling, and wanting. When people-focused companies help their team members strengthen their ability to empathize, those businesses are well positioned to take action that results in customer belonging, engagement, and loyalty. Before we explore other ways that Airbnb hosts enhance belonging and create the foundation for service excellence, let's take a moment to examine opportunities for you to craft your service mindset and active listening skills, as well as to practice empathy on behalf of those you serve.

 ## YOUR TRAVEL PLANNING GUIDE

1. How would you describe your team's overall view of human nature? How does that view affect the way you and your team engage in service relationships? Since service mindsets are not fixed, consider discussing existing attitudes with the goal of fueling an authentic commitment to serve (for example, helping people discuss and shift from mindsets like "customers are a means to an end" to "customers should be celebrated"). Also, consider discussing the personal and business benefits that come from choosing a service mindset.

2. Do you agree with David Augsburger's contention that being heard is "so close to being loved that for the average person

they are almost indistinguishable?" If so, how does that shape your behavior as a listener?

3. What percentage of the time do you and your team ask open-ended questions and actively listen for responses by paraphrasing and asking follow-up clarification questions? What goals will you set for yourself to increase your percentage of active listening over the weeks ahead?

4. Think about a high-value customer segment. Based on what you know about them, what do you think occurs during their typical day? What challenges and joys might they regularly experience? What might they need, think, and feel as they seek and receive service at each stage of their journey with you and your company? Strive to maintain their perspective and discuss insights as a team.

ATTENTIVELY WELCOME

According to Richard Shapiro, founder and president of The Center For Client Retention (TCFCR), within the first 10 seconds of arriving in a store, a customer decides whether they will stay or leave. If the customer isn't greeted in that short time, there is skyrocketing likelihood he or she will pivot and go. Similarly, Princeton researchers found that decisions about attractiveness, likeability, trustworthiness, competence, and aggression are made within one-tenth of a second. First impressions do matter, and customers expect to be greeted promptly.

Airbnb hosts certainly understand the opportunity they have to connect when a guest arrives. Peter Kwan, a Superhost who first listed the lower level of his San Francisco home in 2011, says, "My favorite part of hosting is greeting people. I enjoy welcoming them to my home. Quickly I ask about their journey, their immediate needs, and how I can assist them based on their plans in San Francisco. I am able to show them the layout of the house and make sure they are comfortable." Superhost Peggy J. Sturdivant adds, "I want to greet all of my guests with a smile when they arrive. I'll make a point to stay up even if they are arriving at 1:00 in the morning. I want them to know that someone cares that they made it safely. I want to make sure each guest is welcomed properly." Superhost Adrienne Penny shares, "Not only do I strive to create a sense of belonging in the way I welcome my guests, but I also look for ways to be of immediate assistance such as offering my empty hands to carry their luggage."

Linda Bonugli, a Superhost from St. Petersburg, Florida, notes, "My husband and I became interested in hosting on Airbnb after having so many positive travel experiences as guests. When we began hosting, we wanted guests to have a person-to-person welcome and not simply gain access through a lockbox. We think a personal authentic greeting makes for an elevated travel experience." Warm, authentic greetings foster a sense of belonging for your customers, as does an arrival experience that is as easy as possible. Part of that ease occurs when you attend to the details of your customer's arrival environment.

CREATE INVITING ENVIRONMENTS

It's difficult for someone to feel he or she belongs in an experience or home if little to no effort has been invested in preparing for that guest's arrival. This lack of preparation can be reflected in haphazard cleaning, poor communication prior to the guest's arrival, or not allowing sufficient time between guest bookings (more on these topics in Chapters 6 and 7).

Superhost Javier Lasuncion, who lists his one-bedroom, one-bath home in Barcelona, Spain, notes, "I am here to receive guests, make them welcome, and let them know they are appreciated. I can say those words to them, but for guests to truly feel those things, they must see my intentions become real in my actions. Guests will know if a welcome is genuine when they look at the physical condition of the home. When I attend to details in their room, I am saying *you are a special guest*. If I didn't make my home meticulous and ready for the guests, all welcoming words will ring hollow."

Similarly, Superhost Louise Gotting, who lists a one-bedroom, one-bath luxury apartment near Brisbane, Australia, notes, "I want guests to have the cleanliness of luxury hotels with a homelike quality that hotels can't create. I am a bit obsessive when it comes to cleaning because I think cleanliness speaks volumes about how much you care about a guest's arrival."

Unlike all other Airbnb hosts mentioned in this chapter, Kerrie Dymnycz does not host her home for overnight stays. She hosts a sourdough-bread–making experience held in the kitchen of her home in Brisbane, Australia. Kerrie shares, "I want people to walk into this bread-making experience and know I have been anticipating their arrival. I want my home to feel warm and inviting, have all the necessary ingredients in place, and share my eagerness to put our hands in dough together."

Host Emanuela Marino enhances her personal welcome by adding a visual representation of belonging in the form of a map. "Belong Anywhere means that we are one race, and there should be no boundaries. So, I have a beautiful map in my home that shows the shape of continents but does not have boundary markers. During their stay, I encourage guests to put a pin in the map signifying their journey to this wonderful part of our shared world."

Airbnb hosts understand the importance of a positive arrival experience and an inviting physical environment. Impressions formed when your customers first interact with you will set the stage for whether they will ultimately feel respected, valued, and accepted. How much effort are you and your team expending on a welcome, arrival, or "you belong here" experience? Whether, in person or online, is every customer greeted every time with enthusiasm and warmth? Do you make extra effort to create a physical environment where your customers feel welcome and special?

READ THE INVISIBLE SIGNS

During an interview for CBS's *60 Minutes*, Danny Meyer, legendary restaurateur and author of the book *Setting the Table*, emphasized that "everyone is walking around life wearing an invisible sign that says, 'Make me feel important,' and your job is to understand the size of the font of this invisible sign and how brightly it's lit. So, make me feel important by leaving me alone. Make me feel important by letting me tell you everything I know about food. It's our job to read that sign and to deliver the experience that that person needs." Danny Meyer's invisible-sign analogy encapsulates the refined art of customer experience excellence—reading the cues of your customer.

Airbnb hosts develop skills to infer and read the imaginary signs being displayed by their guests. Superhost Aroha Warburton shares, "When I first started out, I had a lovely girl come and stay. She booked a couple of nights and for two full days stayed in her room. I was a bit worried that she was not comfortable in my home but sensed she just needed to be left alone." Aroha reports that on the last night of her guest's stay, the woman came out of her room, and she and Aroha had a lengthy conversation. "During that talk, she expressed such gratitude for me giving her space because she'd just completed six rough but rewarding months in the Australian Outback. She told me that it was dirty and dry and that she needed a couple of days to be comfortable and get relaxed before she caught a plane back to the United States. In my home, she apparently spent her time soaking in the bath in the ensuite and literally just enjoyed comfort, cleanliness, beauty, and a lack of interruptions. I then realized that my job wasn't to entertain guests but to read their cues."

Similarly, Superhosts Bryan and Charlotte Chaney, who list several renovated historic buildings such as the Barbara Fritchie House in downtown Frederick, Maryland, add, "We just hand-delivered towels to guests this morning, but often guests signal that they'd prefer little if any interaction. We strive to listen to what our guests tell us about their preferences but also seek to infer what they are communicating nonverbally. To the best of our ability, we use our intuition to deliver an experience for them."

Sometimes reading cues means a host should actively and directly engage guests. Superhost Peter Kwan says:

> In my listing, I tell my guests that I live very close to Chinatown in San Francisco and that I go very frequently to do my shopping there, so if they want to come with me, they are very welcome. Sometimes, I sense an interest in joining me but a reluctance to impose . . . so I make the offer very clear. Frequently, the reluctance melts away, and I take them to the stores where local Chinese people shop for our fruits, vegetables, live seafood, live poultry, and other items. From time to time we'll even have a dim sum lunch together. When I sense interest and restate my offer, guests often allow me to show them parts of Chinatown that tourists don't normally see. It is an honor and pleasure when I can address an interest that guests are initially hesitant to share.

In order to read invisible signs like *give me privacy, bring me towels,* or *take me to Chinatown's local markets,* hosts and all of us who create customer experiences must constantly work on nonverbal communication skills.

Customer care comes in many forms. Sometimes it involves doing things for the customer, while other times it involves empowering customers to do things for themselves. There are times when excellent service requires only taking time to listen or "be with" a customer, or learning and respecting a customer's desire to shop, browse, or be left alone.

For two Airbnb guests, caring came in the form of offering comfort during a tumultuous time. Those guests, Rob and Debi Hertert, are Airbnb hosts themselves, and they were attending a 2015 Airbnb conference in Paris. Debi and Rob were staying with Airbnb Superhosts Etienne and Sylvie Couvreur in Monmarte. Upon returning to Etienne and Sylvie's Airbnb at the end of the first day of the conference, Rob and Debi noticed that Etienne's phone began pinging with texts. During the conversation they began learning about the nearly simultaneous terrorist attacks occurring that evening at Parisian restaurants, bars, a stadium, and a concert hall. They experienced the horror of being in a city where 130 people had just died and hundreds more were wounded. Etienne and Sylvie translated French television reports for Rob and Debi, and the two couples stayed up until 3 a.m.

Debi noted, "We FaceTimed people back home to let them know we were okay. We found ourselves crying with Etienne and Sylvie as we were united in our horror." The next day, Debi reported, Paris was essentially closed, and people were home in mourning. Debi added, "We considered leaving the country early, but Etienne and Sylvie were determined to help us not leave Paris without some joy amid the pain."

That afternoon Etienne and Sylvie made lunches for an outing they planned for the next day. Etienne picks up the story there: "Sylvie and I decided to take Debi and Rob in safety to our country home located in the Impressionist Valley. We introduced them to the history and beautiful landscapes overlooking the Seine Valley."

After Etienne and Sylvie served their guests a sumptuous four-course lunch, the couples drove back along the French countryside, and their hosts treated them to an authentic Moroccan dinner at a restaurant owned by a friend.

From Etienne's perspective, "Airbnb gave us the opportunity to make new friends out of a nightmare." Debi concluded, "We left Paris with hugs and tears knowing we had made life-long friends. Tragedy brought us together, but our shared joy of life, people, and traveling keeps us in contact even today. That is the special kind of care I've come to know through Airbnb."

At Airbnb, as is the case with all businesses, the guest or customer is the final judge of efforts to create belonging, welcoming, or extraordinary experiences. In this chapter, Airbnb hosts have offered insights on the behaviors necessary to initiate "creating belonging." Like any guidance, it is only as good as one's willingness to heed it. So, how willing are you to enhance skills to actively listen, practice empathy, attentively welcome, create inviting environments, and read nonverbal cues?

If your efforts result in customers feeling they are welcome or they "belong" with you, they will share positive stories, make future purchases, and refer family and friends. When done well, the belonging behaviors shared by Airbnb hosts will lead to a bond essential to all human relationships and ultimately sustain our next theme: trust!

POINTS OF INTEREST AS
YOU CREATE BELONGING

→ A service mindset reflects learned or developed tendencies to view belonging, caring, and compassion as essential to both the well-being of the service receiver and the service provider.

→ Mindsets are shaped by an individual's personality as well as by life events, and they can be adapted.

→ Service mindsets (and the actions that follow from them) produce marked interpersonal and business benefits such as increased happiness, longevity, a greater sense of purpose, profits, customer retention, and referrals.

→ To reduce the inevitable confusion that comes from varied communication challenges, it is important to develop active communication skills such as using open-ended questions, paraphrasing, and seeking clarification.

→ Effective communication during early service interactions predicts later relationship strength, ease of serving customers, and customer loyalty.

→ In its simplest form, empathy is an awareness of the emotional state of others. At an elevated level, empathy involves assuming the frame of reference of other people so you can understand their feelings, thoughts, and attitudes.

→ Research has shown that within the first 10 seconds of arriving at a retail store, customers are deciding if they will stay or leave. If customers aren't greeted in that short time, there is likelihood they will pivot and go. Similarly, Princeton researchers found that decisions about attractiveness, like-ability, trustworthiness, competence, and aggressiveness are made within a tenth of a second. First impressions do matter, and customers expect to be greeted promptly.

→ It's difficult for clients to feel a sense of belonging with your company if little to no effort has been invested in preparing for their arrival. Enthusiastic anticipation and attention to de-tails should be prioritized.

→ Customers carry invisible signs. The refined art of customer experience excellence involves reading those signs. It re-quires the ability to understand nonverbal communication.

PART II

trust

Design for
Trust and Safety

Trusting you is my decision.
Proving me right is your choice.
—Unknown

Normally, we think about trust as something to be earned. However, in this chapter we will explore trust in the context of "design." As you'll recall from Chapter 1, Airbnb's cofounders Joe Gebbia and Brian Chesky graduated from design school. That educational experience shaped their perspective on the importance of solving human problems by applying principles of sound design. Since Airbnb's business model depends on helping strangers trust one another enough to share personal spaces, invariably design tools come into play. Before we look at how design thinking is deployed to drive trust on the Airbnb platform, let's first make sure we share a general understanding of trust and trustworthiness.

Many conceptualizations of trust explore the topic from either a psychological or a sociological perspective. Psychological models seek to explain how individuals develop their internal perspective on trust. For example, psychologists might examine how being abused as a child affects an individual's ability to trust others in adulthood. Sociological models explore trust in the context of social exchange. They might address what actions need to be taken in a business transaction for both parties to feel that the interchange is fair and warrants continued trust.

Psychologists have generally viewed trust as a disposition. In essence, trust is a collection of attitudes and beliefs about whether people will be honest, cooperative, helpful, and reliable. By contrast, J. David Lewis and Andrew Weigert's views, as they have expressed them in the journal *Social Forces*, reflect the sociological perspective: "Trust may be thought of as a functional prerequisite for the possibility of society in that the only alternatives to appropriate trust are 'chaos and paralyzing fear.'. . . Although trust, in general, is indispensable in social relationships, it always involves an unavoidable element of risk and potential doubt." In business, prospective customers must overcome their doubts about the believability of promises made by companies concerning products and services.

Stephen R. Covey's studies of trust cross both psychological and sociological boundaries and specifically focus on the application of trust to business. In his book *The Speed of Trust*, Covey wrote: "Trust impacts us 24/7, 365 days a year. It undergirds and affects the quality of every relationship, every communication, every work project, every business venture, every effort in which we are engaged. It changes the quality of every present moment and alters the trajectory and outcome of every future moment of our lives—both personally and professionally."

A key takeaway from Covey's work is that we can and should seek to view trust as a measurable and changeable aspect of business. "Contrary to what most people believe, trust is not some soft, illusive quality that you either have or you don't; rather, trust is a pragmatic, tangible, actionable asset that you can create—much faster than you probably think possible." While Covey talks about business trust as an "actionable asset that can be created," Airbnb's cofounder Joe Gebbia talks about trust as something Airbnb has "designed."

DESIGNING TRUST?

In a 2016 TED Talk titled *How Airbnb Designs for Trust*, Joe Gebbia shared a story of his first hosting experience. Gebbia reflected on a yard sale that he held right after he graduated from the Rhode Island School of Design. A man in a red Miata pulled up to the yard sale and purchased a piece of Gebbia's original art. Later Gebbia invited the man to join him for a conversation over a beer. In the course of their discussion, the man shared that he was on a cross-country road trip in advance of going to work for the Peace Corps. As the evening waned, Gebbia asked this veritable stranger if he had a place to stay for the night. The stranger did not.

Let's have Gebbia pick up the story:

> Do I offer to host this guy? But, I just met him—I mean, he says he's going to the Peace Corps, but I don't really know if he's going to the Peace Corps, and I don't want to end up kidnapped in the trunk of a Miata. That's a small trunk!
>
> So then I hear myself saying, "Hey, I have an airbed you can stay on in my living room." And the voice in my head goes, **"Wait, what?"**

Gebbia reports the man took him up on his offer, and the stranger slept on the floor in Gebbia's living room. Gebbia's anxiety prompted him to lock his bedroom door . . . just in case the stranger was psychotic. As it turned out, the stranger, now a teacher, has maintained contact with Gebbia. That teacher now desplays Gebbia's yard sale art piece in his classroom.

Gebbia's story demonstrates his understanding of and empathy for trust issues that guests and hosts encounter when deciding to conduct business on the Airbnb platform. Similar concerns also affected Gebbia and his partners as they initially sought financing for their company. In the early days, many investors were unwilling to gamble on a business where people had to agree to rent out personal spaces (for example, bedrooms and bathrooms) to complete strangers.

In an article for *WIRED* magazine titled "How Airbnb and Lyft Finally Got Americans to Trust Each Other," Jason Tanz talks about his belief that brands like Airbnb faced a stranger danger mindset, which he describes as "a widely held, deeply ingrained attitude—reinforced by decades of warnings about poisoned Halloween candy and drink-spiking pickup artists." Tanz notes that despite our fear of strangers, we trust unfamiliar people every day in traditional commerce. Tanz observes that we provide "credit cards to shop clerks, get into the backseat of taxis driven by cabbies we've never met, ingest food prepared in closed kitchens, and ignore the fact that hotel workers with master keys could sneak into our rooms while we sleep."

Given all the ways in which we routinely trust strangers in conventional business, why is it difficult to imagine a similar transfer of trust in the context of sharing economy options like Airbnb? Tanz believes that the rapid growth of the sharing economy caught industry regulators and most of the population off guard. Tanz notes a change of perspective has occurred: "Many of these companies have us engaging in behaviors that would have seemed unthinkably foolhardy as recently as five years ago."

To facilitate trust in its person-to-person marketplace, Airbnb's founders turned to a discipline they knew well: the tenets of good design. While experience design principles were extremely important to Airbnb, Alice Emma Walker, writing for UXdesign.cc, has shown widespread use of design thinking across brands like Survey Monkey, Royal Mail, Zara, Amazon, and others.

The first step in most design processes involves empathizing with those for whom you seek to create solutions (for example, Joe Gebbia's red Miata story). After stepping into your customer's need state, solid design typically involves the following:

- Creation of a "driving question"

- Gathering relevant inputs

- Looking for breakthrough ideas

- Crafting prototypes for possible solutions

- Testing possibilities to drive improvements

- Communicating findings to inspire others

Airbnb cofounders kicked off their design process with this driving question: "Is it possible to design for trust?"

The answer, as you'll find in the pages ahead, is a resounding yes. To demonstrate some of the breakthrough ideas that surfaced among Airbnb innovators, Joe Gebbia asked audience members at his TED Talk to engage in a live experiment. Gebbia instructed the audience to unlock their cell phones and pass their phone to the person next to them.

In the moments that followed, Gebbia said, "What if we changed one small thing about the design of that experiment? What if your neighbors had introduced themselves first, with their name, where they're from, the name of their kids or their dog? Imagine that they had 150 reviews of people saying, 'They're great at holding unlocked phones!' Now how would you feel about handing your phone over? It turns out, a well-designed reputation system is key for building trust."

Gebbia also acknowledged that like all great design, Airbnb's reputation system wasn't perfect in its earliest form. Rather, Airbnb's approach to sharing host and guest ratings improved through a series of incremental changes.

The concept of reputation and rating systems is not new. Amazon has been deploying customer product reviews on its site since 1995, and its website designers routinely make design improvements to better guide consumer decision-making. Beyond the sharing economy and online marketplaces, consumers are crowd-sourcing rating and review systems to help one another decide virtually everything. Consumers use reputation systems to decide which movies to watch, what to select at a restaurant, which doctor to choose, the best dry cleaner to frequent, and which mechanic to avoid. Before we look at Airbnb's reputation system and explore key learnings involved in designing and improving ways for hosts and guests to trust one another, let's examine the way you approach customer trust in your business.

 YOUR TRAVEL PLANNING GUIDE

1. What's your reaction to Stephen R. Covey's view that business trust is an "actionable asset that can be created" and Joe Gebbia's view that trust can be "designed"?

2. Given that successful design requires understanding of and empathy for those you seek to serve, what fears, uncertainties, and distrust are your customers and prospects experiencing? Where does doubt creep into their relationship with you?

3. What driving question frames your efforts to design trust? For example, "Can we build trust across our service phase?" or "Can we design greater trust at the onset of our relationship?"

4. Where are you gathering relevant inputs on customer trust? How are you encouraging breakthrough ideas, developing prototypes for possible solutions, testing possibilities to drive improvements, and communicating your findings in ways that inspire more solutions?

DESIGNING HUMANITY INTO THE ONLINE INTERACTION

Increasingly customers make decisions about brands and service providers through online interactions. Frequently, these interactions are devoid of important elements needed to drive trust. Airbnb has designed ways for people to make meaningful connections starting with account sign-up. In order to create an Airbnb account, every person must be at least 18 years of age. A person can become a new member of the community via email, Google, or Facebook.

Airbnb requires that each participant complete a profile prior to booking or hosting through the platform (this parallels the example from Gebbia's cell phone experiment where strangers introduced themselves before a cell phone was handed over). Airbnb profile data is used to verify participants' identities, acquire contact details that can be used to communicate with them, and secure payment information. At sign-up, Airbnb requires the following:

- First and last name

- Birthdate

- Email address

- Phone number

- Payment information

Hosts can ask a guest to provide a picture in their guest profile, but the picture isn't revealed to the hosts until the booking is confirmed. This ensures that the picture is not considered in the acceptance process, while still enabling the hosts to know who will arrive on their property. Hosts can also require guests to provide Airbnb with a government ID (such as a driver's license, passport, or visa) before the guests book their listing. The hosts are then required to also provide a verified government ID to Airbnb. Hosts will not see the guest's government ID, as Airbnb simply uses it for verification purposes. Airbnb also verifies users through their profiles on platforms like Facebook.

Most web platform designers seek to reduce user effort, or "friction," needed to complete a user profile. Friction often leads to prospects abandoning the profile creation process. Writing for *Forbes*, tech analyst Theo Miller suggests that platforms do everything to avoid friction: "Most product designers would never force users to upload pictures. . . . If a social network doesn't require a profile picture, why would a home sharing platform? . . . The impact of seeing your host's smile is profound. It's inviting and warm. It's nothing like craigslist. The moment you see a person for the first time, you create a story in your head. You humanize them. This step is essential, if you want to build trust." At Airbnb all of the hosts are required to upload a photo, and they are asked to ensure that it clearly shows their face. The potential friction that comes from this is offset by the benefit of a prospective guest being able to see the face of a person and not just the details of a listing.

Once profiles are established, hosts and guests can list and book on the Airbnb platform. When searching for a property or experience, prospective guests can review ratings provided by other members of the community who have booked and reviewed the listing. For example, at the completion of a stay, guests rate a host's listing on a five-star scale for:

- Overall experience

- Cleanliness

- Accuracy

- Value

- Communication

- Arrival

- Location

Guests are also provided the opportunity to write comments and suggestions.

Once three guests rate a listing, an aggregate overall experience score is calculated, and that very important score appears prominently at the top of the listing. By clicking on this overall experience rating, a prospective guest can see averages on the other six categories (accuracy, communication, cleanliness, location, check-in, and value).

Ratings and reviews of hosts made by past guests determine whether a property will appear during a search by a future guest. These ratings and reviews also guide prospective guests as they finalize their selections. Conversely, since Airbnb hosts provide comments on guest behavior and rate them on a five-point scale in three areas (cleanliness, communication, and observation of house rules), guest ratings by past hosts can affect the willingness of other hosts to accept a guest's future booking requests.

TRUST IN RATINGS

Generally speaking, online reviews, like those posted on the Airbnb site, are perceived as highly trustworthy by consumers. Writing for *Inc.*, Craig Bloem noted, "If you think online reviews get lost in all the Internet noise, think again. Research shows that 91 percent of people regularly or occasionally read online reviews, and 84 percent trust online reviews as much as a personal recommendation. And they make that decision quickly: 68 percent form an opinion after reading between one and six online reviews."

Despite the perceived truthfulness of reviews, many factors can create bias in a reputation management system. Some of the many potential biases include these:

- Strategic manipulation

- Recall bias

- Fear of retaliatory reviews

I will describe these forms of bias and explore how Airbnb's reputation system is designed to address each.

Strategic manipulation bias represents intentional actions taken by a brand or its competitors to falsely influence decision-making. Strategic manipulation often occurs when review sites don't verify that actual customers are writing the posts. In systems where anyone can tender a review, ratings can be positively manipulated by brand advocates or negatively influenced by competitors.

Recall biases occur when rating completeness or accuracy degrades due to delayed evaluation.

Fear of retaliatory reviews happens in two-way rating systems (like that of Airbnb) in which parties are encouraged to rate one another.

From initial design, Airbnb mitigated strategic manipulation bias by ensuring that only verified guests could review hosts and vice versa. Solutions for recall biases and the fear of retaliatory ratings required design evolution. In 2014, Airbnb announced changes that reduced the impact of both possible biases. As leaders announced the changes, they emphasized:

> Both hosts and guests may worry that if they leave an honest review that includes praise and criticism, they might receive an unfairly critical review in response. To address this concern, reviews will be revealed to hosts and guests simultaneously. Starting today, hosts and their guests will only see reviews they receive from a completed trip after both participants have completed their assessment of the experience. We want to make it more comfortable for everyone in our community to provide honest, accurate feedback, and help increase confidence in the reviews they see on listing and profile pages.
>
> And since 90 percent of hosts and guests who leave a review submit one within two weeks, we're shortening the review period to 14 days, so that all of the feedback people provide is based on a recent impression. At the end of the 14-day review period, if only the host or the guest has left a review from a completed trip, we'll make that review public to both the recipient and the community.

By developing a simultaneous reveal of ratings, Airbnb crafted a design solution to reduce the *fear of retaliatory reviews*. By shortening the review period, Airbnb also mitigated *recall biases*. These types of actions taken by Airbnb website designers have helped drive open, accurate, and transparent review processes, and they have application well beyond Airbnb and the sharing economy.

At the outset of every business relationship, service providers want to know if a prospective customer will engage the transaction responsibly. Similarly, future customers want to hear honest and unfiltered feedback from prior consumers. As such, business leaders should look for ways to empower their people and their customers to make decisions guided by information that has the least amount of bias possible.

DESIGNING TRUST THROUGH
PREARRIVAL COMMUNICATION

In Chapters 2 and 3, we reviewed the importance of prearrival communication when creating guest belonging. From a design perspective, Airbnb's secure communication channel also serves to foster bidirectional trust.

In an article for the website *Airbnb Design*, Charlie Aufmann, a member of the Airbnb design team, wrote:

> Our research has shown that these prebooking messages may be a good signal of effort and trustworthiness for guests. A few months ago, I was in Europe on a research trip trying to understand how hosts assess trust and fit in their guests. One participant in our focus group said, "If people take care with their first message to you and say a little bit about themselves, . . . you relax a bit about it. . . . Trust takes effort."
>
> A lot of the information guests submit with their reservation that gets relayed to the host is structured (travel dates, number of guests, check-in time, and so on). The message, on the other hand, is free-form and allows the guests to share more details about themselves and the purpose of their trip. Messages also reveal a bit of the character and personality of the writer, which helps hosts and guests alike begin building a trusting relationship.

Let's connect Charlie's observations concerning the power of open communications from hosts and guests to additional information shared by Joe Gebbia during his TED Talk. Gebbia mentioned that Airbnb has studied and helped design trust building prearrival communications:

> [We] learned that building the right amount of trust takes the right amount of disclosure. This is what happens when a guest first messages a host. If you share too little, like, "Yo," acceptance rates go down.
>
> And if you share too much, like, "I'm having issues with my mother," acceptance rates also go down.
>
> But there's a zone that's just right, like, "Love the artwork in your place. Coming for vacation with my family."
>
> So how do we design for just the right amount of disclosure? We use the size of the box to suggest the right length, and we guide them with prompts to encourage sharing.

The figure that follows shows an example of that box design:

Introduce Yourself to Susan

Giving your host more information will make them more likely to confirm your booking request:

- **Tell Susan a little about yourself.**
- **What brings you to Atlanta? Who's joining you?**
- **What do you love about this listing? Mention it!**

Message your host...

Thanks to design elements like requiring host pictures in profiles, a two-way reputation management system with simultaneous reveals, and a secure messaging system with well-crafted boxes and prompts, Airbnb has helped people who are complete strangers trust one another. Designing the transfer of trust in a person-to-person marketplace serves to overcome the type of fear Joe Gebbia experienced when he first offered his air mattress to the man in the red Miata.

Mareike Möhlmann, assistant professor in the Information Systems and Management Group at the University of Warwick, has conducted research on Airbnb and other companies involved in the sharing economy. Writing for *The Conversation*, Mareike noted, "With the use of some key digital features, trust is being built between people that have never met each other. In fact, research I've carried out shows that, when they are designed well, sharing economy services can build greater trust between strangers than you'd expect between colleagues." Airbnb staked its business model on its ability to design trust, and investors who took the risk have been rewarded accordingly. Chris Lehane, Airbnb's SVP of policy and communication, told me:

> At Airbnb, we know that we would be nowhere without our hosts—we don't succeed unless our hosts succeed. Hosts' success depends on guests succeeding, guest success depends on local communities welcoming them, local communities welcome Airbnb guests because they come to see that their returns are greater with Airbnb than with mass tourism. Trust is at the center of this stakeholder wheel. It all starts with hosts taking the first step of opening their doors. Their guests leave reviews on more than 70 percent of reservations, an accumulation of reviews that cannot be replicated and lets guests book with confidence. Communities benefit from Airbnb keeping more of the returns

of tourism local and are proactively seeking to remit tourist taxes. Trust literally makes that wheel go around.

Much like Airbnb, trust invariably underpins the success and sustainability of your business. Let's take a moment to extrapolate lessons from Airbnb as you design and strengthen the trust between you and the people you seek to serve.

 YOUR TRAVEL PLANNING GUIDE

1. Are you sharing team member profiles or otherwise humanizing your service delivery?

2. How do you use communication platforms to foster a consistent cadence of connection with your customers?

3. How are you helping customers and prospects make well-informed decisions? Are you encouraging transparency through tools like uncensored customer ratings or other metrics by which prospects can realistically consider you?

DESIGNING FOR SAFETY

To earn and maintain consumers' trust, you must ensure their safety. In its person-to-person marketplace, Airbnb must address safety needs for both the guests and hosts. Up to this point in the chapter, we've looked at only trust; however, Airbnb views trust and safety as completely interrelated. As such, Airbnb has named an internal department Trust & Safety, and it has placed a link on its platform with the same name.

As you will recall from Chapter 3, Maslow placed safety and physiological needs at the base of his hierarchy of human priorities. Nick Shapiro, who oversees global trust and safety efforts at Airbnb, understands the foundational importance of physiological and safety needs. Prior to joining the Airbnb team, Shapiro was the CIA's deputy chief of staff and senior advisor to former CIA Director John Brennan. He was a White House spokesman for President Obama and he has served on the National Security Council staff. Nick told me:

> Trust is the fundamental currency of the sharing economy, and it's at the heart of everything we do at Airbnb. Trust is not something you get just because you ask for it, trust is not something you can tell people to do, and trust is not something that can be bought, not even in a multi-million-dollar marketing campaign. At Airbnb, we know we need to earn people's trust. We primarily do this by following three principles, our own version of the hierarchy of needs, if you will. First and foremost is *safety*—people need to be safe while using Airbnb. Second is *education and transparency*—people need to know how to use Airbnb and what to expect while using it. And last but not least is *support*—when something goes wrong, we need to be there to make it right.

Shapiro's description establishes Airbnb's trust hierarchy as having safety at the base, connection and transparency in the middle, and community as well as support at the top.

We've discussed connection in Chapters 2 and 3, and we will address community in Chapters 8 and 9, so let's take the remainder of this chapter to explore how Airbnb creates "Safety by Design" for guests and hosts alike. From a broad perspective Nick shared:

We know that the idea of opening your home to or staying with someone you've never met can feel like a leap of faith. That's why we intentionally designed our community to help earn and build trust within and among our millions of hosts and guests in more than 191 countries worldwide. Society is currently in the midst of an unprecedented crisis of trust, as people's trust in big business, government, the media, and even nonprofits and charities is plummeting. But through Airbnb, people are trusting each other more and more. While nobody can eliminate all the risk in hosting or traveling, we strive to ensure that every host and guest has the best possible experience. We build this trust by focusing on our hierarchy-of-needs approach.

Generally, Airbnb's safety tools and strategies relate to:

- Online activities

- Scam prevention

- Preparedness

- Host guarantees

- Support

Let's begin by examining how Airbnb has designed for security across its global e-commerce platform.

Online Activities

- Account security: Through a series of measures, Airbnb focuses on safeguarding personal information and money. Nick notes, "Airbnb accounts are safeguarded using multifactor authentication, requiring additional verification whenever a login is attempted from a new device, and you should never be asked to pay off of the Airbnb site or app."

- **Risk scoring:** Nick reports, "We use advanced technology and machine learning to assess each and every reservation ahead of time for risk." Through predictive analytics and machine learning, Airbnb is able to flag and prevent suspicious activity. In response to concerns, leaders can take a range of actions (including cancelation of bookings or removal of users from the platform).

- **Watch lists and background checks:** According to Nick, "While no background check system is infallible, we screen all hosts and guests globally against regulatory, terrorist, and sanctions watch lists. For US residents, we also run background checks looking for prior felony convictions, sex offender registrations, and significant misdemeanors."

In keeping with the Community Commitment discussed in Chapter 2, Airbnb used background checks and community input to proactively cancel bookings associated with a white supremacist rally in Charlottesville, Virginia. As you'll recall, that rally, referred to as Unite the Right, was organized in opposition to the removal of a statue of Confederate Commander Robert E. Lee from Charlottesville's Emancipation Park. The rally was marked by acts of intimidation and violence, including an incident in which a self-proclaimed white supremacist drove his car into a group of counterprotesters, killing one person and injuring 19.

According to local news station NBC29, a post on a neo-Nazi website claimed rally supporters used Airbnb to book "seven houses for 80 to 90 people from various alt-right groups." Based on an investigation of that claim, Airbnb officials provided the following statement:

When through our background check processes or from input of our community we identify and determine that there are those who would be pursuing behavior on the platform that would be antithetical to the Airbnb Community Commitment, we seek to take appropriate action including, as in this case, removing them from the platform.

Airbnb leaders took swift action to cancel reservations and remove the booking privileges of individuals who expressed prejudicial and potentially harmful intent. Using their own background check processes and information garnered from social media, Airbnb was proactive in support of their Community Commitment.

Scam Prevention

Airbnb has developed multiple levels of detection and defense against individuals who seek to misrepresent themselves or cause financial harm on the platform. In an interview for *Fast Company*, former military intelligence officer and Airbnb Trust & Safety Manager Phillip Cardenas highlighted how his team identified suspicious indicators on a specific account:

> Through extensive research, our team was able to link this account to a few other accounts that had very similar profiles and similar suspicious characteristics. All of the accounts, it turned out, were linked together and also shared similar information to some scammers that had attempted to use other vacation rental sites in the past. Further investigation revealed that they were scammers, not legitimate Airbnb users. None of their Airbnb listings had been booked, and we were able to quickly remove their accounts from Airbnb permanently.

Whether it is potential physical harm, the possibility of financial loss, or risk for identity fraud, Airbnb understands the importance of maximizing the safety of all users on its social commerce platform. Whether you conduct business through e-commerce, phone sales, or face-to-face service, your ability to protect your customers' financial assets, information, and physical safety will ultimately contribute to your company's longevity.

Preparedness

Leaders at Airbnb are vigilant about designing for trust and safety on their platform, but they can't control the actions of all guests and hosts engaged in millions of experiences and home stays. Nick Shapiro shares, "Our community's safety, both online and offline, is our priority. With hundreds of millions of guest arrivals in Airbnb listings, negative incidents are extremely rare. Even so, we're constantly working to improve our platform, our policies, and our protections because even one incident is one too many."

As you'll recall from our discussion in Chapter 3, there are many ways to care for those you serve. Sometimes you must provide direct care (for example, mitigating the risks you can control, such as website security), and at other times you must help guests and hosts avert risk on their own. In this context, Airbnb offers numerous safety tips for guests and hosts alike. From a guest perspective, those tips include these:

- *Read the ratings and reviews.* Look through feedback from past guests to help find the right fit for you.

- *Get your questions answered.* Our secure messaging tool is a safe and easy way for you to ask potential hosts any questions you have about their home before you book.

- *Always communicate and pay on Airbnb.* Keep yourself, your payment, and your personal information protected by staying on our secure platform throughout the entire process—from communication to booking and payment.

- *Do a safety check.* Once you've arrived at your home, make sure you know where all of the relevant emergency equipment and safety information is located.

- *Research local travel alerts and warnings.* Whether you're traveling with Airbnb or not, it's always a good idea to research your destination ahead of time and check with your local embassy in case there are any travel warnings or special requirements.

Similarly, an abbreviated set of tips Airbnb provides for hosts includes these:

- *Set clear expectations.* Your listing description should let potential guests know about the unique features and amenities of your home. Even small details like the number of flights of stairs to your front door can help make sure guests enjoy their time with you.

- *Set guest requirements.* Every guest is asked to provide their full name, date of birth, photo, phone number, email address, and payment information to Airbnb before booking.

- *Read profiles and reviews.* If you want to know more about a guest before accepting their reservation request, check out their profile or read reviews from past hosts.

- *Get to know your guests in advance.* Our secure messaging tool gives you the chance to get to know guests and answer or ask any questions that come up before or during the trip.

• *Keep safety information and equipment handy.* It's important to equip your home and your guests with the safety essentials they might need during their trip. These include items like a working carbon monoxide and smoke detector, a first aid kit, a fire extinguisher, and information on how to contact local authorities.

Nick also notes, "To help equip our hosts with the latest tools and information, we often lead home safety workshops with local fire and emergency experts and distribute free smoke and carbon monoxide detectors to hosts."

In addition to your direct efforts to ensure and design safety for those you serve, how are you helping them to maximize their security and the security of those around them?

Host Guarantees

In many of the examples listed throughout this chapter, Airbnb leaders practiced proactive design—meaning they anticipated opportunities to enhance trust or safety. In 2011, Airbnb leaders got caught off guard when it came to safety protection involving a host named EJ. In that case, Airbnb had to quickly design a reactive set of safety solutions. A portion of EJ's blog post sets the context for the crisis that ensued after Airbnb guests:

> Smashed a hole through a locked closet door, and found the passport, cash, credit card and grandmother's jewelry I had hidden inside. They took my camera, my iPod, an old laptop, and my external backup drive filled with photos, journals . . . my entire life. They found my birth certificate and social security card, which I believe they photocopied—using the printer-copier I kindly left out for

my guests' use. They rifled through all my drawers, wore my shoes and clothes, and left my clothing crumpled up in a pile of wet, mildewing towels on the closet floor.

One can only imagine how EJ felt in response to these violations of trust, privacy, and personal property. Fortunately, initial interactions between EJ and Airbnb customer service team members were positive, as noted by EJ:

> I would be remiss if I didn't pause here to emphasize that the customer service team at airbnb.com has been wonderful, giving this crime their full attention. They have called often, expressing empathy, support, and genuine concern for my welfare. They have offered to help me recover emotionally and financially and are working with SFPD to track down these criminals. I do believe the folks at airbnb.com when they tell me this has never happened before in their short history. . . . Someone was bound to eventually, I suppose, and there will be others.

While EJ noted that Airbnb's early reaction was acceptable, over time she expressed frustration with Airbnb's efforts to help her gain resolution of her crisis. She also took exception to public statements made by Airbnb's leaders. After thoughtful consideration and admitting that "we have really screwed things up," Brian Chesky announced the creation of the Airbnb Trust & Safety team and started what would become Airbnb's $1 million host guarantee.

Support

In the wake of the EJ incident, Airbnb has continued to design a number of rapid response solutions. Nick Shapiro describes the host guarantee and increased host support by noting:

In the rare event that any issue should arise, our global Customer Service and Trust & Safety teams are on call 24 hours a day, 7 days a week, in 11 different languages to help make things right with rebooking assistance, as well as refunds, reimbursements, and insurance programs. If, for instance, you arrive at a listing and it's not as advertised, all you need to do is reach out to our team. We are here to help. Hosts are protected by our Million Dollar Host Guarantee, which covers listings for up to $1,000,000 USD in damage—and it's free for all hosts and every single booking. In addition, our Host Protection Insurance provides home sharing hosts worldwide with protection against third-party claims of property damage or bodily injury up to $1,000,000 USD at no extra cost.

Similarly, Airbnb provides $1 million in free liability insurance for hosts who are providing Experiences on the platform. This Experience Protection Insurance protects most Experiences hosts against property damage or personal injury claims.

Nick highlights the importance of these solutions:

> When something does go wrong, we need to be there to help support our guest or host. If not, then the person may suffer what I call a second breach of trust, and that second breach of trust can be even more harmful sometimes. People know that we can't prevent all things from happening while traveling, but how we respond, that is completely in our control and we need to get that right. That is a major focus and a major priority for us. People are seeing the value of a trusted community on Airbnb and all of the access it can unlock.
>
> All of this is possible because of the trust we are helping people put in each other and in us. I'm incredibly proud

of the diverse team that's been built across the company and around the globe to help protect and support our community. At Airbnb, we don't just have former national security and law enforcement professionals working these issues, but we have engineers and product managers, designers and data scientists, experts in cybersecurity, fraud, human trafficking, insurance—you name it, we have it on this team, and ... we're keenly focused on the latest advancements in the identity verification space and how we can securely and effectively incorporate new technology to help ensure our users are who they say they are—while still maintaining a quality user experience.

Most of us understand the importance of trust and safety in the context of our service delivery; however, many of us have not approached trust and safety as actionable assets requiring design excellence. In Chapter 5, we will examine how guests and hosts utilize tools discussed in this chapter and how they focus on trust and safety throughout their service relationship.

POINTS OF INTEREST
AS YOU DESIGN FOR TRUST AND SAFETY

→ Stephen Covey describes business trust as an "actionable asset that can be created." Airbnb's cofounder Joe Gebbia talks about trust as something Airbnb has "designed."

→ Joe Gebbia's TED Talk demonstrates empathy for pervasive "stranger danger" thinking and sets the stage for Airbnb's driving question, "Is it possible to design for trust?"

→ After stepping into the need state of your user or customer, solid design processes typically include the creation of a "driving question," gathering relevant inputs, looking for breakthrough ideas, crafting prototypes for possible solutions, testing possibilities to drive improvements, and communicating findings to inspire others.

→ If you are optimizing for efficiency, you will remove user effort wherever possible, but Airbnb designs and optimizes for trust. As such, they require hosts to upload pictures to their profile.

→ Reputation systems are extremely valuable when designing for trust. An exploration of biases that can affect the trustworthiness of ratings should be carried out, and effort should be exerted to design for mitigation of likely biases.

→ Communication is an essential element in trust building, and it should be encouraged and facilitated through interactional design.

→ Safety is a primary need, which is essential to establishing and maintaining trust.

→ Where possible, safety should be designed into online and offline interactions. Offer tools to your team and your customers to help them stay vigilant for their own safety.

→ Trust and safety design come in both proactive and reactive forms. Leadership involves anticipating trust and safety needs and swiftly responding to urgent and emergent needs as they arise.

Practice Helpful Disclosure

Truth is like the sun. You can shut it out
for a time, but it ain't goin' away.

—Elvis Presley, singer and actor

TRUST AND REPUTATION

In Chapter 4 we explored how leaders at Airbnb "design trust" through tools such as rich online profiles, reputation management systems, and secure communication channels. In this chapter, we'll look at how the Airbnb community deploys those tools in ways that foster trust between strangers. In the pages ahead, we will also be highlighting ways you can drive greater trust during your prospective customer's search, consideration, and sales journey.

Amazon CEO Jeff Bezos once observed, "A brand for a company is like a reputation for a person. You earn reputation by trying to do hard things well." In this chapter, you will see how the best Airbnb hosts build their reputations through choices made long before a prospective guest finds them.

Specifically, this chapter will focus on how hosts do the following "hard things well":

- Market accurately

- Make appropriate personal disclosures

- Set expectations

Later in the chapter, we will see how these activities work together to produce heightened guest trust. For now, let's look at how one guest, K. Ford K., described the transformational power of trust creation at Airbnb. Writing for the *Huffington Post*, K. Ford K. explained that she was initially concerned about staying with strangers during an international trip. After spending time looking through reviews from prior guests, she made her selections and was pleased with every experience. K. Ford K. concluded, "While the locations and amenities of Airbnbs are important, the most important thing by far are the people, the hosts who made us feel right at home. We experienced firsthand that we weren't just renting a room. We were making local connections, making true friends, and expanding our community one Airbnb at a time."

Through thoughtful action taken in advance of a guest's arrival, Airbnb hosts enable guests like K. Ford K. to no longer feel "nervous about staying with strangers" and instead feel like they are "making true friends." Let's see how Airbnb hosts plant seeds of trust and how you can do the same.

Market Accurately

Most of us have become cynical of advertising and marketing claims. Despite our cynicism, misleading and puffed-up marketing (often referred to as "puffery") continues to have a mixed impact. In an article titled "Processing Exaggerated Advertising Claims," Elizabeth Crowley, professor and deputy dean of the University of Sydney Business School, found, "Even though consumers can identify a puffed claim as less credible, they still rated the brand more favorably than brands associated with a factual claim." Crowley added that the implication for marketers was clear: "Puffery works. A legally accepted, but misleading claim, results in consumers liking the brand better and not remembering the exaggeration specifically." While Crowley's work suggests that puffery favorably affects initial brand perception, questionable claims also spark consumer wrath on social media and across review sites. Word spreads when brands fail to meet their promises.

Gallup has reported that approximately 50 percent of consumers feel brands aren't living up to advertising promises—which makes trustworthiness an important brand differentiator. According to the 2018 *Reader's Digest Trusted Brand Survey*, trustworthiness could trump many other brand attributes consistently. "Eighty-three percent of consumers would buy from the company they 'trust' more." At the same time, current levels of customer disillusionment and cynicism are making it difficult for any marketing message to be believed. According to the survey, "Roughly half (48 percent) of participants [are] indicating they are less trusting of brands today. In fact, 69 percent of respondents agree with the statement that 'brands need to do a better job of earning consumers' trust.'"

So how can a brand develop a reputation for earning consumers' trust? Outstanding Airbnb hosts suggest that when you tell the truth, reputation takes care of itself. These hosts also indicate that from a business perspective, reputation is everything. Guest Matt Kerr agrees: "I remember looking at the online reviews for one Airbnb host and thinking I really need to stay with her and those reviews were spot on. She is over-the-top with hospitality, and I am a regular repeat guest, and I now encourage family members to stay with her as well." On the Airbnb platform, negative reviews may affect the ease with which future guests can find a host's listing (a result of algorithms in Airbnb's search function).

Negative reviews can also cause prospective guests to skip over a host's listing when it appears in search results. One host noted, "I know every guest who stays at my property will be asked to rate the accuracy of my listing on a five-star scale. It would be silly for me to poorly depict, misrepresent, or omit important information. Not only would I violate a guest's trust but over time I would erode my reputation. Worse yet I would decrease trust in the Airbnb platform. My listing should authentically help every prospective guest consider if my home and my style of hosting are right for them."

Eliminating hype and crafting advertising messages that accurately inform and don't oversell sounds good in theory, but it is far more challenging in practice. Let's look at how hosts put marketing accuracy into practice through their listing descriptions and pictures.

Accuracy of the Written Description

Words matter, and too often sales and service providers think their words must be chosen to "sell their offerings to all people." The best Airbnb hosts emphasize the importance of offering balanced and informative descriptions to their listings, so guests can self-select.

Superhost Kathy Peterman recalled advice that she received at an Airbnb conference: "Chip Conley, the head of hospitality at Airbnb, said our listings should provide the important reasons why a guest would want to stay with us, followed by two reasons they might not find our place suitable. My listing now includes the fact that guests can't cook meat in my kitchen—given my veganism. That serves to help guests make an informed choice."

Here are a few other examples of transparent listings that demonstrate a willingness to offer prospective guests insights on likely suitability:

This is not a luxury loft building and is not priced as such. It is an old factory building converted to lofts and is occupied mostly by artists and musicians. The ceiling is thin, and you can hear my neighbors from time to time. Light sleepers may find this annoying.

Please do not book this listing if you are afraid of nature or its creatures. Understand you are surrounded by thousands of acres of completely untouched nature. You are very likely to hear (or see) coyotes, owls, seals, roadrunners, and bunnies. There is a bobcat in the area, but these are usually very skittish. There are mice in the Santa Monica mountains. About once a month, a guest will complain that they saw a mouse. Said mouse might come into the Airstream if food is left outside the fridge. We do not offer refunds if a mouse comes into the Airstream, but we do have four traps around the Airstream, so the odds are heavily stacked against the mice.

There may be noises and smells that you'd expect from a boat. Pumps, motors, ocean water, etc....We are...tucked behind Drum Island at the base of the Ravenel Bridge, which dilutes almost all the waves from the harbor. There is still a small amount of wave action, and you'll feel a slight rock from time to time, mostly from boats passing by who don't respect the no-wake zone (feel free to yell at them and shake your fist while doing so).

If you are a light sleeper, don't want to chance a visit from a mouse, or don't wish to "shake your fist" at boaters creating a wake, these three properties may not be right for you. However, each of them has appeal for large numbers of prospective guests, and all rate highly for the accuracy of their listing. In the context of Jeff Bezos's quote, these three examples reflect what it looks like to do the hard work of "telling the truth and not selling a fantasy." It is by doing this hard work that these hosts develop and maintain a reputation of trustworthiness. Imagine if more product descriptions were written with this level of openness. Better yet, think about opportunities you have to do the same.

Accuracy in Imagery

If a picture is worth a thousand words, then an overly flattering image is likely to contribute to an amplified level of customer disappointment when reality hits. Many of us have purchased an item that looked great in the catalog or online—only to have it be much smaller, dingier, and certainly not as spectacular as the marketing photos implied. Our reading of thousands of Airbnb reviews suggests that quality Airbnb hosts take photo accuracy very seriously. For example, when photos were mentioned in reviews, comments usually read like this:

> Superb! We found the townhouse is exactly as shown in the pictures and much larger than we expected.

> Judy's condo is way better than pictures indicate. It is tastefully decorated, has a beautiful view, and the location can't be beat.

> Congratulations to the person who designed this place! Looks better than the pictures! I highly recommend to anyone who is looking for a memorable vacation.

Airbnb reminds hosts, "Listings with beautiful photos receive more eyes, more interest, and more bookings, so take some time to make them shine. Draw in potential guests, highlight what's amazing, and set their expectations appropriately." Given the power of photos, Airbnb also cautions hosts to "let guests book with confidence.... Be sure the photo aligns as closely as possible to the actual space when they arrive. Let photos be a true reflection of how guests will find it."

Jasper Ribbers, coauthor of the book *Get Paid for Your Pad*, blogs that the picture section of the Airbnb listing should not only be visually accurate but also provide a correct representation of how guests might experience their stay. Ribbers says pictures "create the perfect visualization of the experience that your guests can have when staying at your place." Ribbers recommends hiring photographers through Airbnb in locations where they are available, removing clutter, bringing in the light, and providing captions "to describe the experience that your guests can have, using what is displayed in the photo."

One host summed up picture accuracy this way: "I want pictures to show my listing at its best but not better than it is. I want photos to be representative of my home and inspire me to keep it as inviting as I made it on picture day. Guests have their own cameras, so what they see on the listing should be what they see upon arrival and what they share for others to see from their mobile devices." Another host said, "Photos on my listing are like dating: you want to put your best foot forward early, but you can't lie about your age, or wear too much makeup. My pictures tell an honest story of my property inside and out. Whatever excitement guests might feel while looking at pictures of my listing, the dating phase if you will, I want them to maintain as their relationship continues into my home."

All business leaders should consider the way they depict and describe products across all marketing materials and customer-facing contact points. The images you present and the words you use serve as a promise to your customers. Irrespective of industry, your promises must be delivered when your customers receive their goods or services.

While product and service descriptions attract customers, consumers are also interested in the people who will be serving them.

Before we look at offering constructive personal disclosure from service providers, let's take a moment to assess your marketing accuracy.

 YOUR TRAVEL PLANNING GUIDE

1. On a scale from 1 to 10, how would you rate the transparency and authenticity of your marketing materials?

2. Is puffery present in your marketing claims? If so, how might those claims be restated?

3. How do you help customers know both the strengths and the limits of your offerings?

4. Does your visual storytelling show your products and physical environment at their best but not better than they are? Does your imagery inspire you to deliver products and experiences that won't belie your photos?

Make Appropriate Personal Disclosures

The Airbnb hosts we interviewed told us that guests typically want to know a little about the person who will be hosting them, and often guests tell them they've looked at their profile before requesting a reservation. This is especially the case for owner-occupied homes (for example, if a guest is sharing a room in a place where the Airbnb host resides). Superhost Javier Lasuncion notes, "When I am invited to someone's home, I want to know something about the person who will be hosting me. I think that's human nature." Host Emanuela Marino shares, "I don't want to be just an unknown brand representative that a traveler might encounter at the front desk of a hotel chain. Those front desk clerks can be very friendly, but they often come off more as a professional and less as a person. I want people to know a little about me as a person, and I want to know a little about them, as well. This is a person-to-person business."

Researchers have studied the importance of appropriate self-disclosure in creating trust and comfort in business. Specific to Airbnb, researchers from Cornell Tech, Stanford University, and Cornell University (Xiao Ma, Jeffrey Hancock, Kenneth Mingjie, and Mor Naaman) published a research article titled "Self-Disclosure and Perceived Trustworthiness of Airbnb Host Profiles." They described the purpose of their research with the following:

> On Airbnb, each host has a profile page that includes photos, a text-based self-description, social media verification status, and reviews (if any) from other Airbnb users who have stayed with the host. These profiles contribute to a guest's decision-making process . . . and help establish perceived trustworthiness. . . . We focus on host profiles, especially the text-based self-description and its role in establishing the perceived trustworthiness of hosts in the eyes of potential guests.

These researchers looked at two key factors: (1) what Airbnb hosts disclose on their profiles and (2) what elements contribute to perceived trustworthiness. While the findings of this study have broad impact, a couple of highlights are particularly relevant to anyone seeking to strike the right trust-enhancing tone on- or offline.

Overall, researchers categorized host profile disclosures into eight categories:

1. **Interests and tastes:** Favorite books; how they spend their weekends

2. **Life mottos and values:** Personal philosophy; inspirational motto

3. **Work or education:** Past or current job; schools attended

4. **Relationships:** Significant others; pets

5. **Personality:** Description of the kind of people they are

6. **Residence:** Where they are from; past and current places they have lived

7. **Travel:** Places they have traveled; favorite destinations

8. **Hospitality:** A welcome; an explanation of their reasons for hosting

Of these eight variables, Airbnb hosts most often disclosed three—residence, work and study, and interests and tastes. The three least disclosed areas were relationships, personality, and life mottos and values. The researchers also assessed perceived trustworthiness across three dimensions:

- **Ability:** Host is able to maintain a clean safe, environment.

- **Benevolence:** Host will give extra effort to help me if needed.

- **Integrity:** Hosts will do what they say.

In conclusion, the researchers found that "hosts should be encouraged to disclose more information and that this information should come from a diverse set of the eight categories."

From our anecdotal perspective, Airbnb guests frequently told us they look at host profiles to get a feel for whether a host will help make their stay a pleasant one. Guest Carmen Allan-Petale relates an example of this sentiment. Carmen and her husband David co-own and run a content creation business in Australia called Red Platypus Creative, and they are high-volume Airbnb users.

Carmen notes, "We started staying with Airbnb hosts in 2013 when my husband and I traveled across the US for six months. From there we ended up traveling the world mostly through Airbnb for just over three years." Carmen adds, "We find hotels to be a bit too impersonal. They feel like big buildings where every single room is the same. We look for opportunities to be hosted by real people who can help us travel as locals. Since we're writers and editors, we pay attention to how hosts write about themselves in their profiles. We look for individuals who have profiles that tell a story. We've found that those people often do a great job at also sharing the story of their community when they host us."

In the spirit of authentic, appropriate, and humanizing disclosure, let's look at a couple of examples of actual Airbnb host profiles that weave various elements of disclosure (from the eight categories highlighted in the research):

Yuki, a host from the Tampa, Florida, area, shares:

> I work in the airline industry as a trainer and learning facilitator. I love to travel. I love great food, great conversations over an adult beverage, a good meditation session.
>
> My favorite condiment is mustard. I love a good cup of coffee. Italy and Japan are incredible places. I've lived in the US, Japan, and Singapore. Spent a summer in Brittany, France, and a few months in Cebu, Philippines. I love unplanned vacations and serendipitous encounters.
>
> I love grandparents for their love and wisdom.

Superhosts Violet and Bill from San Diego offer their personal disclosure statement:

> Building a global community by opening our home and making friends out of strangers . . . one person at a time!

When I was very young, I had a passion to see the world. The only way my parents let me travel was staying at people's homes, either as an exchange student or at friends' houses.

Later on, I traveled a lot for work and stayed at wonderful hotels; however, my most dear memories are the ones I spent with families from other countries.

My dream was to have a home where one day I could re-create the hospitality they so selflessly provided.

Loving and caring hosts, speak several languages, and eager to help. Well-traveled and offer a home away from home. Worked over 18 years at UMASS, UCSD, and SDSU in the academic environment.

Lived in South America, Europe, and the USA. Love meeting new people and hosting.

Guests are not the only ones who find value in appropriate personal disclosure. Hosts report that they pay attention to guest profiles as well, and they can use that information to help them decide about accepting a booking. Yvonne, a host in London, shares, "Because I live in the home where I rent out a room (and am out at work during the day), I like to find out a bit about prospective guests through their profile before I accept the booking. I ask in my profile for guests to provide information about themselves and the reasons for their trip, so I will know if they'll be out or in all the time, when they will arrive and depart, whether they'll be cooking, having visitors, and so on. I need to feel comfortable with them in my home as much as they will need to feel they can trust me."

Adrian, a host from Cooma, Australia, adds, "I think guests should warm up their profiles with more than the mere mention of a first name and the industry in which they work. My listing price is low to give people with limited funds an opportunity to stay with me. I want to get a sense from their profile that they'll value my home and not see it as a cheap hotel."

Across industries, prospective customers are increasingly researching purchase options online and deciding to reach out to potential service providers based only on written descriptions and images. Because of this trend, the e-commerce platform provider Shopify encourages business leaders to create "drool worthy" product pages that immediately convey the value of a product or service.

Once a prospect reaches out to a provider, that prospect often makes final selections based on trust that develops through texts, emails, or online forums. Wendy Burt-Thomas, the author of *The Everything Creative Writing Book*, notes that once a customer chooses to engage your business, it's a matter of "building trust from the very first email." Hopefully the lessons you glean from Airbnb and its host community will assist you with trust creation across every digital communication with your customers. Let's take a moment to apply the trust building lessons shared by Airbnb hosts thus far.

 YOUR TRAVEL PLANNING GUIDE

1. In addition to accurately describing your products or services, how much do you disclose about your service providers' human side (for example, life mottos and values, work or education, personality, and origin or residence)?

2. On a five-star rating of accuracy, would all your customers give you five stars on prepurchase communication? If not, why not? What hard work needs to be done to earn that reputation?

3. How would your customers rate your perceived trustworthiness through the search, consideration, and purchase phases of their journey with you? Assume those ratings are made for dimensions of perceived competence, benevolence, and integrity.

Set Expectations

In addition to accurately describing the benefits, attributes, and limitations of listings and offering trust-facilitating personal disclosure, top Airbnb hosts understand that trust is often won or lost by setting clear expectations up front. The expectations hosts set are bidirectional—meaning they address what guests can expect from hosts and what hosts can expect from guests. The best Airbnb hosts understand that guest satisfaction is often a lagging indicator of the degree to which the host effectively established agreements on expectations at the outset of the relationship.

Often service providers fear they will lose a sale if they reveal expectations they'll place on a prospective buyer. By contrast, the best Airbnb hosts are abundantly clear regarding what guests can expect and what will be expected of them, when it comes to:

- House rules

- Special considerations

- Host interaction style

House Rules

Most of us don't mind rules—as long as we are the ones making them. If we must comply with someone else's rules, we tend to do better if we've had a chance to consider and agree to them before we are expected to comply. When done well, Airbnb hosts spell out house rules and special circumstances on their property listing, which removes surprises and forges agreements necessary to maintain trust. Here are examples of the level of specificity you can find in house rules and noteworthy consideration messages in actual Airbnb listings:

- No parties or events.

- No candles.

- Turn all lights off whenever you leave.

- Please do not eat or drink on or over the pool table.

- Please remove shoes.

- Strictly no smoking inside the apartment. If you would like to smoke, you may do so only on the balcony and the roof deck (please ensure that the balcony door and roof-deck door are closed so that smoke doesn't enter the apartment).

- Out of consideration for our neighbors, the fragility of the property, and the nature of the surrounding wilderness, **only you, the registered Airbnb guest**, may be present at this property. You may not have visiting guests over for any period of time. This is nonnegotiable. If you violate this rule, you will be asked to leave immediately.

- Pets must be declared to the owners in advance, preferably at the time of booking. We ask that if dogs are left unattended that they be crated and that they remain on a leash when wandering the property as they might be inclined to chase a child, cat, or chicken, or wander off.

Special Considerations
- The apartment is equipped with noise-monitoring technology, so please make sure you keep noise to a

minimum after 11 p.m. in order to not activate the alarm.

- From time to time, villagers need to use the river for bathing (naked), washing clothes, and performing ceremonies.

- The Internet is very poor and sometimes not working at all. We recommend being prepared for an off-the-grid experience.

- It is important to know that the last 3 kilometers of the road to the villa are not very good.

- Our property is run as a luxury self-sufficient apartment as opposed to a full-service hotel. We request that you leave it normally tidy (no food lying around).

- Cleaning is on departure only.

- Required excessive cleaning will be charged.

- If you are staying for longer than three nights, extra towels will be provided.

- Booking in the winter, you will need a four-wheel-drive vehicle.

Host Interaction Style

Not only do hosts set expectations regarding service levels, guest behavior, and the realities of getting to or staying at a property, many Airbnb hosts provide details on how they typically interact with guests. Here are three examples of interaction styles ranging from "not available on property" to "highly interactive":

We are very responsive via email, web, text, or phone, but will not be on site. There are plenty of guidebooks and a

welcome book located at the cabin that offer recommendations for places to eat and hiking trails.

We will welcome you and give you the guided tour, then
leave you alone. We are of course available via telephone
or email.

It is not uncommon for us to invite our guests to join us for
a wonderful home-cooked meal. Or we are happy to ac-
company you or just let you know where you can find [our
town's] best green chili restaurants, live music to two-step
to, a local festival or fair, or where you could go watch [NFL
football] on game day. . . . The options could be endless!

Outstanding Airbnb hosts adjust their style to the needs of a
guest, but they also set expectations on the likely range of interactions guests might experience. By offering information about being
unavailable to meet in person, guests can choose if a host is right
for them.

Many other customer-centric brands emphasize the importance of setting easily understandable customer expectations up
front. This is particularly true in areas such as response times, return policies, shipping conditions, and warranties.

Man Crates (a company that sells curated products for men) is
an example of a brand that sets clear customer expectations using
an engaging voice. With regard to limited hours of operations, the
Man Crates website clearly states:

It is not uncommon for us to invite our guests to join us for

While we'd like to be here for you 24/7, we'd like to see the
outside world occasionally so we try to keep pretty regular
business hours.

Our Customer Champions are available to help from
6 a.m. to 6 p.m. Pacific Time, Monday through Friday, and

from 9 a.m. to 6 p.m. on Saturday and Sunday. We may
have adjusted hours if the day you're reaching out is a holiday. Our reply email or phone message will let you know if
you've reached us on one of those days.

How clear, concise, and up front are you with your customers?
What should you be telling them in advance, to avoid confusion,
distress, and disappointment later?

PUTTING IT ALL TOGETHER

Let's take all the elements outlined in this chapter and see how
they affect trust in an example from guest Cheri Perry. Cheri and
her husband Dean founded their credit card processing business
Total Merchant Concepts in 1996. Cheri travels approximately every other month and uses Airbnb whenever possible. Her normal
process for deciding on an Airbnb listing begins by looking at pictures. Cheri explains, "I want a place that doesn't look too good to
be true and that is uncluttered, inviting, and creates an inspiring
environment in which I can work and relax. I also want to see all
the rooms and be able to see the view from the property." She then
reads the description of the listing. "I usually search for properties
where the property owner is not living on site, although my husband and I had such a positive experience with an owner-occupied
property that I may change my search behavior in the future."

In reading the property description, Cheri looks for a balanced
presentation that "accurately presents the strengths and limitations of the property." She adds, "At this point, I am looking at
the house rules and special considerations. In my case, I'm particularly interested in cancellation policies, as my business travel
needs can change quickly." If a listing looks promising, Cheri notes,
"I look at the overall property rating and each of the subratings

and read through recent reviews. I'm looking for how other guests have experienced the home and the host. From there, I click on the host profile to get a sense of the person who is providing the listing. I want to feel like I'm dealing with a person, not a mechanical property manager."

After Cheri has selected viable options, she reaches out to hosts through Airbnb's secure communication channel. "I never make a booking until I reach out to a host and ask a few questions. Normally, I am asking something like how far the property is from where I will be conducting business." She indicates that these questions are not just a fact-finding mission. They also help her establish whether hosts respond in a timely manner, seem personal in their responses, and have a genuine interest in her needs.

As a business owner, Cheri believes that trust is essential: "I know it has to be given to be received. I've made sure I provide helpful information in my guest profile, so hosts can feel comfortable allowing me in their homes. I've listed information about my education, family, personality, and interests." She adds, "I make it a point to always provide honest ratings and feedback at the end of every stay. I love that I get the chance to share openly about my experience—plus, I want to be a highly rated guest!" Cheri sees value in the immediate feedback Airbnb hosts receive from guests and the highly transparent and public nature of the feedback for the consideration and trust of future guests. "I believe everyone in business is and should be evaluated on trustworthiness by our customers and our team members." Cheri should know: her business was selected as one of the 10 best small businesses to work for in the state of Washington by *Seattle Business* magazine.

How is your business being informally and formally rated for trustworthiness by your customers and team members?

This chapter has focused on how hosts foster trust through the search, consideration, choice, and prearrival phases of the guest journey. Of course, trust is ultimately put to the test during actual service delivery (throughout Airbnb experiences or home stays). In Chapters 6 and 7, we will examine how Airbnb and its host community deliver personalized hospitality beyond the arrival experience and how they pay off their brand promise and strengthen trust. We will also examine how you can ensure trust as you deliver on your brand promise and build strong and lasting customer relationships.

POINTS OF INTEREST
AS YOU PRACTICE HELPFUL DISCLOSURE

→ Amazon CEO Jeff Bezos believes, "A brand for a company is like a reputation for a person. You earn reputation by trying to do hard things well."

→ During your customers' search, consideration, and purchase phases, it is important to do the following hard things well: market accurately, make appropriate personal disclosures, and set realistic expectations.

→ While puffed-up marketing claims can favorably affect consumer brand perceptions initially, questionable claims often incite the wrath of customers across social media and review sites when your promises aren't met.

→ Consumers have become cynical about brand promises, but they will pay a premium when brands earn trust.

→ Truth equals trust and reputation—and your reputation is everything.

→ Describe and inform, and avoid the temptation to sell a fantasy.

→ Think of marketing and advertising communication the way you would think of dating. Don't misstate your age or put on too much makeup. Present yourself at your best but not better than you are.

→ Drive trust through appropriate and diverse personal disclosure in areas such as your work background, personal interests, and passion for service.

→ Consider your trustworthiness to be judged as a function of your likely competence, benevolence, and integrity.

→ Most of us don't mind rules—as long as we are the ones making them. If we have to comply with someone else's rules, we tend to do better if we've had a chance to consider and agree to those rules before we are expected to follow them.

→ Be clear, specific, and up front with your rules and expectations of customers.

→ Be clear, specific and up front with what customers can expect from you.

→ Forge alignment on expectations to avoid negative surprises and to deliver satisfaction and maintain trust later.

hospitality

Be a Host

If you knew what I know about the power of
giving, you would not let a single meal pass
without sharing it in some way.
—Buddha,
monk and sage

BROADENING CONCEPTS OF HOSPITALITY AND HOSTING

Words like *hospitality* and *host* are typically applied to a narrow range of endeavors. In fact, the *Merriam-Webster* dictionary defines *hospitality* as "the activity or business of providing services to guests in hotels, restaurants, and bars," and it defines a *host* as "one that receives or entertains guests, socially, commercially, or officially." At Airbnb, however, hosting represents a long-standing practice of forging emotional connections that go well beyond what is traditionally thought of as the hospitality industry.

During a speech titled "Hosts Are Heroes," Airbnb's CEO and cofounder Brian Chesky reflected on the historic elements of hosting this way:

> One of our core values at Airbnb, and it may very well be the most important core value, is to "be a host." . . . Hosting's been around as long as there have been people. It happened thousands of years ago around a warm fire with some strangers and some friendly faces.

Chesky suggested that hosting is not only historically relevant but of increasing importance in modern business:

> There's a lot of talk about technology companies disrupting the way people work and the way people live, but . . . technology is never going to disrupt hosting. Author Tom Friedman . . . says there's three types of jobs: jobs through the hand, jobs at the head, and jobs with the heart. . . . Technology first typically disrupts jobs of the hand, . . . then eventually jobs at the head, but technology can never disrupt jobs of the heart, and hospitality is service with heart.

In this chapter we will look at how Airbnb supports their "be a host" corporate value. We will also examine how Airbnb assists the host community in delivering service with heart. Furthermore, we will clarify how Airbnb's efforts apply to your business no matter how you refer to those you serve ("customers," "clients," "patients," "users"). In the end, those who visit your websites, apps, or physical locations are your "guests." Like Airbnb, you invariably want to host (forge an emotional connection) with your guests and offer them hospitality (service with heart).

Compared to most companies, Airbnb faces a unique set of challenges when it comes to influencing service with heart. Specifically, Airbnb leaders control only those service experiences that occur on their web platform. Yet Airbnb team members must also influence the actions of millions of independent business owners who deliver guest experiences that link back to Airbnb.

To ensure that guests who book on the Airbnb platform receive consistent and emotionally engaging service, Airbnb provides training opportunities and resources directly to hosts to support success within the guest-host ecosystem. For hosts to be successful, Airbnb leaders must help individuals with a wide range of customer service talents learn how to turn homes and experiences into bookings. For guest success, Airbnb drives referrals and repeat bookings on the Airbnb platform.

Airbnb's unique service challenge is a function of a sprawling universe of hosts, interactions, and geography; however, all outstanding customer experience providers must balance the needs of the entire stakeholder ecosystem. For example, if your team members are unreasonably burdened in pursuit of positive customer experiences, over time, those experiences won't be sustained. Conversely, if your customers exert undue effort to make the lives of your team members easier, your customers will churn.

Most leaders who commit to outstanding customer experience delivery seek to first satisfy and ultimately emotionally engage customers in ways that will result in repeat business and referrals. Given changes in expectations, I suggest service providers must meet what I call *The Customer Experience Challenge.* To successfully address that challenge, service providers need to deliver the following:

- What customers want

- When they want it

- Where they want it

- As effortlessly

- Immediately

- Consistently

- Personally

- And as memorably as possible

Let's explore how Airbnb helps hosts satisfy guests through service basics. Later in the chapter we will address the advanced skills required to heartfully engage customers and drive positive memories, loyalty, and referrals.

SATISFACTION THROUGH
BASIC SERVICE

In his foreword to Chip Conley's book *Wisdom@Work*, Airbnb's Brian Chesky acknowledged that when Airbnb started, it was a hospitality business that didn't fully understand how hospitality worked. In partnership with Conley, Chesky affirmed that Airbnb started harnessing "the power of millions of micro-entrepreneurs." He said, "Truth be told, early on, we actually considered *hospitality* a 'dirty word.' Hospitality was what the hotel industry did, where guests are called 'sir' and 'ma'am,' and everything is a transaction, not an interaction." Chesky added, "Chip helped us understand that Airbnb could do hospitality differently. . . . By inviting guests into their homes, Airbnb hosts personify true hospitality by getting to know their guests, learning their stories, and maybe even becoming their lifelong friends."

To understand how Airbnb helps hosts set new standards of hospitality, imagine you have a spare room in your home, and you want to generate extra income by sharing it. Let's also assume you have no background in hospitality, and you've never worked in a customer service–related job. In that scenario, how would you begin your journey to be an effective Airbnb host?

Laura Chambers, general manager of Homes Hosts at Airbnb, notes, "We want to help our hosts be successful entrepreneurs. So, when hosts complete a listing on our platform, they will begin getting emails with business and hosting tips. Those emails continue on a monthly basis and help connect new hosts with online and offline community support. Online support includes the Airbnb Community Center, and offline opportunities involve Host Groups, which Airbnb supports. Our efforts are designed to drive host success and excellent guest experiences."

Hosts are encouraged to strive for service excellence. For example, on the Hospitality page of the Airbnb website (a resource prominently available to hosts), Airbnb asserts, "We want to give you clear guidance so you know what's expected and can provide a 5-star stay every time you share your home." Receiving 5-star guest reviews every time is a lofty aspiration. To achieve that goal, Airbnb helps hosts focus on the following:

- **Responsiveness:** Providing immediate guest service and communication—"when they want it"

- **Convenience:** Offering effortless experiences—the "way guests want them"

- **Needs fulfillment:** Meeting guest needs consistently— "giving them what they want and how they want it"

Before we look at the guidance Airbnb provides hosts to enable them to deliver "a 5-star stay every time," let's consider how changing customer behavior and hospitality delivery affect your business.

YOUR TRAVEL PLANNING GUIDE

1. How is hosting guests relevant to your business? Consider having a team discussion about your current strengths and opportunities when it comes to delivering hospitality—service with heart.

2. Looking at your service ecosystem, are there places where team members are unreasonably burdened in pursuit of positive customer experiences? Conversely, are there areas where customers must exert undue effort to make the lives of your team members easier?

3. What opportunities help you meet your Customer Experience Challenge? Where can you do a better job to give customers what they want, when they want it, where they want it, and as effortlessly, immediately, consistently, personally, and memorably as possible?

Responsiveness

Imagine that you are eager to purchase a product or service. You email the seller to get more details before you decide to buy. Imagine further that you wait and wait for a response. You check your inbox, you check your spam filter. Most likely at this point, your only remaining decision will be whether you will write a scathing review before or after you seek out a more competent service provider.

Since mobile technology allows us to instantaneously interact with one another from virtually anywhere on the planet, consumers have come to avoid businesses that can't address their inquiries and needs immediately.

Jeff Toister, author of *The Service Culture Handbook*, conducted a study that looked at customer expectations for the timeliness of responses to emails, Twitter direct messages, and Facebook inquiries. Toister noted, "A one-hour email response time will meet the expectations of 89 percent of your customers." For both email and Facebook responses, he suggested, "Companies aiming for world-class customer service should respond within 15 minutes or less." Similarly, when it comes to a response to a direct message on Twitter, Toister warned: "Anything slower than 15 minutes risks disappointing a large portion of customers."

Being time urgent is a large part of the responsiveness picture, but it is not the *entire* picture. Toister found, "The pressure to respond quickly causes many people to skim and scan emails from colleagues. They then send partial responses which generates a lot of unnecessary back and forth. One study found that the average email conversation at work includes 4.5 messages." In essence, responsive communication is not simply a function of communication urgency. To be responsive, a company must track the speed of its communication and service delivery—as well as the *quality* of responses.

Management consultant Peter Drucker once wrote, "What gets measured gets improved," but to truly get things done, people have to also be held accountable for the things being measured. Quite often leaders don't understand the importance of measuring service elements like response speed, and when they do, some leaders fail to hold individuals accountable for performance on those measures.

The ultimate marketplace example of business accountability was shared by former AT&T Chairman C. Michael Armstrong in something I've termed the "tremble effect":

The ancient Romans had a tradition: whenever one of their engineers constructed an arch, as the capstone was hoisted into place, the engineer assumed accountability for his work in the most profound way possible: he stood under the arch.

While I am not sure there is an actual historical record that supports Armstrong's claim, his example evokes images of trembling architects awaiting the ultimate proof of their competency. It also conveys a morbid Darwinian flair whereby only the best architects survived.

Airbnb emphasizes the importance of responsive communication through a variety of online and offline training tools that we will explore later in the chapter. These leaders also create metrics to measure communication speed and evoke their own version of Darwinian accountability through publicly shared performance metrics and unedited customer feedback.

Airbnb holds hosts accountable with transparent metrics that drive responsiveness and rapid communication behavior. On each host's profile, Airbnb provides two pieces of information about communication speed. One reports the host's overall response rate within 24 hours of inquiry, and the other indicates the host's average recent response times. For example, most hosts with whom we've interacted have 100 percent response rates and respond to inquiries within an hour.

Let's take a moment to analyze the value hosts and guests derive from publicly posted data on response rates and response speeds. Hosts receive useful feedback that helps them track performance against a basic Airbnb service standard. That data is also factored into Airbnb's search algorithms. Responsive hosts benefit as prospective guests consider communication performance (for example, if you want to book on short notice, you'd probably skip over hosts who typically have been slow to respond). Guests can also use information about communication times to develop realistic expectations for responses to their inquiries.

Chip Conley shared that early on in Airbnb's efforts to assist hosts with hospitality skills, "We realized we had to help hosts understand what they were missing when it came to hospitality. Often hosts would have high ratings on most but not all important areas of service excellence, so we would send those hosts emails with relevant and helpful information based on opportunities in areas like responsiveness." Imagine being a host for Airbnb and receiving an email with tips targeted to help you elevate your ratings on an area of opportunity like your check-in process. That email would demonstrate customized care consistent with what Airbnb leaders want every guest to experience.

Airbnb Superhost Harry in Athens, Greece, offers advice to new hosts through posts on the Airbnb Community Forum, suggesting you should "reply as soon as possible." He continues, "I have found that replying within four to five minutes to a message surprises the guest. . . . Even if you don't have something to say to your guest, write a quick 'Thank you for your interest, I am driving at the moment, I will come back to you with more info ASAP within less than an hour of the original message.'"

Along with information on response rates and response times, Airbnb posts additional accountability data concerning each host's overall communication. As you'll recall from Chapters 4 and 5, guests are asked to rate each Airbnb experience and provide feedback on six subcategories, including communication, which enables a guest to evaluate the host's overall communication effectiveness from the first contact to well past the booking process. The comments section further enables guests to describe a host's response speed and effectiveness. Prospective guests can type keywords like "responsiveness" into the search box above each host's comment section and find all the information that is relevant to the query.

Being responsive is important, but often it is better to anticipate customers' needs rather than having customers reach out in a way that requires a response. For example, by focusing on customer convenience, Airbnb gives hosts the opportunity to let guests book without an inquiry—so immediate host responses aren't as essential. Before we look at this type of customer convenience, let's explore the role convenience plays as a customer experience differentiator.

Convenience

In his book *The Convenience Revolution*, Shep Hyken writes "Convenience is relevant to your business, no matter what your business happens to be. . . . It would be a strategic catastrophe to assume you are 'convenient enough' for your customer, and it's a potentially huge marketplace advantage to make what you offer the customer a little more convenient."

Making customers' lives easier and making your service delivery more convenient aren't novel business concepts. The core success of Airbnb is linked to how the founders crafted a convenient way for people to find and share available spaces. A 2010 *Harvard Business Review* article titled "Stop Trying to Delight Your Customers," written by Matthew Dixon, Karen Freeman, and Nicholas Toman, emphasized the importance of brands becoming "easy to do business with." Those authors encouraged leaders to track customer effort through the *customer effort score* (CES).

The CES is the average of customer responses to a single question that asks them how much effort was required to use a product or service. Respondents answer using a five-point scale ranging from very easy to very difficult. Research findings validate CES as a valuable tool in predicting customers' future purchase behavior and their future spend. As a customer experience consultant, I encourage my clients to evaluate customer effort in the context of metrics involving customer engagement, loyalty, and advocacy.

Airbnb continually looks for ways to remove customer effort and enhance customer convenience at important moments along the Airbnb booking journey. Greg Greeley, president of Homes for Airbnb, told me one of the reasons he left his position as vice president of Amazon Prime to join Airbnb because of Airbnb's mission and demonstrated commitment to customer convenience: "At Airbnb we have an opportunity for a tremendous amount of innovation to continually encourage and reward hosts who use tools that drive guest convenience and ease."

Airbnb, for example, gives hosts the opportunity to remove a step in the booking process. Rather than having guests look at a property's available dates and then make a booking request (requiring a host's response and approval), hosts can choose to give prospective guests the option to instantly book the property. Once the guests click on an instant booking, their request is immediately accepted, and the reservation is confirmed. Prospective guests on the Airbnb platform can filter their searches so they see only those listings where hosts have selected the Instant Book option. An *Airbnb Blog* post explains how instant booking positively affects a host's status during a guest's search:

> The main goal of the search algorithm is to facilitate bookings. And if a guest has an excellent experience booking and traveling on Airbnb, they're highly likely to use Airbnb again in the future. This helps travelers and hosts alike. We've seen for many years that—all other things being equal—travelers prefer to use Instant Book because they can book quickly, skip the wait time for hosts to respond, and avoid possibly being rejected. Because of the high booking success for hosts and guests, Instant Book gives your listing a boost in searches.

Instant Book is not required of all hosts (since some hosts want to interact with guests prior to agreeing to let them stay in their home). By offering the choice to hosts, Airbnb seeks to strike a delicate balance in the host-guest ecosystem. A host we talked to who uses Instant Book remarked: "I am committed to Airbnb's vision of Belong Anywhere, building trust, and of making the lives of my guests as convenient as possible. By allowing guests to book instantly, I am accepting everyone and increasing guest convenience. After guests book with me, I reach out to them via the Airbnb platform and start building rapport and trust in advance of their visit. Thus far Instant Book has been a win on all fronts."

Airbnb guest Dru Johnson commented, "I like having options to book instantly or to interact with a host before I make a decision to book. Sometimes I am in a rush to get a short-term booking secured so I want to be able to book immediately. Other times, like when I traveled to Europe during the warmest days of the summer, I wanted to make sure air-conditioning units were fully operational, so I reached out to prospective hosts before I booked their properties." Creating options for customers and service providers is often the best way to maximize convenience for all parties in a service ecosystem.

As you look at your business, where have you enhanced customer convenience while also making service delivery manageable for your team? Where else might you reasonably expand customers' options to drive convenience?

Airbnb's commitment to driving convenience is also reflected in the ease by which individuals can list properties on the site. New hosts are onboarded swiftly by moving through a series of screen prompts (user-friendly templates) that guide them through the listing process:

- Creating a property description
- Listing amenities
- Taking photos
- Setting guest requirements

- Selecting house rules

- Deciding if they want to use the Instant Book option

- Building an availability calendar

- Establishing a base, minimum, and maximum pricing (using recommended and Smart Pricing tools)

- Considering a special offer to encourage initial guests to book a property, so the listing receives reviews

Airbnb offers tools for both hosts and guests to reduce effort, and it is driving customer experience success by asking the question: how can we make this easier for the people we serve—for employees, customers, and other stakeholders? Of course, ideas that emerge from asking that question must receive follow-up as demonstrated by instant booking and onboarding templates.

Laura Chambers notes that Airbnb's commitment to innovate ways to help hosts deliver easier experiences for guests starts with Airbnb's overall approach to hosts: "We focus on helping our host community by taking a three-step approach. The first step involves engaged communication and active dialogue with the community. The second involves prioritizing improvements our hosts desire, taking action on those priorities and building trust by consistently delivering on what we promise. Finally, we strive to streamline the host experience with us in ways that reflect very personalized creativity." Laura's comments reflect the importance of treating those you serve in the way you wish them to treat those they serve.

Fulfilling Needs

In my book *Leading the Starbucks Way: 5 Principles for Connecting with Your Customers, Your Product, and Your People*, I suggest that above all else, service providers must meet functional needs. To make that point, I cited Roger Sant, vice president of Maritz Research, who observed, "Nobody enters into a service interaction without having a functional need to fulfill. People never say, 'I don't want anything. I just want to see if you're nice.' It just doesn't happen." Guests want their Airbnb hosts to be nice, but a guest's primary concern is to secure a clean place that meets their functional need for shelter.

Airbnb leaders emphasize functional need fulfillment and guide hosts to provide a clean and tidy home consistent with a listing's photos. Through tips on the Host section of the Airbnb website and articles written for the host community, Airbnb encourages hosts to allow enough time between bookings to ensure that the space is ready for each next guest. The company recommends that hosts consider charging a cleaning fee to be used to purchase cleaning supplies or hire professional cleaners. Airbnb reminds hosts that in response to these high-priority service behaviors, "guests will have the opportunity to rate the cleanliness of your space, and the average of your ratings will appear on your listing page. If you consistently receive low cleanliness ratings, you may be subject to penalties."

Chip Conley, Airbnb's first global head of hospitality and strategy, suggests that many functional guest needs are addressed through an accommodation's "hardware" while emotional needs are met through a host's interpersonal skills, or "software." Let's look at how Airbnb offers guidance on delivering the right hardware or amenities needed to satisfy guests.

Airbnb requires hosts to provide what the company refers to as "essential amenities" in the form of toilet paper, soap, linens and sheets, and at least one towel and pillow for every guest. Hosts who fail to provide these essentials are subject to penalties that include having their listing removed from the platform.

Airbnb dedicates an entire section of its blog site (blog.at airbnb.com) to information and posts about hospitality. One of the blogs posted there encourages hosts by saying:

> Why stop at this bare minimum when by offering just a little bit more, you can make your guest's stay even more enjoyable? For starters, use those essentials as a springboard to more noteworthy hospitality. Raise the bar on that bar of soap by also treating your guests to some fabulous shower gel or bath salts—and source from local makers. And how about a sweet on the pillow as a finishing touch for those freshly laundered sheets? If you think toilet paper can't be kicked up a notch, we beg to differ. Spending a few seconds folding back the corners of that first sheet on the roll—or mastering [toilet paper] origami—has the power to make someone say, "Hey, honey, check this out!"

In addition to offering suggestions to hosts to slightly elevate beyond the basics, Airbnb encourages hosts to provide highly desired amenities and to list them in their property's description. These types of items include Wi-Fi, a TV, a hair dryer, and an iron. Airbnb's suggestions for other hardware enhancements are voluminous and include simple ideas like creating a welcome basket or setting up an in-room beverage station stocked with bottled water, an electric tea kettle, coffee maker, and a selection of teas and coffee.

Airbnb has taken need fulfillment, amenities, cleanliness, and convenience to another level with Airbnb Plus. As you'll recall from Chapter 1, Airbnb Plus is a program available to highly rated hosts who meet exacting standards and a 100-plus quality inspection rating. Airbnb Plus listings are well equipped. For example, a kitchen in an Airbnb Plus home must be stocked with the following:

- Large knife for food prep, bread knife, and paring knife

- Cutting board

- Four utensil sets (set containing a fork, knife, and spoon)

- Four plates, bowls, glasses, and mugs

- Two pots and two pans of any size

- Spatula

- Sponge or cleaning brush

- Dish soap

- Garbage can with garbage bag

- At least one roll of paper towels

- Bottle opener and wine opener

Airbnb Plus homes must also be stylish, well maintained, and offer an effortless check-in with either a "lockbox, keypad, doorperson, smartlock, or nearby host."

As an added encouragement strategy, Airbnb profiles Superhosts who provide outstanding service basics and amenities in videos on various social media sites. Leaders also highlight these types of hosts in feature articles on the Hospitality tab of the *Airbnb Blog.*

Cleanliness and the presence of basic—as well as desired—amenities are necessary elements of Airbnb service, but they don't guarantee that a guest's experience will be infused with heart. Before we look at how leaders at Airbnb inspire the host community to deliver emotionally engaging and memorable travel experiences, let's first reflect on how Airbnb's basic service approaches apply to you.

YOUR TRAVEL PLANNING GUIDE

1. How are you measuring and driving accountability for responsiveness as well as communication speed and quality?

2. Consider using the customer effort scale (CES) to assess the convenience level of your business. What average score do you think you would receive today concerning the effort customers must expend to do business with you (with 1 being very easy and 5 being very difficult)?

3. Are you continually asking and taking action on the question: how can we make our service delivery easier for the people we serve (employees, customers, and other stakeholders)?

4. Have you established minimum service standards related to your customers' basic needs? How do you respond to team members who consistently fail to meet those standards?

MORE THAN SERVICE BEHAVIOR

Take a moment to recall a positive service experience. As you think about what made that interaction memorable, it's likely that the event stands out because of how that service made you feel. The importance of emotion in memory formation is alluded to in a quote often errantly attributed to Maya Angelou but that came from Carl W. Buehner in 1971: "They may forget what you said, but they will never forget how you made them feel."

In the intervening decades since Buehner's observation, researchers and behavioral economists have validated the role of emotion in shaping memory. Writing in the journal *Frontiers in Psychology*, Chai M. Tyng and colleagues assert:

> Emotion has a substantial influence on the cognitive pro-
> cesses in humans, including perception, attention, learning,
> memory, reasoning, and problem solving. Emotion has a
> particularly strong influence on attention, especially mod-
> ulating the selectivity of attention as well as motivating ac-
> tion and behavior. This attentional and executive control is
> intimately linked to learning processes.

Given that emotion strengthens memory, how can we understand and engage positive emotions during quality service delivery? Throughout my career, I've worked with leaders who have
taken the time to explore what they want customers to feel and
how they want their company to be remembered by customers.
I've come to call the by-product of these explorations a "way we
serve" statement that defines the optimal emotional experience of
customers.

In the context of Starbucks, for example, that desired emotional state is reflected in this "way we serve" statement: "We create
inspired moments in each customer's day." In the case of Mercedes-
Benz, the "way we serve" statement is captured in the title of my
book *Driven to Delight: Delivering World-Class Customer Experience the Mercedes-Benz Way*. Inherently, Mercedes-Benz wants
to deliver delight, and Starbucks wants to create moments of
inspiration.

The Starbucks "way we serve" statement not only focuses on
the emotion of inspiration but also on the importance of delivering inspiration during moments of interaction. This approach is
in keeping with Dan and Chip Heath's summary of research on
memory and emotions, in their book *The Power of Moments*. Dan
and Chip refer to these brief interactions as "flagship moments":

What's indisputable is that when we assess our experiences, we don't average our minute-by-minute sensations. Rather, we tend to remember flagship moments, the peaks, the pits, and the transitions. This is a critical lesson for anyone in service businesses—from restaurants to medical clinics to call centers to spas—where success hinges on the customer experience.

Essentially, our memory for service is based on emotions at peaks, valleys, transitions, and end points in our interactions with a brand or service provider.

Influenced in part by Neal Gabler's *Walt Disney: The Triumph of the American Imagination*, Brian Chesky captures the emotional essence of the optimal Airbnb experience in a single word: magical. The Airbnb "way we serve" statement could be reflected in delivering memorable and magical experiences. For example, in an interview for *Fortune* magazine, Chesky noted, "We call all this 'magical trips'—basically trips that are just amazing, memorable, end-to-end experiences. This is what we want to be doing in the next 10 years."

To inspire these experiences, Airbnb offers webinars, and it invites hosts to regional training events and workshops. It has also conducted three Airbnb Open events that provide training and networking to hosts from across the globe. Attendance at the last Airbnb Open involved thousands of hosts from over a hundred countries.

In some markets like China (where Airbnb announced it had more than 10,000 Superhosts as of March 2018), Airbnb has created formalized hosting programs. For example, Airbnb created China's Airbnb Host Academy (AHA). Leaders describe AHA as "an innovative program leveraging online and offline efforts to provide relevant educational content to hosts." In advance of AHA's launch in 2018, Airbnb conducted offline sessions across

Beijing, Shanghai, Chengdu, and Guangzhou. During these workshop sessions, Airbnb employees provided face-to-face host training. Airbnb has continued to develop AHA, describing it this way: "We offer offline workshops, live chats through our official Airbnb Host WeChat account, and a series of inspirational and educational videos." Airbnb leaders note that through AHA, "hosts will be able to access the right level of education for the various stages of their host journey. The Airbnb Host Academy's offline programming also provides access and valuable networking opportunities to other hosts in the community."

Chip Conley provided me insights into Airbnb's initial journey helping hosts provide what he calls "the generous spirit of hospitality": "In the early days I did a series of road trips across the world to 26 different markets where I would literally run two-hour workshops. That travel allowed a few hundred hosts in each market to immerse themselves deeper in hospitality skills."

Conley and Airbnb's dive into the generous spirit of hospitality has fueled the type of personal and memorable guest experiences reflected in an article for the *Tourism Management Perspectives* journal titled "Exploring Tourists' Memorable Hospitality Experiences: An Airbnb Perspective." In that article, researchers Erose Sthapit and Jano Jiménez-Barreto explore factors that make an Airbnb stay truly memorable:

> Today, offering memorable experiences are pivotal when attempting to gain a competitive advantage. . . . Memorable tourism experiences (MTEs) have recently attracted the attention of researchers and practitioners. . . . [MTEs are defined] as tourism experiences that are positively remembered and recalled after the events have occurred. Several studies have indicated that MTEs are the best predictors of tourists' future behavior.

These researchers interviewed Airbnb guests, coded their responses, and analyzed data looking for factors that contributed to memorable Airbnb stays. Sthapit and Jiménez-Barreto concluded:

> Given that memorable Airbnb experiences were related to the social interactions with the host, the attitude of the host, and the location of the accommodation, this study calls for a shift in the Airbnb host's role from offering cheap rental accommodations to being memorable experience cocreators. . . . Airbnb hosts should consider interaction as a resource that helps guests to make the optimum use of the time spent at the destination and increase the value. To create a more memorable experience, hosts should treat their guest in a friendly manner throughout their stay. Furthermore, hosts should resolve any unexpected problems faced by the guest.

Airbnb encourages hosts to share best practices in the spirit of being experience cocreators and as a way to swiftly resolve guest concerns. For example, at the time of this writing, Airbnb has dozens of videos providing tips to hosts on its YouTube channel https://www.youtube.com/airbnb. Additionally, there are countless other tips provided in host-specific interviews throughout Airbnb's social media channels. These videos include a Q&A session with Brian Chesky asking a panel of Airbnb hosts to share their best hospitality insights, as well as activity-specific videos like one titled "Making Your Guest's Stay Special." (To see both videos, go to airbnbway.com/book-resources.) In the latter example, Airbnb host Joy shared that while staying at an Airbnb in Portland, Oregon, her host provided an array of local treats that made her trip memorable. Joy added, "My stay got me thinking to do the same at my Airbnb. I have a few friends who own local businesses here. So sometimes I get to throw in their treats."

Through access to hospitality leaders, webinars, blogs, workshops, regional training, formal hospitality programs, peer-to-peer sharing, and a clear articulation of Airbnb's desired magical and memorable experiences, Airbnb has defined their *what* and *how* of emotional engagement. How might you do the same at your business?

In Chapter 7, Airbnb hosts share how they are delivering five-star hospitality for their guests. Airbnb guests will also share what makes stays and experiences memorable. You will see how service at Airbnb is elevated to service with heart. Most importantly, you will get a glimpse into how anyone can make service experiences memorable and magical.

POINTS OF INTEREST
AS YOU SEEK TO BE A HOST

→ Hosting has been around for thousands of years and will likely be around for thousands more. Hosting is resistant to technological disruption.

→ Hospitality transcends specific business sectors. It can be described as "service with heart."

→ Basic service drives customer satisfaction. Basic service plus emotional engagement drive loyalty and referrals.

→ Basic service requires responsiveness, providing convenience, and meeting needs.

→ Customer expectations for service speed have greatly increased, prompting a need to measure and drive accountability on responsive communication and action.

→ *Customer effort* is an indicator of how convenient it is for a customer to engage a business.

→ A customer's memory of a service experience is shaped by peak, valley, transition, and end moments along their journey with a brand.

→ Memorable experiences often drive repeat business and referrals from customers.

→ *Service with heart* can be facilitated through a variety of means including webinars, blogs, workshops, training academies, and, peer-to-peer sharing.

→ Successful brands define their optimal customer experience (their "way we serve" statement) and help team members understand how they can and should deliver that experience for every customer, every time.

Think Magical and Memorable

*Sometimes you will never know the value of
a moment until it becomes a memory.*

—Theodor Seuss Geisel ("Dr. Seuss"),
children's author and cartoonist

In Chapter 6, we explored how Airbnb seeks to support a service ecosystem that delivers magical and memorable travel experiences through responsiveness, convenience, needs fulfillment, and personal care. In this chapter, we will look at how Airbnb's hosts deliver service with heart. But before we get into host stories, let's put hospitality excellence in context.

Throughout the mid- to late 1980s, professors of retail and marketing from Texas A&M University (A. Parasuraman and Len Berry) and a marketing professor from Duke University (Valarie A. Zeithaml) developed a comprehensive model of service excellence that identified 10 factors associated with quality service experiences:

1. Reliability

2. Responsiveness

3. Competence

4. Access

5. Courtesy

6. Communication

7. Credibility

8. Security

9. Knowing the customer

10. Tangibles

Through subsequent research, these marketing and retail thought leaders compressed the 10 drivers into five dimensions of service excellence, which they described as follows:

- **Responsiveness:** Helping customers with prompt service

- **Reliability:** Efficiently delivering on promises

- **Tangibles:** Appearance of virtual and physical property, equipment, people, products, and communications

- **Assurance:** Courtesy, knowledge, thoughtfulness, and anticipation of emotional needs

- **Empathy:** Personalized care

The first three of these dimensions closely align with the service components outlined in Chapter 6 (responsiveness, convenience, and needs fulfillment), and the last two relate to emotional or heart elements needed to achieve memorable and magical experiences.

Measuring customer perceptions across these five dimensions, Parasuraman, Zeithaml, and Berry developed a tool they referred to as SERVQUAL that measures service quality in the context of the following model:

$$SQ = P - E$$

where

SQ is the *service quality*.

P is the individual's *perception* of the service rendered.

E is the individual's *expectation* for that service.

SERVQUAL calculates service experience quality by assessing how well providers meet or exceed customer expectations when it comes to responsiveness, reliability, tangibles, assurance, and empathy. When gaps are large, customer satisfaction and engagement are low. When customer expectations are met or exceeded, customer engagement and satisfaction are high.

In the pages that follow, we will look at how Airbnb hosts deliver experiences that exceed guest expectations based on the host's *responsiveness* (prompt communication and service), *reliability* (providing what is promised), *tangibles* (meeting needs through physical elements), *assurance* (courtesy and thoughtfulness), and *empathy* (personalization and anticipation of needs). Since responsiveness, reliability, and tangibles are "table stakes" for service today, we will also focus on behaviors required to anticipate and personalize connections with guests and customers. More importantly, we will look at how you and your team can drive service quality that delivers magical and memorable experiences for those you serve.

RESPONSIVENESS
AND RELIABILITY

Outstanding Airbnb hosts understand the importance of service urgency and accuracy. They appreciate that in business today, time has become a form of currency.

Most customers are calculating the cost of an experience based not only on how much money they pay but also on how much time and effort they must expend to receive their goods or services. Airbnb hosts report that service speed is a significant factor in delivering value and maintaining guest trust. These hosts suggest they must communicate and take action *before* guests begin to worry about being forgotten. Superhost Peter Kwan notes, "If guests have to wait a long time to hear back from a host about a booking inquiry, they start to wonder if future needs will also receive a slow response. Once a person starts doubting, it can become all consuming." Irrespective of industry, customers associate a slow response with service incompetence, neglect, and a lack of appreciation of their patronage. In many cases, that perceived neglect can lead to customer churn.

Guest Brooke Ashley Johnson shared, "We've stayed in a lot of Airbnbs and have had amazing experiences with one exception." In that instance, Brooke and her husband were booked for two nights in Berlin. Upon their arrival, the couple began to have Wi-Fi problems, and Brooke needed the Wi-Fi to complete a work project. Brooke added, "The host wasn't responsive to our request for help, and we started to feel uneasy. As luck would have it, the unit's air conditioning also wasn't working. Even before we reached out to the host on the air-conditioning issue, we braced for a poor response, and sadly our prediction came true. She made excuses but took no action to help us."

After one night without the Wi-Fi and air conditioning, the couple began exploring other options. Brooke continued: "Fortunately, we contacted Airbnb's customer service. They helped us get out of the second-night commitment and did an outstanding job with service recovery. If Airbnb hadn't helped us, I'm not sure we would have kept booking through them. Given how they handled the situation, we're probably more loyal to Airbnb now." Brooke left an unfavorable yet honest review to encourage the host "to step up to meet guest needs" and also to warn others that this host was not delivering on expectations.

Airbnb's 24/7 help center serves an important function when travelers like Brooke feel they aren't receiving timely communication or service, but ultimately Airbnb must rely on hosts to be responsive and reliable in ways that don't require service recovery.

As is the case with a lot of individuals in business, Airbnb hosts can demonstrate resistance to a change even when that change creates convenience for guests. For example, Superhost Kathy Peterman shared how she was slow to embrace the Instant Book function discussed in Chapter 6: "I had been reluctant to allow the Instant Book option because I was proofing every single person before they came in my home. Finally, I decided to try instant bookings for a month to see how it would work. I have not turned it off since." Kathy now recommends guests take advantage of Instant Book and other convenience features provided by Airbnb noting, "I encourage each guest to make sure they have the Airbnb app loaded on their phone as it will allow us to communicate during their stay and it will enable me to function like a concierge at their fingertips."

Debi Hertert, cofounder of Host2Host, a networking and resource organization, notes: "Generally hosts realize that when they make the lives of their guests easier, they also make their own lives easier." She adds, "Most seasoned hosts understand that you need to communicate quickly, do what you promise, and reduce guest effort. Those are basic elements of a successful stay. The Airbnb platform also gives rich feedback on how we are doing in those areas. Unmet basic service expectations show up in ratings and reviews."

To back up Debi's point about the transparency of customer feedback, here are candid guest reviews (with host names removed) concerning missed, met, or exceeded expectations with regard to responsiveness and convenience:

Missed

No air conditioning when we arrived at about 6 p.m. There was a fan by the bed, but it didn't work. We contacted [the host] about this because A/C is one of the amenities in the listing, and it was very hot in the apartment. He told us there was a window unit in the basement and another fan downstairs. He said we could either set it up ourselves, or he'd do it when he arrived home at 10:30 or 11 p.m.

We thanked him and then opted to go for dinner . . . to give him time to come put the window unit in. I texted him at 11 p.m. letting him know we would be back in about 30 minutes and that we still needed it put in. He replied at about 11:30 p.m. saying he'd be back in 30 minutes. . . . My fiancé finally caved at around 12:30 a.m. . . . and went to put the unit in himself but couldn't get the screen out. At 12:50 a.m. my fiancé called the host, this time pretty upset. The host did not apologize, only said he was pulling in now. It was past 1 a.m. when it was finally resolved.

Met

We had some noise issues in the beginning, but the host took prompt care of them and we had no further issues.

Exceeded

From the beginning, communication was frequent and direct. [Our host] offered great recommendations and was hospitable beyond compare. Once we arrived, the house and room were impeccably clean, gorgeously decorated, and conveniently located. They provided us with everything we could need and more. . . . We could not recommend this place more! . . . We will definitely be back!

When service providers lack urgency in responsive communication or action, customers often experience a gap between expectations and reality. Similarly, when service professionals forget the importance of making their customers' lives easier, customers consider other options. When providers are responsive and deliver convenience, they often make their own lives easier and hear more customers say, "We will definitely be back."

MEETING NEEDS THROUGH PHYSICAL ELEMENTS

Sociologist Martha Beck encourages people to "stop fixating on stuff you can touch and start caring about the things that touch you." While her comment reflects the importance of making emotionally touching connections with customers, it does not negate the importance of focusing on the touchable elements of your business— your service tangibles.

Thanks to the proliferation of cameras in smartphones, flawed service tangibles are often posted on social media. In an article published on *Mylio* in 2017, Eric Perrett estimated that consumers were taking more than 1.2 trillion digital photos annually. Customers are poised to snap pictures of poorly presented meals at restaurants, cluttered waiting rooms, or customer service missteps.

In some cases, an image is so frequently shared and reposted that it achieves negative virality. Such was the case for a picture taken by Michelle Cehn, which prompted a phenomenon that came to be known as "orangegate." On a blog at her website worldofvegan.com, Michelle Cehn explains she walked into a Whole Foods in Oakland, California, and "saw these naked mandarin oranges sitting in plastic jail cells." Michelle noted, "I had to pause, pull out my phone, snap a photo, and post it to Facebook."

Before long, Michelle's photo had thousands of shares. The Plastic Pollution Coalition tweeted the picture, and a day later Whole Foods permanently pulled the plastic-packed oranges. Shortly thereafter Michelle's photo was part of widespread, global news stories on television, in print, and on websites. Michelle concluded, "Take notice when things aren't right, and do something about it! All it takes is one voice, one photo, one email, one tweet, one action to make a change in the world."

Whole Foods apologetically tweeted: "Definitely our mistake. These have been pulled. We hear you, and we will leave them in their natural packaging: the peel." Whole Food's skillful management of the potential PR issue tamped down the negative impact of the image, but other brands like United Airlines have had substantially greater fallout from customer-generated photos and videos. In 2017, United experienced a $1.4 billion stock drop in the aftermath of a viral video that captured a passenger being bloodied while forcibly removed from an overbooked plane.

Airbnb Superhost Wendy Needy puts it this way: "I want my guests to post pictures and videos of the fun they are having during their stay. It's my job to make sure they aren't touching, tasting, seeing, or hearing anything unpleasant that would make them want to grab their camera to share a negative picture. Because I am focused on the details of our guests' visits, I am not worried about what our guests will post."

While there are ample Airbnb customer photos and videos posted across social media, depicting magical and less-than-magical service tangibles, I'll let you conjure your own images of expectations missed, met, or exceeded based on actual reviews involving *tangible service elements:*

Missed

First impressions are lasting. I was shocked by the state of the door leading into my room, which looked dirty, had peeling paint, and a length of wire hanger to use instead of a doorknob. The rug next to the bed, although it may be clean and just stained, looked filthy. All window and door frames and moldings were peeling and/or looked dirty.... Made me want to spend as little time as possible in the unit, as it felt squalid.

Met

Clean. Detailed. Complete. Spacious. Beds were really comfy, and each room had a personal refrigerator!

Exceeded

The casita is a great size.... Within the casita is beautiful artwork and effects that we truly appreciated.... The casita was clean with fresh linen.... The bathroom was clean, and I loved the mirrored walls—modern and gorgeous. A very good supply of towels were provided for our stay. There is a handy hairdryer and iron for guest use. There is a small fridge filled with water provided. There is also a coffee maker. . . . The TV has cable and Netflix. . . . Access to the casita is via the side gate, allowing for privacy. . . . The accommodation is in a lovely, quiet neighborhood, and the view to the golf course is gold class! . . . Communication with host was efficient and open. We would definitely stay again. . . . Five stars, Clean, Comfortable, Private access, Parking with ease. You won't be disappointed.

When customers upload pictures or post comments, service providers are given the gift of customer feedback. Sometimes that "gift" can seem unfair and hard to process. Host Amanda Lankford suggests, "By listening to guests, I've learned the importance of setting and keeping high standards and making sure you communicate with guests before a problem occurs." Amanda explains that she had a part break on a fire pit, and she ordered the replacement component immediately. "I also reached out to my next guests to let them know that the part might not get there before they arrived. If they expected to feel the warmth of the fire, I wanted to help them reset their expectation or help them find a place with a working fire pit."

Writing for *Value Penguin*, host Andrew Pentis cited that he learned a lot by asking guests for feedback and taking their reviews seriously. As for tangible service improvements, Andrew listed the following:

- *Put a small garbage can in the bedroom.* We made the mistake of forgetting that guests would have trash and that respectful guests would not be comfortable leaving it on the floor.

- *Put a powerstrip in the bedroom.* Given there were only four outlets in the room, a powerstrip now gives visitors the opportunity to plug in as many as seven devices. The electric bill goes up, but so does their satisfaction.

- *Deep clean the bathroom before arrival.* Multiple guests have complained about the condition of our bathroom. To make them feel more comfortable, ... we now make spraying down our shower and wiping away toilet grime a matter of practice. It's more work for us, but the guests appreciate it.

Andrew listened to and learned from customers. He also did additional work. In turn, that work likely saved him from having to resolve customer complaints or respond to negative reviews.

Basic service skills do take work, problem-solving skills, and patience in the face of challenges. As such, business philosopher Jim Rohn's wisdom applies: "Don't wish it was easier, wish you were better. Don't wish for less problems, wish for more skills. Don't wish for less challenges, wish for more wisdom." I would add to Jim's comments that great service brands do more than wish for improvements, wisdom, or skills. They take action.

Let's take a moment to plan actionable improvements related to your service basics.

 YOUR TRAVEL PLANNING GUIDE

1. What do your customers expect when it comes to communication speed? How are you performing against those expectations?

2. What are the most important tangibles your customers encounter during their journey with you? Where are you vulnerable for negative virality from customer-generated videos or images?

3. What processes have you developed to ensure performance against quality standards?

4. How do you leverage the voice of your customer to guide improvements in service delivery? What specific service elements or tangibles have you changed because of customer feedback?

EMOTIONALLY CONNECTING BY ANTICIPATING NEEDS

Jeff Bezos, the CEO of Amazon, suggests the best customer experiences occur when the "customer doesn't need to call you, doesn't need to talk to you. It just works." Outstanding Airbnb hosts understand that they must take steps to anticipate guest needs in order for everything to work for the guest. Often, that anticipation requires little more than thoughtfulness.

Superhost Soniya Ahuja from Bellevue, Washington, says she tries to think of things guests might forget while traveling. She makes sure she always has personal items like toothbrushes and toothpaste on hand. Soniya says, "My guests are grateful for not having to run to a store to grab these items." Since guests often lose a sense of control while traveling, Soniya stocks cold drinks and healthy snacks so "guests who check in late after a long flight won't go to bed hungry."

Airbnb Experiences guests also notice when their unstated needs are anticipated. For example, a guest who participated in a batik-making activity noted her host created a "very beautiful, comfortable, and friendly atmosphere." She continued, "I really enjoyed the whole experience! They took good care of me from my arrival. They offered delicious homemade gluten-free jackfruit cakes with a pot of tea! . . . I would highly recommend and would go for other classes if I had more time."

Amanda Lankford, both an Airbnb host and frequent guest, shares how a host couple in Fairbanks, Alaska, anticipated her physical comfort needs. Amanda timed her visit so she could take a sled ride with the hosts and their sled dogs: "I definitely brought warm clothes, but my hosts thoughtfully provided special waterproof and windproof gloves and footwear to make sure I was warm. That's just a small example of their kindness, and it has drawn me back to their place in Alaska about five times in the last four years." Amanda proves that when you anticipate customer needs, you often earn repeat business.

Airbnb hosts go beyond anticipating physical needs of guests by thinking about what guests might encounter before and after their Airbnb visit. Superhost Debi Hertert shared, "I've gone to Airbnb conferences in San Francisco, Paris, and Los Angeles as well as having worked directly with the Airbnb team in my home city of Portland. Through those experiences and interactions with other hosts, I've come to think about my guests' end-to-end travel experience—not just their time with me."

In keeping with Debi's comments, guest reviews often highlight how a host demonstrates thoughtfulness particularly related to transportation, directions, or other travel considerations. One guest responded, "Our host arranged our transportation to and from the airport, and when we forgot our bag in one of the cars, they immediately got on the phone with the company and had the driver come back. It was above and beyond."

A couple participating in a city tour experience shared this about their host:

[She] was very efficient in communicating through Airbnb's messenger, and we met up quickly. She was very thoughtful and notified me before the tour that it was raining in the area and that we should bring an umbrella for the trip. . . . She was also thoughtful and consistently asked if we needed help to take photos or have drinks. . . . She didn't mind extending her services for an additional hour, and we had so much fun bonding over food and her knowledge of Chinatown's history. She took care finding a good diner for our lunch, as we are vegans. Not only did the dishes fit our dietary restrictions, but the food was very delicious. . . . Overall, we enjoyed ourselves thoroughly and will highly recommend to friends!

Superhost Kathy Peterman uses handwritten messages and signs in personal ways: "I try to personalize things with signs. For example, I have a sign that welcomes my guests and uses their name. I try to add a personal touch to messages I place to help guests when they need to know what is expected or how to use something. So, when you come in my door, you will see 'Leave your worries and your shoes at the door.'"

Superhost Debi Hertert notes, "I think about what I would need if I was traveling and try to provide those things even if my guest has not specifically asked for them." Debi's perspective is in keeping with the thinking of Steve Jobs from Apple when he said, "Get closer than ever to your customers. So close that you tell them what they need well before they realize it themselves."

How well are you demonstrating your thoughtfulness and anticipating the unstated needs of your customers? Are you so close to them that you're providing for their needs before they're aware they exist?

HOW DO YOU WANT THEM TO FEEL?

In Chapter 6, we looked at how major customer service brands like Starbucks, Mercedes-Benz, and Airbnb define the experience they want customers to have in every interaction, every time. For Airbnb, I suggested the desired experience is to deliver memorable and magical travel. In reality, each Airbnb host is a microbusiness and represents a brand within the Airbnb host community. Superhost Kathy Peterman puts it this way: "I think of myself as an entrepreneur as opposed to expecting Airbnb to take care of everything. I feel that I can create my own brand and my own following while using their platform. My brand is built on my words, photos, and guest reviews."

Kathy's brand, as well as the brand of all hosts, should define the way they want customers to feel (their "way we serve" statement) throughout their interactions with guests. The "way we serve" statements of individual hosts will invariably differ, but they should still result in guests leaving with a sense that they've had memorable and magical Airbnb experiences. Let's look at Kathy Peterman's "way we serve" statement and compare it to that of Superhosts Wendy and Doug Needy.

Kathy Peterman is a Superhost who lists a bedroom and private bath in her home in Portland, Oregon. Kathy's Airbnb profile includes "I am 'very Portland' with a vegan diet, being ecoconscious, loving all the great food we offer and embracing creativity and diversity as a good thing. I am a retired RN manager, now gone blogger, who's exploring minimalism and creating a life well lived!"

Kathy told us she wants every guest to feel "uncluttered, refreshed, and peaceful." She seeks to create a memorable stay by being respectful of every guest while also setting an example of how every person can thoughtfully be a good steward of the planet.

Examples of Kathy's effectiveness in delivering her desired experience can be found in these representative guest reviews.

> Kathy's home is so peaceful and is the perfect place to retreat to after a day of exploring the city.

> Staying at Kathy's is a gift. Her home is so very peaceful and lovely, spotless and welcoming.

> Kathy creates a welcoming and calm energy, and staying in her home made my trip to Portland that much more enjoyable.

By contrast, Wendy and Doug Needy cohost an Airbnb private apartment in a converted grain silo located between Sedalia and Green Ridge, Missouri. Wendy shared, "We want everyone who visits to feel like they are part of our family. We hope they will savor the joys of rural life." Doug added, "Since many of our visitors come from St. Louis, Kansas City, and the suburbs, we want to help them reconnect with the farm and experience delight as their children climb into an old barn looking for kittens or help us milk a goat."

To deliver their desired emotional state, Wendy and Doug commit to meet every guest personally: "We always bring a farm ambassador with us when we welcome our guests. Sometimes we bring a kitten, other times a goat or miniature burro. We also greet our guests with freshly made treats to eat or drink because they've usually traveled some distance to join us. We also let them know they are always welcome to visit and spend time with us at our main house."

It's clear that guests feel like members of Wendy and Doug's family, savor farm life, and experience delight. Here is typical guest feedback posted on their listing:

This was our very first time using Airbnb, and I'm so happy we chose to stay here. The stay was absolutely PERFECT! Upon arrival, Wendy had in hand fresh lemonade for us in cute little mason jars. My boyfriend and I got to feed the goats, play with the farm cats. We also were able to catch a ton of fish. My boyfriend caught two really good-sized bass. Wendy also had breakfast ready in the refrigerator for the next day (although we ate that for dinner instead, lol . . . super yummy!). Wendy makes soap from goat's milk that smells so good, I can't wait to see what other scents she comes up with. Wendy and Doug are such GREAT people! This place is so cozy and super cute! We will definitely be staying here again. . . . Can't wait to return!

Superhost Kathy and Superhosts Wendy and Doug have defined distinctly different optimal experiences for their guests and seek to make those optimal experiences a reality for everyone they serve. Wendy notes, "We couldn't have made this happen without help and guidance from resources at Airbnb, and we are grateful for the successes we've had—particularly the way guests feel about their time with us." The success of these Superhosts lives in reviews and stories their guests share.

Are your customer reviews consistent with the desired experience you want them to have?

Before we look at how Airbnb hosts deliver personal care, let's take a moment to explore "anticipation of needs" and a "way we serve" statement for your business.

YOUR TRAVEL PLANNING GUIDE

1. What needs do your customers have before and after they interact with you? How might you anticipate and meet those needs?

2. What is your "way we serve" statement? In other words, what is the emotional experience you want for every customer? Are customers providing feedback that shows they are feeling what you hope they will feel?

3. If your team members were asked how customers should feel when they interact with your brand, would they all provide the same answer? If not, how can you assure consistency of awareness and action?

PERSONALIZING TO CREATE
MAGIC AND MEMORIES

In Chapter 2, I asserted that all business is personal and that technology can provide personalized information but *not* personal care. For care to be personal, it must be delivered by a person in a way that is tailored to another person. While human needs can be broadly anticipated (people will be hungry and tired, and they will predictably forget items), personal care involves customizing service to the specific needs of the individual you are serving at any given moment. Customized service can be easily planned (for example, Soniya from Bellevue, Washington, keeps extra tooth-brushes and healthy snacks on hand), but personalized care must be crafted.

A simple example of this type of crafting is reflected in a post by Michele Robson, in her *Turning Left for Less* blog. Michele describes the actions of a Superhost this way: "[She] was very helpful in advance. . . . When I contacted her to ask if they had a cocktail shaker in the flat, she kindly offered to buy one if I sent her the Amazon link. Sure enough, when we arrived, there was a brand-new cocktail shaker."

While personalization can be as simple as making a single item purchase, often it involves close collaboration with the customer. Superhosts Dabney Tompkins and Alan Colley list an extremely popular Airbnb property atop a 40-acre meadow on 160 acres of private land near the Umpqua National Forest in Oregon. The property is so desirable it appears on the wish lists of 20,000 Airbnb guests and gets booked for the entire season within a few minutes of opening their annual calendar. The home is modeled after fire lookout towers built by the US Forest Service, with considerable modern upgrades. Despite all of the property's modernization, guests still have to traverse four flights of stairs to get from the ground to the living area, and toilet facilities are primitive by flush toilet standards.

Limitations notwithstanding, the peaceful, off-the-grid nature of the listing is a large part of the fire tower's appeal. An equally important attractant is Dabney and Alan's commitment to personalized guest care. Dabney and Alan choose to live on the 40-acre parcel so they can be available to guests. Cell service is provider dependent, so Dabney and Alan supply two-way radios for communication with guests. They also keep guests informed if they go off-property for supplies.

These hosts are actively in communication with guests before, during, and after their visits. They also collaborate with guests to help them, in Alan's words, "listen to the wind giving voice to the trees and to create lifelong memories."

Dabney told us, "We are aware of 12 marriage proposals that have taken place on this property. It's a very popular place because it's so remote, and we are eager and willing to do whatever we can to make a visit special." Alan gave a specific example of one of those proposals and the way the hosts partnered to personalize the experience. The man began involving the hosts in his plan for his proposal as soon as he secured a booking for his return visit. When the guest and his girlfriend arrived, Alan recalled, "We met them at the base of the tower and asked if we could reveal to them the major renovations we had made in the home since they last visited. To do so, we asked if we could blindfold them before we led them into the living space. They agreed, and we took the boyfriend in first.

"The room had been staged for the event, and he swiftly went to one knee with his ring in hand. We then escorted his girlfriend in and removed her blindfold. We videotaped her surprise and her acceptance of his proposal." Dabney added, "When we were discussing the arrangements, I said, 'This is a personal moment. Are you sure you want us there?' And our guest said, 'You guys are like family to us.' So, we enjoyed the honor of sharing that moment."

Airbnb hosts who are committed to creating personalized and memorable experiences often find themselves sharing powerful moments with guests. Airbnb Superhost April Brenneman has compiled many examples of the deeply poignant connections she has experienced through Airbnb. Before we relate one of her stories, let's explore April's first Airbnb listing.

April and her husband Donald are the parents of five children. Their youngest child, Josh, was four when he developed Ewing sarcoma. Prior to his diagnosis, the tight-knit family would do sleepouts on the deck of their home. April shared, "We'd throw pads and blankets down and had this tree right by the deck that I called the Bilbo Baggins party tree with lights hanging in it. We'd read books and turn down the lights."

While going through treatment for his rare form of cancer, many people asked Josh if he had a wish that he would like fulfilled. Josh repeatedly responded that he wanted to sleep with his family in a "house in the trees." Through the efforts of members of the Brennemans' church, Josh and one of his sisters helped draw plans for that house, integrating a tree from the family's backyard. Soon, a host of volunteers (some friends and some strangers) built Josh's house. A video of the treehouse construction can be found at airbnbway.com/book-resources. The "house in the trees" not only served as a safe and sacred place during Josh's treatment to remission but also through his ongoing battles with post-treatment pain.

As Josh got older, the treehouse was used intermittently, so the family mitigated financial challenges by listing Josh's House in the Trees on Airbnb. As the Brenneman children grew and moved, other rooms in the family home were listed as well.

Many of April's most personal host experiences link to guests in Josh's treehouse. April recalls, "One most precious guest was a little girl who had cancer. It was very important to her and her parents that they stay at Josh's House in the Trees, and the family cherished their time here. Sadly, they contacted me about a year later as their daughter was losing her battle. At that time, her wish was to return to the treehouse, and we immediately made the space available to her and her family at no charge." April told me she wished she could have done more than sit with, offer understanding, and provide that special space for the family. It's hard to imagine that more could have been done—certainly nothing more memorable or personal.

Josh's House in the Trees is a special and memorable place thanks to the generosity of those who built it and thanks to the gracious hosting of the Brenneman family. In truth, every home, product, or service interaction can also be memorable. Unfortunately, from the business side of interactions it is easy to get lulled into repetitive and routine aspects of service, forgetting our opportunity to infuse "heart" into each customer encounter.

Some time ago, I got into a heated discussion with a mentor of mine, Horst Schulze, the founder of the modern-day hotel company. Horst was talking about "perfect" service experiences, when I interjected, "Shouldn't we be encouraging excellence—since perfection isn't possible?" Horst responded, "If you settle for making connections with 90 percent of your customers and call that excellent, I hope one of your family members isn't among the 10 percent that leave your business disappointed." Point taken Horst: when it comes to magical and memorable human connections, perfection should be the goal.

American philanthropist Melinda Gates notes, "Deep human connection is . . . the purpose and the result of a meaningful life—and it will inspire the most amazing acts of love, generosity, and humanity." From the perspective of Airbnb hosts, deep personal connections inspire both guests and hosts alike.

As a business leader, your path to achieving meaningful customer connections requires you to meet expectations for responsiveness and consistency. You and your team must address your customers' stated needs and anticipate ways you can help them before and after each interaction with you. Ultimately, you will differentiate yourself from your competition through service that is personal, magical, and memorable. When you master these components of service delivery, you foster customer connections rich with love, generosity, and humanity. By attending to practical and emotional elements of service delivery, your business will continue to succeed, grow, and stay relevant.

POINTS OF INTEREST AS YOU THINK
MAGICAL AND MEMORABLE

→ A. Parasuraman, Valarie A. Zeithaml, and Len Berry developed a comprehensive model of service excellence that focuses on five factors associated with quality service experiences: *reliability, responsiveness, tangibles, assurance,* and *empathy.*

→ Parasuraman, Zeithaml, and Berry developed the tool SERVQUAL to assess service quality across their five service factors. The tool measures the gap between customers' expectations and their perceptions of actual service.

→ Responsiveness, reliability, and tangibles are table stakes for service today and represent the basics of service delivery.

→ Assurance and empathy can be linked to service experience behaviors like personalization and anticipation of customer needs. These behaviors represent higher-level experience-creation skills that drive emotional connections with customers.

→ Most customers calculate the cost of an experience based not only on how much money they pay but also how much time and effort they must expend to receive their goods or services.

→ Customer experience excellence involves taking care of customer communication needs and service requests before customers start to worry that their needs won't be met.

→ Irrespective of industry, customers associate slow response with service incompetence, neglect, and a lack of appreciation of their patronage. In many cases, that perceived neglect can lead to customer churn.

→ Unmet basic service expectations often show up in customer ratings and reviews.

→ Thanks to the proliferation of cameras in smartphones, breakdowns involving the tangibles of service are prominent in social media posts.

→ In customer reviews, it is often easy to determine whether customers felt their needs were missed, met, or exceeded.

→ Customer feedback and online posts should be viewed as gifts that can help guide transformative service improvements.

→ Business philosopher Jim Rohn advised: "Don't wish it was easier, wish you were better. Don't wish for less problems, wish for more skills. Don't wish for less challenges, wish for more wisdom." Great service brands do more than wish for improvements, wisdom, or skills. They take action.

→ Jeff Bezos, the CEO of Amazon, suggests the best customer experiences occur when the "customer doesn't need to call you, doesn't need to talk to you. It just works."

→ In addition to products and services that just work, most customers also want service providers to take extra steps to anticipate their needs. Often, that anticipation requires little more than thoughtfulness.

→ Needs anticipation often involves issues like hunger, thirst, rest, and comfort. It also requires you to consider your customers' transition into and out of your service interactions.

→ Steve Jobs said, "Get closer than ever to your customers. So close that you tell them what they need well before they realize it themselves."

→ Reading customer reviews can often help determine how well you are delivering the experience you want customers to have (your "way we serve" statement).

→ While human needs can be broadly anticipated (people will be hungry, tired, and will predictably forget items), personal care involves customizing service to the specific needs of the individual you are serving at any given moment.

→ Service providers committed to creating personalized and memorable experiences often find themselves sharing powerful moments with customers.

→ Melinda Gates notes, "Deep human connection is . . . the purpose and the result of a meaningful life—and it will inspire the most amazing acts of love, generosity, and humanity." Those connections also produce magical and memorable experiences, as well as business success.

empowerment

Maximize Impact

*It turns out that advancing equal opportunity
and economic empowerment is
both morally right and good economics.*
—William J. Clinton,
forty-second president of the United States

In earlier chapters I've outlined how Airbnb leaders aspire to create belonging, trust, and hospitality. We've explored how Airbnb is positioned to be a "people business aided by technology" and how it's dedicated to a mission of creating a world where anyone can Belong Anywhere. We've also reviewed Airbnb's meteoric financial success as evidenced by profitability that was attained well before Uber or Lyft.

Harsh critics of capitalism might argue that a company like Airbnb can't achieve rapid economic success and authentically pursue a lofty social mission concerning human acceptance and belonging. In their book *Conscious Capitalism*, Whole Foods CEO John Mackey and Professor Raj Sisodia note, "Capitalism and business are all too frequently vilified as the bad guys and blamed for virtually everything our postmodern critics dislike about the world. Capitalism is portrayed as exploiting workers, cheating consumers, causing inequality by benefiting the rich but not the poor, homogenizing society, fragmenting communities, and destroying the environment.... This is a fundamentally misguided view."

In this chapter we will explore how Airbnb leaders are challenging negative portrayals of "for-profit" businesses. Chapter 10 will examine how Airbnb is seeking to strengthen communities, protect the environment, and provide humanitarian relief.

Since this is a chapter about Airbnb's efforts to drive entrepreneurship, economic opportunity, and employee engagement, let's frame our discussion in the context of social capitalism. Tristan Claridge, founder of Social Capital Research and Training, defines social capitalism as a "socially minded form of capitalism, where the goal is making social improvements, rather than focusing on accumulating capital in the classic capitalist sense. It is a utilitarian form of capitalism with a social purpose."

In the pages ahead, we'll look at Airbnb's "social purpose" from the perspective of how it has improved economic opportunities for it's employees and the host community. In Chapter 9, we will hear from Airbnb hosts and employees who have been empowered and who empower others.

So what is the meaning of "empowerment"? The origin of the word *empower* dates as far back as the 1400s and can be found in John Milton's 1667 classic poem *Paradise Lost*. Despite a lengthy history, the concept of empowerment started to gain traction in a broader social context less than 50 years ago. In an article for the *Journal of Extension* titled "Empowerment: What Is It?," authors Nanette Page and Cheryl Czuba define it this way:

> Empowerment is a construct shared by many disciplines and arenas: community development, psychology, education, economics, and studies of social movements and organizations, among others.... The meaning of the term

empowerment is often assumed rather than explained or defined.

As a general definition, however, we suggest that empowerment is a multi-dimensional social process that helps people gain control. . . .

It is a process that fosters power . . . in people, for use in their own lives, their communities, and in their society, by acting on issues that they define as important.

For our discussion, we will briefly touch on economic and social empowerment factors in the sharing economy, then examine how leaders at Airbnb develop processes that foster power for the people served by Airbnb. This chapter will also address economic and employee empowerment in your business.

SHARING INTERESTS, ASSETS, AND OPPORTUNITIES

In Chapter 1, the sharing economy was defined as offering goods or services through an online marketplace, whether those are business-to-business (B2B) or peer-to-peer (P2P) markets. To be fair, the sharing economy is far too complex to be captured by a single-sentence definition. It actually represents an array of business variations carrying descriptors like the "gig economy," "platform economy," "peer economy," or "on-demand economy." In an article for the World Economic Forum, April Rinne, an adviser to sharing companies, broadly describes the sector this way:

The sharing of idle assets, usually via tech platforms, in ways that produce economic, environmental, social and practical benefits. . . . Sharing rather than owning helps people—and increasingly organizations as well—save money, earn income, lower carbon footprints, increase social capital, boost community, meet new people, build trust ... and even enhance choice and convenience. Indeed, few if any other business models can profess so many benefits at once. This is an incredibly powerful proposition for individuals, companies, and society at large.

Given its impact, commentators and researchers study the sharing economy's benefits and risks. Similarly, policy makers try to cope with and regulate this burgeoning marketplace.

A 2015 PricewaterhouseCoopers (PwC) report examined participation, impact, and trends associated with the sharing economy in the United States. At that time, 19 percent of respondents reported they had engaged in a sharing economy transaction. Respondents who had done business in the sharing economy reported that it made life more affordable (86 percent), increased convenience and efficiency (83 percent), strengthened communities (78 percent), and was good for the environment (76 percent).

PwC projected that global revenues across the five core sharing markets (travel, transportation, content streaming, staffing, and finance) would spike from $15 billion in 2015 to $335 billion in 2025. If PwC's projection is accurate, the sharing economy of 2025 will generate revenue equaling that of the entire retail sector. In support of their projections, PwC highlighted how consumers are favoring "access" over "ownership":

Only one in two consumers agree with the statement that "owning things is a good way to show my status in society." Four in five consumers agree that there are sometimes real advantages to renting over owning, and adults ages 18 to 24 are nearly twice as likely as those ages 25 and older to say that access is the new ownership. Happiness studies show that experiences increase contentment far more than purchases do, and young people's intrinsic understanding of this is fueling an experience economy.

While trends toward increased product and service sharing seem unstoppable, the sharing economy is not without critics. While many of those who speak against the sector come from established businesses that are being threatened by the sharing economy, others fear unintended consequences or unmanageable negative impact. In an article for the *Journal of Cleaner Production* titled "Is Sharing the Solution? Exploring public acceptability of the sharing economy," researchers Catherine E. Cherry and Nick F. Pidgeon encapsulate concerns raised about sharing platforms noting they "have been repeatedly criticised for exploiting regulatory loopholes, eroding workers' rights and creating a race to the bottom that shifts most of the risks, but few of the benefits, onto the individuals using the system."

Since comprehensive reviews of the benefits and liabilities of the sharing economy can be found in books like *Shareology* and *The Rise of the Sharing Economy*, we will instead focus on how Airbnb seeks to maximize the economic and social benefits of its platform and how those empowerment efforts can relate to any business operating within or outside of a sharing marketplace. Before we look at Airbnb's economic empowerment efforts, it is important to understand how revenues from an Airbnb booking are distributed.

When a host lists a property or service on the Airbnb platform, no listing fee is charged. Hosts set the price for their listing. Each host can choose to use Airbnb's Smart Pricing tool. According to Airbnb, Smart Pricing allows hosts to set "prices to automatically go up or down based on changes in demand" for similar listings. "Smart Pricing is based on the type and location" of a listing and "the season, demand, and other factors." Once a guest pays, Airbnb collects a 3 to 5 percent fee from the host. Put differently: hosts keep 95 to 97 percent of their booking charge. Airbnb does not garner any additional fees from the host for credit card processing or to cover the $1 million of insurance the company provides.

Airbnb's compensation structure is designed to empower hosts to engage in business without the additional high costs of marketing, payment processing, or customer service support. Airbnb's revenue is principally derived from the fee guests pay to cover their easy access to accommodations and experiences across wide price points and in locations closest to their desired destination (according to Airbnb, the majority of listings are outside of hotel districts).

The guest service fee for homes ranges between 0 and 20 percent of the booking subtotal (the nightly rate plus cleaning fee and additional guest fee, if applicable, but excluding Airbnb fees and taxes). This service fee is calculated using a variety of factors— these include the reservation subtotal, the length of the stay, and characteristics of the listing. In general, the service fee gets lower as the reservation cost gets higher. Guests see this fee on the checkout page before they book a reservation.

Irrespective of the service fee, guests often report that traveling on Airbnb enabled them to take trips they would not have been able to afford if they had to stay in hotels. Work teams and families also report team building and social benefits of renting an entire home as opposed to being divided across multiple rooms or floors in a hotel.

The home sharing marketplace continues to grow based on the options and benefits it provides to both hosts and guests. Airbnb, in turn, benefits by supporting the health of the marketplace. Let's continue to explore economic empowerment by looking at how Airbnb supports the host community.

AIRBNB AGENDA AND IMPACT

When it comes to helping individuals leverage their interests and their homes to achieve financial well-being, Airbnb literally has an agenda. In 2017, Airbnb advised hosts about a new set of initiatives called the Airbnb Economic Empowerment Agenda. The announcement posted on the Airbnb host website, *Airbnb Citizen*, explained the purpose of Airbnb's new initiatives by first outlining social trends and citing data on Airbnb's financial impact for hosts.

Before we look at the items that constitute the Airbnb Economic Empowerment Agenda, let's review how Airbnb summarized the relevant social and economic trends that prompted new goals. According to Airbnb:

> At a time of growing economic inequality, Airbnb is democratizing capitalism and creating economic opportunities for the middle class, using technology to help connect and empower our community—not replace it. Our people-for-people platform allows ordinary people to use their house—typically their greatest expense—to generate supplemental income to pay for costs like food, rent, and education for their children.

During a conversation with Airbnb's president of Homes Greg Greeley, he put it this way: "The community is first and foremost the foundation of Airbnb. Hosts have various reasons why they choose to list on Airbnb. For some, the choice emerges from a passion to meet or help people. For others, it is a matter of paying the rent. In any case, we want to democratize capitalism and enrich the lives of everyone on our platform."

In support of Airbnb's goal to democratize capitalism and create economic opportunities, Airbnb shared statistics from 2017 in their announcement on *Airbnb Citizen*. Globally, Airbnb achieved the following:

- Contributed to an estimated 730,000 jobs (as stated in an NERA Economic Consulting study), in a subset of 200 highly booked cities

- Supported more than $60 billion in economic output in the 200 cities evaluated in the NERA Economic Consulting study

In North America in 2017, Airbnb reported:

- US hosts on the platform earned an average of $6,100 annually.

- 62 percent of US hosts noted home sharing helped them afford their home.

- 12 percent of North American hosts claimed home sharing saved them from foreclosure or eviction.

In 2017, Airbnb also stated, "African-American, Latino, and other minority communities were among Airbnb's fastest-growing host areas in US cities." At that time, research on Airbnb's New York host community "found that the number of Airbnb guests grew 78 percent year-over-year in the 30 city zip codes with the highest percentage of black residents, compared to 50 percent city-wide." Similar studies in majority-minority communities of Chicago and Washington, DC, found even greater growth rates.

As part of the foundation for the Airbnb Economic Empowerment Agenda announcement, Airbnb shared studies showing that hosts living in immigrant-rich New York, Los Angeles, and Chicago metropolitan neighborhoods earned more than $24 million by sharing homes on Airbnb. Those neighborhoods also saw a 65 percent growth in active listings within a year.

Despite these findings, leaders at Airbnb explained that they were not content with the progress they had made on behalf of economically challenged ethnic communities, women, and seniors. Their desire to "do more" prompted the creation of the Airbnb Economic Empowerment Agenda, which Airbnb kicked off with two overarching initiatives:

- A living wage pledge

- An aggressive growth target for urban hosts in predominantly minority areas

As it related to living wages in 2017, Airbnb pledged to pay at least $15 per hour "to all contractors and vendors whose personnel provide a substantial amount of work to Airbnb in the United States" by 2020.

In addition to extending Airbnb's Living Wage Pledge to contractors and vendors, Airbnb encouraged the host community to pay their employees and vendors accordingly. For example, Airbnb asked hosts to pledge to pay individuals who clean their properties at least $15 an hour. Hosts who make that commitment can post their support of the Living Wage Pledge on their property listing. This allows prospective guests to consider a host's commitment to provide a living wage when they book a listing. In Chapter 9, you will hear from hosts who've made this pledge.

As for Airbnb's commitment to minority neighborhoods (often referred to as "majority-minority" areas), leadership announced, "We are setting a goal of doubling the size of our host community in urban majority-minority districts and underserved areas around the United States in the next two years. We will do this through a new effort, partnering with national and local organizations and holding on-the-ground, in-person events and trainings to help more people understand the economic opportunity provided by hosting." One such Airbnb partnership is with the National Association for the Advancement of Colored People (NAACP).

Through their partnership with Airbnb, the NAACP website notes:

> [We] conduct targeted outreach to communities of color to help more people use their homes to earn extra income. By increasing the number of travelers to communities of color, the partnership will spread the economic benefits of tourism. The partnership also includes a unique revenue sharing model: Airbnb will share 20 percent of its earnings from this partnership with the NAACP. The NAACP and Airbnb will also collaborate on a series of projects to support Airbnb's ongoing efforts to increase workforce diversity, as well as support Airbnb's supplier diversity goals.

By setting measurable goals to increase opportunities in economically challenged areas, Airbnb is taking action consistent with what the Department of International Development within the Organisation for Economic Co-operation and Development (OECD) describes as "the most powerful tool for reducing poverty and improving the quality of life." Airbnb employees in those regions understand they are helping to provide new economic opportunities and that meeting growth goals for hosts creates a virtuous cycle of micro-entrepreneurship and increased travel revenues in those regions.

In 1948, the United Nations crafted the Universal Declaration of Human Rights that outlines and champions the rights of individuals across the globe. One of the rights delineated in that document reads, "Everyone who works has the right to just and favourable remuneration ensuring for himself and his family an existence worthy of human dignity, and supplemented, if necessary, by other means of social protection." Since the late 1990s, large multinational companies have embraced this concept of a living wage and have pledged to provide responsible compensation as part of their social contract with employees. On its website, Novartis, a global healthcare company based in Sweden, shares its commitment and process for ensuring a living wage:

> In 2000, Novartis was one of the first international companies to implement a commitment to pay a living wage to all of its employees. "Living Wage" is a Novartis initiative and commitment to associates, which usually is above minimum wage requirements. Living Wages are updated annually for Novartis . . . adjusting for changes in inflation, food prices, and other market conditions. Living Wages focus on meeting basic living needs for associates and their families, where legal minimum wages tend to focus on poverty levels for individuals.
>
> Each year, Novartis Group companies review salaries for all associates and adjust salaries that fall below the living wage level.

The Living Wage Network (a certification agency) reports 2,500 small and medium-sized businesses have also taken the pledge. The network focuses on two fundamental reasons that companies should seek to drive economic growth and the quality of life for their employees. From the perspective of economic well-being, the Living Wage Network reports:

> When consumers buy products, companies and their workers profit and the economy grows. But when the vast majority of families have limited wealth, they cannot afford to buy goods and services. Widespread inequality

creates an economy that lacks consumer demand. This lack of demand weakens economic growth, thereby causing the economy as a whole to stagnate and decline.

In his seminal book *Good to Great: Why Some Companies Make the Leap . . . and Others Don't,* Jim Collins writes about a "flywheel effect" where the momentum of change becomes a force for future change. A similar flywheel effect occurs when employees and business partners are paid a living wage. Meaningful compensation turns a flywheel that spins the axle of consumer spending and worker productivity. According to the Living Wage Network, increased productivity occurs through the following:

- Enhanced worker morale
- Better employee health
- Improved service quality
- Lower turnover

In addition to getting employers to pledge to pay a living wage, organizations like the Living Wage Network encourage consumers to pledge to shop at businesses that pay employees sustainably.

Airbnb's Economic Empowerment Agenda was a public declaration of Airbnb's commitment to improving the well-being of members of its host community and those who work with them. The agenda has the added benefits of letting guests know that the company is focused on these important social issues and that Airbnb has a blueprint for initiatives to drive economic growth for majority-minority communities.

A company's willingness to pay a living wage and promote economic well-being to marginalized sectors is more than socially responsible behavior. It is an important component in attracting millennial workers. A 2017 study conducted by Achieve, titled *The Millennial Impact Report,* states the following:

- Millennials are showing significantly increased interest in causes that impact minority, marginalized, or disenfranchised groups or people.

- Millennials are most interested in causes that promote equity, equality, and opportunity.

- Millennials' attention often is drawn to issues outside themselves or their groups.

When Airbnb, or your company for that matter, defines business initiatives that go beyond profit creation, a series of indirect economic benefits can occur. These benefits include overall economic growth with attendant increases in consumer demand, improved worker morale, greater workplace productivity, reduced poverty, and a work environment that attracts emerging generations of candidates. Before we examine how Airbnb actively seeks to empower historically marginalized groups, let's pause to consider your economic empowerment opportunities.

 YOUR TRAVEL PLANNING GUIDE

1. Have you taken the Living Wage Pledge and/or encouraged your business partners to pledge the same? How does your wage structure help attract quality talent, increase employee retention, enhance worker health, or improve service quality?

2. Do you share your economic empowerment objectives publicly? If so, how are they shared (for example, through an "economic empowerment agenda" or by publishing your Living Wage Pledge on your website)?

3. What goals have you set to enable economic growth for communities in which you do business?

SUPPORTING FEMALE
BUSINESS GROWTH

Airbnb proactively seeks to foster female entrepreneurship (women represent 55 percent of the overall population of hosts). Women made $10 billion cumulatively on the Airbnb platform from 2008 to March 2017. Extend that timeline to March 2018 and that cumulative number skyrockets to $20 billion in total revenue for women. In other words, female Airbnb hosts earned as much revenue year-over-year from 2017 to 2018 ($10 billion) as they had in the preceding nine years. (*That should serve as a cautionary tale when considering Airbnb data in the context of the company's hypergrowth.*)

For many leaders, the economic empowerment of women is fundamentally the right thing to do. It also happens to make great financial and social sense for the global economy. A 2018 World Bank Group report written by Quentin Wodon and Bénedicté de la Brière, titled *Unrealized Potential: The High Cost of Gender Inequality in Earnings*, showed that women across the globe account for only 38 percent of capital wealth when compared to 62 percent for men. This disparity is greater in lower-middle income and low-income countries. Assuming women should be paid equitably with men, the researchers estimated existing income disparities are producing a human wealth loss of $160.2 trillion across the 141 countries analyzed in their study. That number is roughly twice the global GDP.

In their report, Wodon and de la Brière outline several steps that business leaders can take to empower women. These include providing access to business networks, developing training tools, and encouraging connection through social networks. The report notes:

> Business associations, networks, mentors, and role models
> hold promise for both women entrepreneurs and farmers as
> they complement and reinforce the effects of interventions

such as business training, cash transfers and agricultural extension. The complementarity seemingly arises from acquiring both information and social support. . . . Self-help groups in particular foster increased solidarity between peers, independent financial decision-making, and greater respect for the women within their households and communities.

In keeping with the World Bank Group report, Airbnb offers "business and social support" to drive global female entrepreneurship, through programs like ikhaya le Langa in the Langa Province of Cape Town, South Africa, and the Self Employed Women's Association (SEWA) in rural India.

ikhaya le Langa NPC (the house of Sun) is a nonprofit organization, serving the oldest historic black township in the Western Cape of Africa. According to the ikhaya le Langa website, the organization is "revitalizing the Langa Quarter, an area of 13 streets comprising five hundred homes housing approximately 7,000 people. This community has languished at the bottom of the racialized socio-economic order in Cape Town for generations." Airbnb partnered with ikhaya le Langa to offer tourism training to women in the Langa Quarter. That training prepares women to be Airbnb hosts by helping them learn the township's history as well as hosting skills.

Similarly, Airbnb leaders partner with the Self Employed Women's Association (SEWA). SEWA's mission is to "organize workers to achieve their goals of full employment and self-reliance through the strategy of struggle and development. The struggle is against the many constraints and limitations imposed on them by society and the economy while development activities strengthen women's bargaining power and offer them new alternatives."

Airbnb supports development efforts by training rural women in India to be Airbnb hosts. In an article for the Thomson Reuters

Foundation appearing in the *Bangkok Post*, Reema Nanavaty, a director at SEWA, said, "At first, we weren't sure how the women would fare and if people would respond to homestays in these areas.... But once they began getting guests, the women invested in upgrading their homes and started using Google Translate to communicate with guests. It has become a significant source of income for them." In both Africa and India, Airbnb has maximized impact by partnering with organizations that are well positioned to empower women. While not all businesses are able to leverage global organizations like SEWA or ikhaya le Langa NPC, every leader can forge partnerships with local agencies.

Airbnb helps many other groups convert unused space into an economic resource and microbusiness. For example, Airbnb specifically focuses on a segment that often struggles in the context of fixed incomes. That group is senior citizens.

SHORING UP SENIORS

From 2007 to 2010 (around the time Airbnb was gaining traction), the US mortgage crisis was mounting. In the aftermath of that crisis, Lori Trawinski issued a report on behalf of the AARP Public Policy Institute, titled *Nightmare on Main Street: Older Americans and the Mortgage Market Crisis*, in which she noted, "This is the first study to measure the progression of the mortgage crisis and its effect on people age 50 and older.... Despite the perception that older Americans are more housing secure than younger people, millions of older Americans are carrying more mortgage debt than ever before, and more than 3 million are at risk of losing their homes.... As the mortgage crisis continues, millions of older Americans are struggling to maintain their financial security." Subsequent reports have maintained concern for housing losses among seniors, particularly in the context of seniors defaulting on reverse mortgages.

Increasingly, US seniors and their counterparts across the globe are turning to Airbnb to help them keep their homes and pay monthly bills. According to Airbnb, senior citizens (ages 60+) have been the fastest-growing host demographics. In 2017, 78,000 seniors shared homes in the United States (that was an increase of 45 percent over the prior year). The average US-based senior host earned $7,000 in 2017. Almost half of them reported that they used hosting income for monthly expenses. And 41 percent of them indicated the revenue from the Airbnb platform helped them remain in their homes.

Airbnb conducts research on the benefits of hosting for seniors and shares those findings with policy makers, leaders of senior organizations, and the media. It also posts relevant content on its *Airbnb Citizen* site and supports media inquiries that feature the stories of senior hosts. This content frequently gets picked up by senior organizations such as the AARP. In turn, Airbnb enrolls large numbers of senior home hosts and senior experience hosts. In 2018, Airbnb reported the number of seniors who were hosting Airbnb Experiences based on their interests, knowledge, and passions, had increased 1,100 percent over the prior year. In Chapter 9, you will meet Airbnb senior hosts and read about the economic and social benefits they derive.

While Airbnb's platform, host training programs, Living Wage Pledge, and goals to grow "majority-minority" host communities are all important to global economic empowerment, not every business is able to effect social change on a scale like Airbnb. However, you and your business can address economic inequalities through your recruitment, hiring, compensation, and promotion of women and minorities. In the section ahead, we will explore how Airbnb addresses these workforce behaviors.

As a business leader, you can also empower employees with decision-making that fosters their engagement, discretionary effort, and loyalty. Since Gallup research shows that only 34 percent of US workers are engaged, enthusiastic, and committed to their workplace, effective employee engagement approaches can offer you a competitive workforce advantage. As such, we will close the chapter with a review of how Airbnb leaders create their culture of employee autonomy and engagement.

INCLUSION AND DIVERSITY AT AIRBNB

The underrepresentation of women and minorities among US technology firms is well documented. A 2018 *WIRED* magazine article written by Blanca Myers, titled "Women and Minorities in Tech, by the Numbers," cites that in 2014, "just 31 percent of Facebook's employees are women. Same at Apple.... One of the reasons for this may be the way companies try to recruit talent. Stanford researchers observed . . . and identified countless seemingly obvious ways recruiters might be alienating female recruits, from sexist jokes to presentations displaying only slides of men." According to Myers, when women and minorities enter into science, technology, engineering, and math (STEM) careers, they receive substantially less compensation. Women on average make $16,000 less than men, and minorities make $14,000 less than Caucasians.

At Airbnb efforts to increase diversity in positions like data science are having an impact. For example, around 2015, according to an article for *Medium* coauthored by Elena Grewal, the head of data science at Airbnb, "Only 10 percent of our new data scientists were women.... This was not the team we wanted to build. Homogeneity brings a narrower range of ideas and gathers momentum to a vicious cycle where it becomes harder to attract and retain talent within a minority group." Through concerted effort, Airbnb has sought to root out unconscious biases, Grewal reports, "Results have been dramatic: 47 percent of hires were women, doubling the overall ratio of female data scientists on our team from 15 percent to 30 percent."

In addition to seeking to attract more women and minorities to technology positions, Airbnb looked for ways to drive greater diversity and economic empowerment across its entire workforce. Those efforts have included but are not limited to:

- Implementing a Diverse Candidate Slates rule, which requires every open position at Airbnb to have women and underrepresented minorities on the slate of candidates presented to hiring managers prior to those managers being allowed to make a selection

- Expanding recruitment from colleges with large black, Latinx, and female student populations

- Forging partnerships with organizations that seek to advance minority career development and gender equality

- Improving interviewing, hiring, performance reviews, and career enhancement policies to mitigate biases against women and minorities

Each year, Airbnb sets diversity goals and measures the company's performance against them. For example, in 2017, Airbnb sought to increase the overall percentage of employees from underrepresented populations in its US workforce from 9.97 to 11 percent. Airbnb hit and exceeded its number by achieving 11.31 percent minority population representation. In 2017, Airbnb also reported that its overall workforce was made up of 41.15 percent women.

From September 1, 2016, to December 1, 2017, Airbnb's African-American employee population increased by 46 percent and Latinx employees increased by 43 percent.

Airbnb is making substantial progress bringing underrepresented groups into the Airbnb family. Despite these advances, Airbnb has ample opportunity to drive greater diversity inside the walls of its business. As is the case when leaders increase inclusion, Airbnb stands to gain broader competencies, varied perspectives, greater sensitivity to evolving markets, and enhanced innovation. Before we look at Airbnb's efforts to engage and empower all employees, let's reflect on your journey to workforce inclusion.

 YOUR TRAVEL PLANNING GUIDE

1. Are you working to avoid "homogeneity," which reduces innovative ideas and "gathers momentum to a vicious cycle where it becomes harder to attract and retain talent within a minority group"?

2. How are you seeking to drive an inclusive workforce? What partnerships have you forged to aid in recruitment of underrepresented segments?

3. What goals have you set for workplace balance? How are you progressing toward those goals?

EMPLOYEE AUTONOMY AND ENGAGEMENT

To this point in the chapter we have exclusively explored economic empowerment—since money is foundational to employee satisfaction and global financial well-being. In his book *Drive: The Surprising Truth About What Motivates Us*, business author and behavioral scientist Daniel Pink highlights the importance of building employee empowerment on a firm financial base. Daniel suggests, "People have to earn a living. Salary, contract payments, some benefits, a few perks are ... 'baseline rewards.' If someone's baseline rewards aren't adequate or equitable, her focus will be on the unfairness of her situation and the anxiety of her circumstance. . . . You'll get very little motivation at all. The best use of money as a motivator is to pay people enough to take the issue of money off the table."

Researchers like Caihong Zhang and Canqiu Zhong, writing in the *Open Journal of Social Science*, suggest that leaders who drive employee empowerment enjoy significant benefits for "innovation . . . performance . . . customer service level and employee satisfaction. . . . Empowerment originates from the separation of powers that managers delegate to their subordinates. This means that leaders empower rights to the employees by delegating the decision-making power, implementing job enrichment and transforming more available and helpful information and resources to the grass root employees." Through communication, delegation, and shared decision-making, leaders position employees to experience autonomy, mastery, and optimum performance. Through these leadership behaviors employees feel more valued and invested in their jobs.

Airbnb's leadership has implemented a variety of job enrichment strategies, including replacing the traditional human resources department with an "employee experience division." Rather than looking at people as "resources" like finances or physical supplies, the employee experience division focuses on everything that touches and can improve the lives of employees. In a *Forbes* article by HR journalist Jeanne Meister, Airbnb's former Global Head of Employee Experience Mark Levy suggested that Airbnb's job enrichment approach involves "creating memorable workplace experiences which span all aspects of how we relate to employees, including how we recruit them, develop them, the work environment we create with them, . . . and the food we share together."

Airbnb's physical environment also enhances the employee experience, enabling employees to work from diverse physical spaces inspired by different city themes and materials imported from Amsterdam, Kyoto, Buenos Aries, and Jaipur. Specific work areas are modeled after actual Airbnb listings to create an authentic home-like feel. For example, meeting and work spaces include a Mexican log cabin environment, and comfortable living room settings from Portici, Italy, and Rio de Janeiro. In Mark Levy's words, Airbnb employees can work alone or "congregate with the folks they are working with to create the sense of belonging, rather than working from a closed-in cube, office, or dedicated desk."

Leaders at Airbnb are continually innovating ways to engage their employees. Dave O'Neill, Airbnb's Values & Culture senior manager notes, "We expect our people to connect with and understand both the host and guest's experience, and we offer a $500 travel credit every quarter. We're also constantly telling Community stories, and we use travel credits as a form of recognition. Right now, we are running a pilot where the entire leadership team, over 200 people, are expected to regularly use and post about home stays and Airbnb experiences."

From the perspective of communication openness for Airbnb employees, information sharing efforts have included:

- A monthly World@—held in person in San Francisco and joined globally via livestream.

- Team meetings at local and global levels on a regular cadence.

- Prompt release of notes from weekly Airbnb executive team meetings provided to all employees.

- An Airbnb internal network that hosts individual employee information and team pages. This intranet is sourced by the employee engagement team and communicates events, birthdays, anniversaries, and other celebrations.

Airbnb leaders also encourage active employee participation in work-related decision-making. Examples include how:

- Airbnb uses a team-based approach to goal setting, tactics, and implementation.

- Employees are asked for their ideas on ways to improve the workplace culture.

- Employee input is incorporated in Airbnb's approaches to strengthening its mission, vision, and values.

- Employee input guides the selection of training and benefits.

- Employees are given choices in how they will use four hours of monthly paid volunteer time.

- The employees themselves select where they will stay using their quarterly travel stipend, which Airbnb provides to encourage global citizenship and active engagement with the Airbnb host community.

Airbnb's employee empowerment efforts are paying off in three noteworthy ways: (1) ease of recruitment, (2) employee recommendations, and (3) third-party recognition. According to Culture Amp (an employee engagement measurement company), Airbnb can have as many as "180,000 CVs submitted for 900 positions." (CV is short for curriculum vitae, a specialized version of a résumé.)

In an article for *Medium*, WERKIN—a tech company that helps leaders manage diversity and career development programs—reports, "90 percent of Airbnb employees recommend Airbnb as a great place to work." Airbnb has also been chosen for Glassdoor's Best Places to Work list in 2016 and 2017 (ranking as high as the number 1 position in 2016). Airbnb's CEO Brian Chesky has made Glassdoor's Highest Rated CEO Employees' Choice List. Airbnb also ranked sixth among 252 companies on The Future of Organizations' Employee Experience Index.

While Airbnb has achieved success empowering stakeholders, many business leaders do not pursue a similar path. As you think about your own business, ask yourself how honestly and regularly you engage in two-way conversations with employees. In what ways do you enrich your employees' work life or involve team members in business decision-making? What kind of employee experience are you providing?

Martin Luther King, Jr., once said, "An individual has not started living until he can rise above the narrow confines of his individualistic concerns to the broader concerns of all humanity." From my perspective, a business cannot experience the fullness of success until its leaders rise above the narrow confines of profitability to address the broader concerns of employee enrichment.

POINTS OF INTEREST
AS YOU MAXIMIZE IMPACT

→ A focus on profits can overshadow the importance of a company acting for the social good.

→ The word *empower* dates back to the 1400s, but it began to gain traction in a broad social context less than 50 years ago.

→ Empowerment can be thought of as a multidimensional social process that helps people gain control in important areas of their life.

→ Leaders at Airbnb see their business as democratizing capitalism and creating economic opportunities for the middle class.

→ PwC research suggests US customers view the sharing economy favorably—based on affordability (86 percent), convenience and efficiency (83 percent), community (78 percent), and the environment (76 percent).

→ PwC expects global revenue from the sharing economy will rise to $335 billion in 2025.

→ According to the Living Wage Network, workers' compensation is linked to employee morale, health, and retention, as well as the quality of service that team members provide.

→ Millennials are showing significantly increased interest in causes that affect minority, marginalized, or disenfranchised groups of people.

→ Millennials are most interested in causes that promote equity, equality, and opportunity.

→ According to a global study conducted by the World Bank Group, women account for only 38 percent of capital wealth when compared to 62 percent for men. This disparity between men and women is producing a human wealth loss of $160.2 trillion. That is roughly twice global GDP.

→ High employee engagement correlates with a company's overall performance, innovation, and customer service levels.

→ Employee engagement increases as a function of bidirectional communication, shared decision-making, and an improved work environment.

→ A business cannot experience the fullness of success until its leaders rise above the narrow confines of profitability to address the broader concerns of employee empowerment and inclusion.

Claim and Share Your Value

The more we share, the more we have.

—Leonard Nimoy,
actor, director, and author

In Chapter 8, we explored how Airbnb empowers hosts, host communities, and Airbnb's employees. Implied in the concept of empowerment is the idea that one party (in this case, Airbnb) enables the other (for instance, hosts) to use a power they had previously not claimed. In this chapter, we will look at how hosts leverage the power of their knowledge, interests, skills, and properties to create various types of value for guests. We will also look at how hosts use the economic power of their microbusinesses to empower others.

POWERING A BUSINESS

In his book *The Personal MBA*, business coach Josh Kaufman identifies five parts of any business:

1. *Value creation:* Discovering what people need or want, then creating it

2. *Marketing:* Attracting attention and building demand for what you've created

3. *Sales:* Turning prospective customers into paying customers

4. *Value delivery:* Giving your customers what you've promised and ensuring they're satisfied

5. *Finance:* Bringing in enough money to keep your business going and make your effort worthwhile

From Josh's perspective, if you fail in any of these areas, you aren't running a business. Let's say you make highly popular chocolate chip cookies but can't produce a profit: Josh would describe your effort as a hobby.

In many ways, Airbnb has enabled people to transform hobbies or unoccupied physical spaces into bona fide business enterprises. Airbnb's major contributions to this transformation process include guiding people in product presentation, helping them establish pricing, and supporting value delivery. Airbnb also makes the marketing and sales process effortless and economical.

Airbnb, however, wouldn't exist unless hosts recognized the value of their physical space, or in the case of experience hosts, the value of their knowledge. Airbnb Superhost Merrydith Callegari describes it this way: "Before I could list my home on Airbnb, I had to recognize that people would find value in staying here and that I could charge for the room. I've hosted a lot of family from my husband's region of Italy, but I had to shift my thinking to imagine I could receive paying guests."

Many Airbnb hosts report they experimented on the Airbnb platform to determine if it would be worthwhile to list an experience or property. Darren Guyaz, who offers an intimate concert experience, notes, "I remember inviting four friends to attend my first concert in case no one else signed up. Quickly it became clear that Airbnb would help me reach a large audience. I am having great success, and I've never looked back."

Writing for *Entrepreneur* magazine, David Rusenko, CEO of Weebly, shared results from a study his company commissioned related to the type of fear business owners must overcome to bring their ideas or products to market. The researchers found that "one-third of Americans are more afraid to start their own business than to jump out of a plane." David noted that this underlying fear has resulted in a 65 percent decrease in new business creation since the 1980s, and he suggested it's all about "finding the courage to take the first step, wholeheartedly commit to your idea and believe in yourself."

The courage needed to claim one's value extends well beyond business owners. In every sales conversation, there is a moment of truth when salespeople—having communicated the value of their product or service—must courageously ask for the sale. Customer service providers must have confidence that their solutions will have value in order to offer them to customers. An Airbnb Experiences host says, "At first I even doubted whether people would find the same level of joy I find in the activity I lead."

In the movie *We Bought a Zoo*, actor Matt Damon's character, Benjamin Mee, turns to his son and says, "All it takes is 20 seconds of insane courage and great things will happen." While the duration of courage required for business success exceeds 20 seconds, there is resonance in the notion that insane courage is required to achieve great business outcomes. Superhost Linda Litehiser, who lives in the San Francisco area, shares, "I suspect some of my friends thought I was crazy when I told them I was going to rent my room out to strangers. The funny thing is, three or four of them are now Airbnb hosts themselves." Linda's comments reflect how the courage of one host can inspire friends and family members to see the value in their own property.

Airbnb recognizes the unique impact hosts make when they inspire and educate their networks and neighbors about the power of hosting. This network effect has been harnessed and institutionalized through the Airbnb Community Center and Airbnb Host Clubs. Laura Chambers, general manager of Homes Hosts at Airbnb, notes, "We seek to assist online and offline host communities. From an online perspective, hosts gather in a number of places including the Airbnb Community Center and in online communities like Facebook groups. We're deeply engaged in the Airbnb Community Center, and we want to be as helpful as possible for the leaders of other online groups. We want to ensure that all online host communities are empowered, connected, and have lots of tools and insights to do wonderful work."

From an offline perspective, Laura shares:

> We have over a hundred people on our mobilization team that sit in a region and work with regional leads and communities on the ground. This team helps build community through Airbnb Host Clubs. We have 300 Airbnb Host Clubs, which are different based on their local passions and interests. Generally, these groups get involved in policy work, share information like how to get more five-star reviews, and participate in activities that benefit their communities. In essence, our Airbnb Community Organizers partner with local hosts to equip them with online tools and in-person trainings needed to successfully lead and drive outcomes for their local Host Club. Overall, some hosts love being on the Airbnb Community Center, others prefer to be in a Facebook group, and some enjoy being in an offline group. We want to help hosts

based on the community that is right for them. We want to assist them where they feel the strongest sense of community and support.

Airbnb Host Clubs are self-governing, host-led organizations that help people muster the courage to start sharing their homes while upskilling the existing community around safety, compliance, and hospitality. Clubs create a space for locals to come together not only to unite around the values of home sharing but also to better their neighborhoods through service initiatives. Most clubs have multiple Host Leaders, who are inspiring and dedicated hosts that volunteer their time to engage and activate their local host community, and also Airbnb guests, small business owners, and tourism partners.

Many of the hosts I've met are actively involved in their local Host Clubs. Superhost Merrydith Callegari, who helped establish the first Airbnb Host Club in Tasmania, says, "I've always been involved in the broader community where I live, and I meet a lot of people. Quite a few have let me know that they've been considering being an Airbnb host and have asked if I could give them a hand. I invite them to our Host Club, and they are assisted in setting up their listing and get to learn what home sharing is all about."

When Airbnb Superhost Lorell Miller was considering hosting, she attended the Airbnb Meetups. She shares, "I met monthly with my group and was active on the group's web page for about a year while we were building an addition to our home. Long before I actually listed my property, I learned how to present my listing in words and pictures. I also received helpful input on how to set up my space on everything from furnishings to linens. I can't tell you how empowering that group was for me. A year and a half after we listed that property, I am still active with the host group and want to make sure I pay forward what I learned."

Coaching is an essential tool at Airbnb and for all business settings. Often, business leaders need to create only the infrastructure for coaching success (technology communication platforms and administrative support) and then let participants craft their own peer-to-peer community.

At the time of this writing, there are more than 3,000 hosts meeting in over 300 Host Clubs globally. Approximately 40 percent of Host Clubs are running outside of the United States, and many of them have active interactions occurring online as well as offline. The DC Home Sharing Club has 592 hosts involved in more than 800 conversations on their online Airbnb Community Center page.

Virgin's CEO Richard Branson said, "Overcoming fear is the first step to success." In business, overcoming fear comes from encouragement and guidance offered by those who have already taken that first step. Coaching and peer support groups help entrepreneurs through the sharing of information and experience.

IS KNOWLEDGE POWER?

In 1597, Francis Bacon published the Latin words "*Nam et ipsa scientia potestas*," which translates to "For knowledge itself is power." Over the intervening centuries, social scientists and business leaders have come to understand knowledge itself is not enough. Knowledge must be acted upon for its full power to be realized.

In his book *Organizations Don't Tweet, People Do*, social media strategist Euan Semple writes that knowledge "is only valuable if it is going somewhere—if it is flowing and being shared. . . . Think of all the movement-related words we apply to money—currency, transfer, exchange, etc. Knowledge is like any other form of value— it has to be moving to be valuable. . . . The more we all open up and share our thinking, leaving a trace of our passing, the more we will all learn."

The types of information shared by Airbnb hosts differs considerably, depending upon whether the guest is booking an Airbnb Experience or a home stay. Airbnb Experiences, in general, are typically pursued to receive what social psychologists call a "hedonic payoff." In an article for *Advances in Experimental Social Psychology* titled "We'll Always Have Paris: The Hedonic Payoff from Experiential and Material Investment," Cornell University Professor Thomas Gilovich and doctoral candidate Amit Kumar explain: "We live in a consumerist society in which large increases in wealth have not brought corresponding increases in well-being." Research shows "experiential purchases (such as vacations, concerts, and meals out) tend to bring more lasting happiness than material purchases (such as high-end clothing, jewelry, and electronic gadgets)."

Dr. Gilovich's conclusions on the hedonic payoff of experiences are best captured in comments he provided for *Fast Company* magazine. He shares, "Our experiences are a bigger part of ourselves than our material goods. . . . You can really like your material stuff. You can even think that part of your identity is connected to those things, but nonetheless, they remain separate from you. In contrast, your experiences really are part of you. We are the sum total of our experiences."

Since experiences fuel well-being and become a part of us, experience hosts often talk about the importance of giving guests "a story to tell" or to share with their friends. Benjamin Bressler, who hosts an Aerial Tram and Rooftop Excursion in Portland, Oregon, notes, "People often feel time pressured, and when they invest their time in an activity, they want to walk away feeling that they made a great choice. My job is to have them leave feeling they've changed in some small way. It might be that they are more knowledgeable or more relaxed or have developed a new skill or insight."

There is great diversity in the hedonic payoffs received by Airbnb guests. Some experiences are more entertainment focused, like participating in a bar crawl in Madrid or attending a comedy show in Shanghai, but many involve classes, workshops, or elements of information sharing in areas like the arts, history, or nature. To get a sense of how hosts transfer insights and passion through Airbnb Experiences, let's look at a couple of examples from the more than 20,000 experiences listed on the Airbnb site.

In Japan, Tenshin Ito offers a brush and ink calligraphy class in which he shares knowledge gained from 45 years of practice that has earned him the highest rank ("*Shihan*," or master) of Japanese calligraphy. Despite the brevity of the class (2½ hours), students report a lasting impact that changes their self-perception and fuels an eagerness for ongoing learning.

For example, one student shares:

> Tenshin is a patient, kind, and compassionate person who loves to teach others about Japanese culture and Shodo calligraphy. I was nervous about taking this class because I am not artistic nor am I the greatest in calligraphy, but Tenshin's patience and positive feedback helped me become more comfortable and eager to learn more about Shodo calligraphy. I expected to learn only about calligraphy, but Tenshin also taught us about Japanese culture and Japanese phrases that were helpful to use for the rest of my 10-day trip in Japan. . . . He is a wonderful person because all proceeds go to his nonprofit organization where he hand-delivers donations to Vietnamese children with HIV. There was a sentimental surprise at the end, and it made this experience one of the highlights of my 10-day trip in Japan. Tenshin also takes pictures of you while you practice your calligraphy, and

he will send it to you so you can treasure the experience forever.

Tenshin's class is an Airbnb Social Impact Experience, meaning that all proceeds go to a nonprofit organization and Airbnb doesn't charge any fees from either Tenshin or his guests. We will talk more about Social Impact Experiences in the context of the theme "Community," addressed in Chapters 10 and 11.

Diane Wong from Somerville, Massachusetts, offers six different Airbnb Experiences including one workshop called Create a Podcast: Find Your Own Voice. Diane notes, "I've had a rich, full life. I'm 72 and a post–World War II baby. I use Airbnb opportunities to teach skills for how to move through your life and realize that you have responsibility for your life." Based on feedback, guests report that their time with Diane represents an important transfer of life skills:

> This experience was phenomenal! It was a tutorial on how to podcast AND a wonderful discussion of ideas, desires, and vision. Diane also helps you conquer the two main things that have been preventing you from podcasting: (1) Not knowing what supplies, software, and other tools you need. (2) Fearing diving right in because of doubt or a lack of confidence. She gives you what you need, helps you produce one to two podcast episodes of the topic(s) that you want to talk about, and nurtures your vision. I'm really glad she created this experience and that I got to partake in it with her. Any other intro to podcasting would likely have left me wavering, or at least not as nurtured in my vision. Thanks, Diane! I hope to send you my creations in the near future.

According to a study by the Interactive Advertising Bureau (IAB) and PwC, the US podcasting industry generated $314 million in revenue in 2017, up 86 percent from the prior year. Who knows? Diane's Airbnb Experience might open up revenue-generating possibilities for her guests.

Tia L. Clark hosts an Airbnb Experience in her hometown of Charleston, South Carolina. Tia is passionate about crab fishing and views it as an activity that has transformational qualities. "I began crabbing after a health crisis and as part of my overall commitment to health. I quit smoking, took up crabbing to lose weight, and am more than 100 pounds lighter. Crabbing became a life-changing form of exercise and a peace-creating part of my life." Before she became an Airbnb Experiences host, Tia shared details of her crabbing adventures online. Soon enough, her friends asked her to take them along. Tia was reluctant, stating, "Crabbing was mine, and I was concerned that sharing it would diminish my joy." Tia took a chance and found "sharing crabbing just made it better."

With the encouragement of her wife, Tia applied to Airbnb to have her crabbing experience offered on the Airbnb platform. Tia notes, "despite my concern that crabbing with strangers might be less positive than crabbing with friends, Airbnb Experiences has been such an amazing gift. I feel like I am living a dream life and I don't want to wake up." Tia shares that she wants to empower her guests by teaching them about responsible crabbing, showing them how to throw a cast net so they can feed their families, and helping guests feel the healing power of being near the water.

Tia knows that by offering her knowledge and love of crabbing, she is changing lives. She continues, "One example is a special ecology-minded 10-year-old girl named Raya. For her birthday, Raya didn't want presents but instead asked to spend the day cleaning up trash on the beach. Given Raya's passion for the beach, her mom knew Raya would also like my crabbing experience. Not only did she enjoy it but she was also eager to bring her catch home so she and her mother could cook the crabs." According to Tia, Raya's only disappointment was that her best friend wasn't there to also learn how to crab. In response to that disappointment, Raya's mom bought a cast net and arranged for the two girls to go out crabbing the next day. Tia adds, "Raya let me know she and her friend caught a bunch of shrimp in their nets and fed both families for days. I live to have people leave my experience with a passion to invest in a $15 casting net—so they can crab or fish for life."

In the context of Airbnb Experiences, sharing knowledge expresses the power implied in the Chinese proverb, "Give a man a fish and you feed him for a day. Teach a man to fish and you feed him for a lifetime."

Everyone in business can transfer knowledge, which creates value for customers. Knowledge can be mobilized and imparted in a variety of ways, including in-person training, blogs, podcasts, articles, or information shared online.

ADDING VALUE WITH INFORMATION

For most classes and workshops, information is the product. However, in other settings, like home sharing, the physical space is the product but information still adds value. Home hosts provide informational value in a variety of ways, with the most notable being their knowledge of their community. This information is typically offered through the Airbnb app, in-person interactions, and guidebooks.

Hosts we've met view themselves as more than providing a safe and comfortable space. They consider themselves to be local travel guides sharing information that meets the needs of a traveler. On their *Forget Someday* blog, travel writers Sam and Tocarra Best note, "While many travelers are still content with simple sightseeing and checking boxes at top attractions, the New Age traveler is looking for deep and authentic travel experiences around the globe.

They seek experiences to create memories that will last a lifetime, rather than just adding a picture to the scrapbook that will eventually end up on a shelf to collect dust." Superhost Lorell Miller says, "We typically don't see guests when they arrive, but I want them to reach out so I can help them find special places in my community. Whether we chat in person or they ask me questions through the app, I love to share the part of my town that typically only locals get to see."

The appreciation for authentic local travel experiences is common in guest reviews, as well:

> He then gave us a wonderful information session on all the local surroundings.

> We asked about local restaurants (we went to the one she recommended, and it was fabulous!)

> [They] were very helpful in recommending local places for us to eat, hike, explore, drive, etc.

In the host section of the Airbnb website, hosts are encouraged to create guidebooks that "suggest local spots, like restaurants, grocery stores, parks, and attractions." Hosts can post these guidebooks on their listings and supplement them with a bound book in the home. Airbnb host, entrepreneur, author, and founder of *Get Paid for Your Pad*, Jasper Ribbers, offers blogs and instructional videos on topics like creating an effective guidebook. During a discussion with Jasper, he recommended sharing the guidebook before the guests arrive, so guests can anticipate their trip and begin their planning process. He also suggested that at the beginning of a guidebook, the host should offer information to help guests find the location. Jasper says, "I am not only talking about directions but pictorial information including an image of your front door and/or the keyless lock they will use to get in."

In addition to community information, Jasper reports guests find value from being educated on how to use items in the home. "Since guests usually want to connect to Wi-Fi shortly after arriving, I have that displayed in their digital guidebook and the physical guidebook in my home. I also have a prominent sign with the Wi-Fi password displayed right near the entry." His guidebook, which is approximately 20 pages in length, also lists his favorite bars, restaurants, coffee shops, and businesses in his neighborhood. The addresses of these locations are provided, along with pictures and short descriptions. The last page of the book contains all other important information (such as Jasper's contact information and local emergency phone numbers).

When shared thoughtfully, information is either a product unto itself or a substantial value-add. Well-placed information enables customers to learn and grow and helps them achieve success. Let's take a moment to see how information sharing creates value for your business.

 YOUR TRAVEL PLANNING GUIDE

1. Assess your business's performance across Josh Kaufman's five components: value creation, marketing, sales, value delivery, and finance. Where are your strengths and opportunities?

2. How have you participated in or helped set up peer-to-peer coaching? How does or will this coaching empower team members or customers?

3. Dr. Gilovich's findings suggest, "Experiences are a bigger part of ourselves than our material goods." Does that finding relate to your customers and your business? How can you make your offerings more experiential?

4. In what ways are you using information to empower customers? What transformational effect is your knowledge having on them? Where have you gained more value with information?

BUSINESS OPPORTUNITIES: THE ULTIMATE EMPOWERMENT

Many Airbnb hosts have launched successful companies to improve the hosting experience. Jasper Ribbers, for example, took expertise he gained as a host and built a business helping other hosts. Jasper shares, "When I started hosting back in 2012, I wanted to optimize my Airbnb hosting business so I could support a lifestyle of travel. I had quit my finance career and was searching the Internet for hosting tips and resources. There wasn't much information available at the time, so I gathered what I could and learned from experience. I started sharing what I learned in the spirit of helping others, and before you know it, that information organically turned into a business."

Soon, Jasper was podcasting, writing a hosting tips book, and publishing blogs. Having developed a sizable following, Jasper used his blog to review new technology solutions created for hosts. In turn, Jasper's company, Get Paid for Your Pad, receives reimbursement for the traffic he generates for solutions he endorses. Jasper also offers paid hosting courses and individual consultation services for hosts.

Jasper estimates that 50 technology companies emerged quickly after Airbnb gained popularity. These businesses offer tools for Airbnb hosts in areas such as:

- **Automated pricing:** These companies seek to maximize revenue generated by hosts through dynamic pricing software.

- **Automated messaging:** With these solutions, hosts can instantly respond to guest inquiries. Some of these providers add artificial intelligence to recognize questions like "How fast is your Wi-Fi?" and provide relevant and informative answers.

- **Market research:** Providers offer software that helps hosts identify optimal areas for opening an Airbnb and likely revenue they can make.

- **Online guidebooks:** Hosts can create a nicely designed online guidebook that guests can access on a mobile device or download before they begin a trip.

- **Advanced payments:** These providers offer loans and other cash flow assistance based on projected Airbnb revenues. These funds enable hosts to improve their properties and grow their business.

- **Other useful tools:** Options in this area include software that tracks indoor and outdoor noise levels so that a remote host can be alerted. (It should be noted that these items are considered surveillance devices by Airbnb. Under Airbnb policy, hosts must "disclose all surveillance devices in their listings." Airbnb also prohibits "any surveillance devices that are in or that observe the interior of certain private spaces—such as bedrooms and bathrooms—regardless of whether they've been disclosed.") When appropriately disclosed and used, a host can respond to a noise level notification (for example, contact the guest with a reminder to reduce the noise level and/or take action to have the guest's stay terminated).

Solution providers also offer local concierge services on a mobile device. This service combines a digital guidebook with scheduling software so guests can book reservations for such things as meals, tours, and transportation. These types of solutions create a triple win. Guests benefit from information about community activities and services. Community partners benefit from the bookings, and hosts benefit from referral incentives.

In addition to inspiring the emergence of new technology businesses, Airbnb hosts foster business creation in allied people-to-people companies. Airbnb Superhosts Charity and Maylene Kuahiwinui had backgrounds in operations, entrepreneurship, and web design before they explored hosting on the Airbnb platform. Charity explains, "After hosting for a while, we noticed we weren't able to leave our area and still keep our Airbnb running. There weren't any formal coverage options available at the time, and that business opportunity matched our combined skillsets." Maylene and Charity wondered, "What if we helped Airbnb hosts cover or run their listings?"

Around 2013, Charity and Maylene created the company Ensourced to assist Airbnb owners with turnovers. According to Maylene, "We came in to clean and stage a home so it was ready to welcome the next guest. Soon we were hosting on behalf of other people." She adds, "We now manage communication, schedule bookings, prepare the home for the next guest, make sure amenities are in place, do the laundry, and thank the guest. If hosts are new to the business, we will help them set up their space and their hosting profile. We will commission their photos and have the listing ready to be successful from the first day on Airbnb."

Charity and Maylene credit Airbnb's easy user experience, social mission, and effective marketing for their success as hosts and for the success of their host support business. Charity reports, "We are proud to provide jobs for upwards of seven people depending upon the season, and for being able to pay a living wage. We are happy we can provide a work environment where we've retained our very first employee while also offering a positive experience for hosts and guests. In fact, we've also retained our first host client, and all our eligible hosts have achieved Superhost status."

Most of the hosts we met were providing meaningful employment opportunities and supporting their communities. Superhost Jill states, "I took the Living Wage Pledge because when I am away I want to pay cleaners and co-hosts well. We are all in business in one form or another, and we need to support, encourage, and empower one another."

Superhost Majo Liendro creates economic opportunities for artists in her community by showcasing purchasable items on the walls of her Airbnb listing. Majo shares, "The central idea is to be able to offer something more to the tourist who visits the city. There are many places to sell typical crafts of the region, but I feel there is a great absence of places to buy art." Majo put a callout to artists and photographers in her community of Salta, Argentina, to exhibit their work in her home. Majo's goal was to envelop her guests in the local culture, expose them to her community's talented artists, and create a marketplace for the artists' works.

Like Majo, Airbnb hosts create direct and indirect income opportunities in the communities in which they do business. They generate employment opportunities and successful partnerships with local business owners. This collaborative approach to wealth creation is becoming the new normal in commerce today. Paul Parisi, the president of PayPal Canada, says it best in an article for the *Globe and Mail*: "The reality of today's business landscape . . . means that partnerships are key to better serving customers by merging talent, expertise, technology, and purpose. While the rewards are great, strategic partnerships require thoughtful consideration to ensure success is achieved."

Savvy business owners "thoughtfully consider" partnerships and build helpful alliances. For example, a florist might develop a relationship with a caterer to cross-refer customers. A pediatric dentist might secure a relationship with a local children's consignment store owner to make each other's brochures available for access by their customers or to offer relevant discounts on one another's social media pages. In the spirit of these types of alliances, let's take a moment to thoughtfully consider the partnerships you might forge and the products you might create to serve your industry.

 YOUR TRAVEL PLANNING GUIDE

1. What challenges do you face in your business? How might you craft solutions that not only meet your needs but address the same needs for others like you?

2. How can you leverage your expertise to create a business opportunity or new information-based product line?

3. Where are you strategically partnering with other service providers or community businesses to create win-win economic benefits? Which product or services complement yours? What partnerships will create meaningful synergies for your business?

THE RECIPROCAL BENEFITS OF EMPOWERMENT

Early in my career, I coined and trademarked the sentence "Service Serves Us" to capture the reciprocal benefits derived from creating service experiences that create value for others. For example, Starbucks baristas build strong relationships, and the brand benefits from high-frequency customers. Contact center employees at Mercedes-Benz report satisfaction from developing personal emotional connections with callers seeking to have a problem resolved.

The *Service Serves Us* concept is experienced through the Airbnb platform as well. When Airbnb hosts provide quality guest experiences, their guests return to the Airbnb platform to book future stays, thus serving Airbnb's profitability and growth. Hosts also report that through guest service, their financial and social needs are met.

Hosts like Peggy J. Sturdivant credit Airbnb with helping them survive extremely difficult financial circumstances. Peggy and her uncle purchased their home in Los Angeles, and they had no difficulty affording it until her uncle started to show signs of dementia. According to Peggy, "Finances became very tight, and I was dealing with my uncle's disease through the time of his passing. I struggled to keep up with the mortgage and the bills. I didn't know what I was going to do." Peggy continues, "I'd heard a little bit about Airbnb, but it wasn't well known in my African-American community." While watching a television program, Peggy heard a Beyoncé interview during which Beyoncé mentioned she was staying at an Airbnb. Peggy shares, "I thought if Beyoncé trusts Airbnb, I should learn more about it." Peggy went on to explore Airbnb and listed her property. Moreover, she says, "Airbnb saved my house, and the experience has been a wonderful ride. I've been an ambassador for Airbnb ever since."

Similarly, Ana Ramirez and her husband lived in a large home in Seville, Spain, which they inherited from her husband's grandfather. After both she and her husband lost their jobs and Ana's small clothing shop closed, the couple had no income. Ana shares, "Those unforeseen life events helped us clarify our values and reinvent ourselves. In 2012, Airbnb became our way out of our income crisis." Ana suggests her success is linked to "trying something new, trusting in one another, and sharing our most valuable asset." She adds, "I don't want to think about where we would be if we hadn't chosen to share our home." Subsequently, Ana and her husband returned to full-time jobs but continue to list on Airbnb "as much for the lifestyle as the extra income. We love sharing our home and our time with the people we are fortunate to meet through Airbnb."

While financial circumstances hadn't gotten as dire for senior Superhost Linda Litehiser, she readily acknowledges how Airbnb provides lifestyle benefits for her and her husband: "I'm 68 and my husband is 71. We married about six years ago, and each of us came to the marriage with homes in the area. We also have four children and 15 grandchildren and wanted to have a place for the family to visit. We hoped we could keep our second home and not list it as a long-term rental."

Linda notes that she and her husband have a mortgage that needs to be paid and that "without Airbnb, I don't think my husband would have been able to retire when he did. We renovated our home where we share space so it is ADA Compliant, and that will help us when accessing stairs becomes more difficult." Linda also sees Airbnb as a way of warding off feelings of isolation that some seniors experience.

Javier Lasuncion, from Barcelona, validates the social engagement benefits seniors receive from home sharing. He notes, "I have been a civil engineer involved in designing Olympic buildings and played a leadership role in Barcelona's Olympic Museum. I didn't need money in my retirement, but I needed to continue to make a difference." Javier reports that hosting on Airbnb allows him "to add value and share the knowledge I have acquired throughout my life. The revenue I generate also enables me to contribute to a family member's education." Javier adds, "Through sharing, I receive so much."

Javier's words remind me of an Italian proverb my mother told me: "A candle loses nothing by lighting another candle." In the context of business sharing, our light, our resources, and our insight with others create a stronger light to guide shared success. Airbnb Superhost Yui Yamaguchi, who cohosts with her mother Taeko Kan, puts it this way: "My family has made much-needed money through Airbnb, but sharing is about more than getting rich—it is about creating a rich life." How has service served you? Where has sharing your light helped to create a better-lit path for your business?

By enriching the lives of others, the lives of Airbnb hosts are reciprocally enriched. Similarly, by empowering hosts, Airbnb leaders have fueled their company's meteoric success. Empowerment and service require you to create value for others. The value you offer will invariably be the greatest determinant of your success. As leadership expert and author John Maxwell noted, "Most people don't lead their life; they accept their life. People who lead their life intentionally add value to others." In the next chapter, we will broaden our discussion of "adding value" and look at how Airbnb leaders give back to the communities in which they do business and serve hosts and guests in need.

POINTS OF INTEREST
AS YOU CLAIM AND SHARE YOUR VALUE

➜ Josh Kaufman defines a business as requiring value creation, marketing, sales, value delivery, and finance.

➜ Entrepreneurship requires the ability to create value and the courage to present that value to the marketplace.

→ One-third of survey respondents reported that they were more afraid to start their own business than to jump out of a plane.

→ Insane courage is often required to achieve great business outcomes.

→ Peer-to-peer coaching is an important empowerment tool that typically involves company leaders providing infrastructure (technology communication platforms and administrative support) and then letting participants craft their own community.

→ Knowledge must be acted upon or shared for its full power to be realized.

→ Research suggests that "our experiences are a bigger part of ourselves than our material goods."

→ Everyone in business can transfer knowledge, which creates value for customers. Knowledge can be mobilized and shared in a variety of ways, including in-person training, blogs, podcasts, articles, or information posted online.

→ When shared thoughtfully, information is either a product unto itself or a substantial value-added benefit. Well-placed information enables customers to learn and grow, and it helps them achieve success.

→ Business opportunities can occur by marketing solutions you have crafted for your own business to others in your industry.

→ Partnerships are key to better serving customers and require thoughtful consideration to ensure success.

→ Service Serves Us!

community

Serve Your
Neighbor

If you want to go quickly, go alone.
If you want to go far, go together.
—African proverb

In 2018, Airbnb founder Brian Chesky wrote an "Open Letter to the Airbnb Community About Building a 21st Century Company." In that letter, Chesky shared a vision of Airbnb serving all stakeholders and changing the world.

Chesky said Airbnb would adopt an open mindset with an infinite time horizon. In so doing, Airbnb could be more audacious, could assume greater social responsibility, and could commit to lasting change that improves society. Chesky views Airbnb as shaping a world "where every city is a village, every block a community, and every kitchen table a conversation.... This is the magical world of Airbnb."

Airbnb cofounders Joe Gebbia and Nathan Blecharczyk have expressed similar views concerning Airbnb's future impact. Gebbia believes, "It's our responsibility to take what we're incredibly good at—hospitality, facilitating trust between strangers, building scalable software—and help the world and leading organizations . . . solve the most difficult challenges of our time." Blecharczyk adds, "Airbnb illustrates and reminds . . . us about the power of thinking differently and of a supportive ecosystem. Airbnb went from an off-the-wall idea to a transformative company as a result of assembling the right team—cofounders, mentors, investors, and later employees—and now we want to help others pursue unconventional ideas that can make the world a better place."

Airbnb's success can be linked to pursuing an unconventional idea that led to improved travel experiences, but can Airbnb's leadership leverage that success to help others innovate on behalf of social improvements? While it's easy to talk about social change, making it happen is a daunting task. Author and social activist Grace Lee Boggs notes, "You cannot change any society unless you take responsibility for it, unless you see yourself as belonging to it and responsible for changing it." Clearly leaders at Airbnb see themselves as "belonging" to a global community and feel responsible for contributing to the advancement of broad social concerns.

This chapter will examine how Airbnb leaders put action behind intentions like improving society, solving the most difficult problems of our time, or making the world a better place. Specifically, we will explore how those leaders serve their neighbors (whether employees, hosts, guests, or civic leaders). In turn, we will examine how Airbnb leaders help hosts, guests, and community partners maximize their positive social impact. In the pages ahead, you will see Airbnb's efforts to:

- Strengthen communities

- Increase global volunteerism

- Drive sustainability

- Respond to crisis

- Foster social impact

- Enable accessibility

WALKING THE TALK

In 2016, *Forbes* listed the 14 youngest (under age 40) American billionaires. All three Airbnb founders (Chesky, Gebbia, and Blecharczyk) were on the list. On the 2018 *Forbes* 400 list (which *Forbes* calls "the definitive ranking of the wealthiest Americans"), each of the Airbnb founders had an estimated net worth of $3.7 billion.

In keeping with their stated desire to have a substantive social impact, each founder (along with Nathan's wife Elizabeth Blecharczyk) has taken the Giving Pledge originated by Bill and Melinda Gates and Warren Buffett. That pledge is a commitment to philanthropy encouraging the world's wealthiest individuals and families to declare they will "dedicate the majority of their wealth to giving back." In an article for *Fortune* magazine, assistant managing editor Leigh Gallagher points out that the Giving Pledge made by these three leaders "marks the first time all the cofounders of a company have pledged at the same time" and that "while the founders are united in joining the pledge, their giving will be individual."

In his book *An Integrative Theory of Leadership*, University of California–Santa Cruz Professor Emeritus Martin Chemers defines leadership as "a process of social influence through which an individual enlists and mobilizes the aid of others in the attainment of a collective goal." By that definition, the Giving Pledge made by Airbnb's founders reflects active leadership. By committing to return more than 50 percent of their accumulated wealth to address social needs, these donors are socially influencing, enlisting, and mobilizing others to do the same.

In addition to personal philanthropy, Airbnb leaders have explored ways to offer the organization's host community an equity stake in Airbnb. In a letter filed with the US Securities and Exchange Commission in September 2018, Airbnb asked for an amendment to commission Rule 701, which "as currently written and generally interpreted, does not allow companies to grant equity to sharing economy participants who are not otherwise affiliated with the issuer." In other words, hosts are not eligible to receive a portion of Airbnb's equity because regulations limit that profit sharing to employees and investors in Airbnb. In making a case for a rule change, Airbnb's leaders said this:

> Twenty-first-century companies are most successful when the interests of all stakeholders are aligned. For sharing economy companies like Airbnb, this includes our employees and investors, but also the hosts who use our marketplace to list unique accommodations and experiences. As a sharing economy marketplace, Airbnb succeeds when these hosts succeed. We believe that enabling private companies to grant hosts and other sharing economy participants equity in the company . . . would further align incentives between such companies and their sharing economy participants to the benefit of both.

Airbnb's petition for host equity reflects both a desire for stakeholder alignment and a willingness to share the wealth that has been generated by hosts. That wealth sharing would provide extra income to hosts and even possibilities for hosts to upgrade the quality or quantity of their listings. In a letter to digital news platform *Axios* concerning Airbnb's requested rule change, Brian Chesky put it this way: "Airbnb is a community-based company, and we would be nothing without our hosts. We would like our most loyal hosts to be shareholders but need these policies to change in order to make that happen."

Along with personal giving and efforts to provide equity to Airbnb hosts, the company's leaders demonstrate the importance of caring for others through their direct involvement with the Airbnb community. In 2017, during a six-city, two-week trip to meet with and celebrate Airbnb hosts, Chesky shared, "Our product is our community. It's you. It's people, and people will always be at the center of what we do." Chesky emphasized that his title as CEO signifies that he runs the business side of Airbnb, but he also considers himself the "leader of the community. How could you lead the business and not lead the community at Airbnb? They have to be one and the same. . . . So I'm going to change my title from CEO to CEO and Head of Community. This is not an expansion of title as much as an expansion of accountability. . . . I want to be held accountable not just for the business but to the community."

At the same time Chesky announced a series of initiatives to strengthen the relationship between Airbnb leaders and the hosts, guests, and local officials they serve. These actions included the creation of a host advisory board, regularly scheduled Facebook live events facilitated by Brian Chesky, and a formal mechanism for hosts to give input to the Airbnb board of directors.

My father once said, "If you want to know what a person values, look at where he spends his money and watch where he puts his feet." To determine the importance of people and social giving at Airbnb, one need only look to the founders' Giving Pledge, the pursuit of host equity, and examples like Chesky's direct involvement in Airbnb communities.

Beyond the actions of the founders, Airbnb has formalized commitments to its entire stakeholder community by developing numerous departments and initiatives that are outlined in this chapter.

Strengthen Communities

Throughout this book, you've read about many commitments, pledges, and public goals set by Airbnb leaders. In addition to pledges we've discussed in this chapter, in Chapter 9 we cited progress on Airbnb's inclusion goals. In Chapter 8 we shared Airbnb's extension of their Living Wage Pledge, and in Chapter 2 we mentioned how Airbnb had taken the White House Equal Pay Pledge and the White House Tech Inclusion Pledge.

Pledges, goals, and other forms of public commitments are an important part of business and interpersonal life. In a *Hypothesis and Theory* article titled "The Sense of Commitment: A Minimal Approach," cognitive science professors John Michael, Natalie Sebanz, and Günther Knoblich offer empirical findings on the benefits of making a commitment:

> The phenomenon of commitment is a cornerstone of human social life. Commitments make individuals' behavior predictable in the face of fluctuations in their desires and interests, thereby facilitating the planning and coordination of joint actions involving multiple agents. . . . Moreover, commitment also facilitates cooperation by making individuals willing to contribute to joint actions to which they wouldn't be willing to contribute if they, and others, were not committed to doing so.

During an interview with Chris Lehane (Airbnb's SVP of policy and communication), he shared one example of a commitment Airbnb made to a stakeholder group that is often forgotten by business leaders:

> In practical terms, we focus a lot of work on seeking to engage responsibly with communities. In 2015, we released

the Airbnb Community Compact which articulated a series of principles that guide our engagement globally, including sharing data, helping to pay our communities' fair share of taxes, and identifying specific solutions to meet the needs of a particular community. Because housing is typically a derivative of history, politics, culture, and economics, it's important to recognize that every community is unique and faces different sets of challenges.

The Airbnb Community Compact addresses civic leaders in communities where Airbnb has a significant presence. The compact reflects Airbnb's promise to:

- Provide personal attention to each local area

- Assist hosts pay their fair share of hotel and tourist taxes

- Provide transparency and openness regarding hosting activities

- Strengthen local communities by promoting responsible hosting

By publishing location-specific information for community residents and city leaders, Airbnb informs sound public policy in support of responsible home sharing. A 2018 Airbnb press release exemplifies the results of these efforts:

At Airbnb, we've made the commitment to treat every city personally and help ensure our community pays its fair share of hotel and tourist taxes (TOTs). Through this work, we're proud to have partnered with more than 400 governments around the world to collect and remit taxes.

Because of this continued commitment to our host community, we're excited to announce that we have collected and remitted more than $1 billion in TOT taxes to date, helping cities and our host community around the globe.

It's unlikely that you will need to generate hundreds of economic impact reports for leaders in cities where you do business. You probably will also not need to ensure tax collection between parties transacting business across your marketplace. However, the Airbnb Community Compact does have broad relevance. Specifically, it demonstrates that cities and city leaders can and should be viewed as an important stakeholder group. Additionally, the compact reflects how business leaders can make commitments to foster cooperation and joint action in support of shared benefits. What commitments have you made or are you making in the villages, towns, or municipalities in which you do business?

Increase Global Volunteerism

Volunteerism has likely been around since the beginning of human civilization. In the United States, volunteerism can be traced back to 1736 when Benjamin Franklin established the first volunteer firehouse.

While corporate philanthropy has a long history (with prominent spikes in corporate giving occurring during the Industrial Age and after World War II), employee volunteer programs (EVPs) and employer-supported volunteering (ESV) have become increasingly popular since the early 2000s when brands like Pepsi, IBM, and Pfizer launched international corporate volunteer initiatives.

In 2013, Airbnb joined the growing ranks of companies supporting employee volunteerism by launching Airbnb's Global Citizenship Champion program in which Airbnb employees receive four hours of paid time per month to volunteer in their communities. In an article for *Airbnb Citizen*, Airbnb expands on the concept behind the program: "Our host communities are regularly invited to volunteer alongside our employees ... so we can be good neighbors in the cities we have offices. Our Champions organize volunteer activities for employees and hosts, lead charitable drives, and make charitable contributions to causes important to their local communities."

Jenna Cushner, the head of Airbnb's Ground Control team, told me, "Employees of Airbnb partner with hosts to do good things in our shared communities. We approach these efforts in very coordinated, diverse, and interesting ways across our community offices around the world." In Chapter 11, you will discover the personal impact of Airbnb's Global Citizenship program.

As of May 2018, Airbnb employees accompanied by host partners participated in over 250 volunteer projects across 50 cities—contributing more than 11,000 hours of volunteer time. The Chief Executives for Corporate Purpose (CECP), a CEO-led coalition, produces an annual *Giving in Numbers* report on more than 300 of the world's largest businesses. According to 2018 findings, 65 percent of large multinational companies offered a paid "release time program" similar to Airbnb's Global Champion Program.

While large companies have significantly embraced employee volunteerism, small and midsized businesses are trailing their larger counterparts. In an article for the *Ivey Business Journal*, professor Kelly Killcrease reported:

> Many small business owners do not turn to the option of volunteerism. . . . Cost-related factors are the main deterrent to increasing volunteerism in small businesses. The three volunteer costs that must be addressed are worker productivity loss, employee compensation, and organizing the volunteer effort.

Countless studies have demonstrated the social and business impact of employee volunteer programs, which include these benefits:

- Attracting top candidates

- Developing broad professional and leadership skills of employees

- Increasing employee engagement and productivity

- Enhancing team function and camaraderie

- Retaining employees

If you are considering creating an employee volunteer program for your business, CyberGrants has a helpful 10-step guide that you can find at airbnbway.com/book-resources.

Whether your business creates a paid volunteer program like Airbnb's, supports an annual day of employee volunteerism, or organizes intermittent employee volunteer opportunities, there is no shortage of community need. By organizing team members to address social needs, you help them serve their neighbors, enhance relationships with one another, and strengthen their connection to your business. Before we explore Airbnb programs designed to address sustainable travel, emergency needs, and travel accessibility, let's take a moment to consider philanthropy, commitments, and volunteerism in the context of your business.

YOUR TRAVEL PLANNING GUIDE

1. How are you and other leaders demonstrating your commitment to personal and corporate philanthropy? Where would your team members say you spend your money and place your feet?

2. What commitments have you made to your stakeholders? How are your commitments facilitating the planning and coordination of joint action?

3. Which community leaders are important stakeholders for your business? How are you helping them strengthen the communities you serve?

4. How does your business help employees contribute to their communities? How effective are your efforts to encourage and/or support employee volunteerism?

Drive Sustainability

Since Airbnb leaders have committed to be a twenty-first-century company that operates on an "infinite time horizon," they focus both on the long-range sustainability of their business and the importance of mitigating unintended negative environmental impacts. Historically, business leaders began considering the need to balance business success with environmentally sustainable practices toward the end of the industrial revolution (which began in Great Britain in the mid-1700s and spread across the world for roughly the next hundred years).

The commonly agreed-upon impact of the Industrial Age includes urbanization (as people left rural life for jobs near factories), population growth (with improved living standards and medications), increased ease and breadth of travel, and expanded production capabilities for housing and food. With increased demand for source materials to fuel industrial production, the by-products of the production process, and growing numbers of humans sharing the planet, industrialization has had demonstrable environmental effects.

Since the impact of production and consumption threaten the quality of life for consumers and the supply of resources needed to run businesses, leaders are increasingly seeking sustainable consumption. Roughly defined, sustainable consumption minimizes environmental impact of a business while maintaining economic viability. In a foreword to a 2018 Airbnb report titled *Healthy Travel and Healthy Destinations*, Jonathan Tourtellot (founder of the National Geographic Center for Sustainable Destinations) sets the frame for sustainable consumption issues in the travel industry:

> Tourism is the ultimate double-edged sword. If done well, it can do a lot of good. It can boost economies and provide jobs; it can educate both locals and visitors; it can promote international understanding; it can motivate conservation and preservation, and it can be a lot of fun. Tourism done poorly, on the other hand, can do plenty of harm—overdevelopment, cultural and environmental degradation, commercial blight, social stress, and crowding to such an extent that a new word has been coined for it: overtourism.

Throughout the years, Airbnb has taken a number of steps to create sustainable travel—or as Airbnb refers to it, "healthy tourism." In 2018, the company formally announced Airbnb's Office of Healthy Tourism with a focus on driving "local, authentic, and sustainable tourism . . . for hosts, guests, and cities around the world." Along with creating a new department at Airbnb, leaders also announced an Airbnb advisory board consisting of global travel industry experts. These industry advisors are charged with helping Airbnb develop a long-term approach that counteracts the impact of overtourism.

Tourist destinations have a carrying capacity—not unlike the safe carrying capacity of an elevator or an airplane. The United Nations

World Tourism Organization (UNWTO) defines *tourism carrying capacity* as "the maximum number of people that may visit a tourist destination at the same time, without causing destruction of the physical, economic, and socio-cultural environment and an unacceptable decrease in the quality of visitors' satisfaction." Airbnb's marketplace, by its very nature, offers tourist options well beyond mass travel destinations. In 2018, Airbnb looked at travel patterns across eight global destinations (Amsterdam, Bali, Bangkok, Barcelona, Japan, Mallorca, Queenstown, and Venice) and found:

> Airbnb travel largely takes place outside of traditional tourist districts. In each of our eight local case studies, at least two-thirds of all guest arrivals take place outside of traditional tourist areas. Across all eight, between 71 and 91 percent of host-recommended places and activities are located outside of traditional tourist areas. Moreover, 31 to 96 percent of Airbnb Experiences are hosted beyond well-worn tourist neighborhoods.

In addition to the naturally occurring dispersion of travel activity across Airbnb listings, leaders actively encourage authentic off-the-grid travel through programs like its €5 million (about $5.6 million) Community Tourism Program that provides grants for innovative projects to drive healthy tourism in Europe. Applicants can apply for up to €100,000 (about $118,000) for "creating, raising awareness, and celebrating not-yet-trending destinations . . . re-imagining tourism and travel by sparking entrepreneurship and strengthening local economies" or "preserving or celebrating local festivals and events while introducing them to a broader, appreciative audience."

Grant recipients as of the time of this writing included the Weg der Münchner, a newly created trail route around Munich, Germany. The trail covers over 62 miles of green spaces, small businesses, neighborhoods, and historic sites that deliver an authentic and local experience beyond the traditional Munich tourist attractions. In addition to encouraging travel to areas with greater tourist capacity, Airbnb also offers hosts and guests guidance on how they can minimize the environmental impact of tourism.

Airbnb has put together companion guides for sustainable hosting and sustainable traveling. Hosts are encouraged to use the sustainable hosting guide to reduce their environmental footprint. They are also encouraged to share the sustainable traveling guide with their guests to help them partner in conservation. The host guide has a myriad of tips related to topics like driving energy efficiency, avoiding single-use products, cleaning with environmentally friendly materials, and recycling or composting. The complimentary guest guide encourages those who use Airbnb accommodations to explore public transportation, resourcefully reuse household items like towels and dishware, and rate their hosts on eco-friendliness.

In a 2014 study conducted for Airbnb by Cleantech Group, a company that works to drive clean technology innovation, it was clear that hosts and guests were working together to have a positive environmental impact. The Cleantech study concluded that per guest night, Airbnb properties consumed substantially less energy than hotels (78 percent less in Europe and 63 percent less in North America). Subsequently, Airbnb updated this information:

A 2018 analysis using the Cleantech model finds that when guests stay on Airbnb, significantly less energy and water are used, fewer greenhouse gases are emitted, and waste is reduced. By staying in Airbnb listings rather than hotels in 2017, Airbnb guests in Europe achieved energy savings equal to that of 826,000 homes and reduced water usage equal to 13,000 Olympic-sized swimming pools. Airbnb guest stays in North America resulted in lower greenhouse gas emissions equal to that of over 354,000 cars and waste reduction of 64,000 tons.

Independent researchers have also evaluated Airbnb's impact on healthy tourism. In an article titled "The Sharing Economy and Sustainability: A Case for Airbnb," published in the *Small Business Institute Journal*, Professors Chelsea Midgett, Joshua Bendickson, Jeffrey Muldoon, and Shelby Solomon conclude that Airbnb is an innovator that provide:

A new and trendy way to incorporate sustainability into lodging options while also allowing local people in destinations to become quasi-entrepreneurs, allow customers an easy and efficient resource for finding affordable accommodations, and provide users with the opportunity to develop social ties. . . . Users of the site have the opportunity to create and enjoy memorable and unique tourism experiences, increase monetary savings, make a positive impact on the local economy and community, and reduce negative environmental impacts to a greater extent as opposed to traditional accommodation types.

Irrespective of industry, conscious consumption and eco-friendliness matter—for the sustainability of your business, for the health of the planet, and for positive customer perceptions. Surveys of Airbnb guests indicate 66 percent report the environmental benefits of home sharing affect their decision to book through the Airbnb platform. Ecoconscious leadership is no longer optional in business. A short-term view of profitability must balance with long-term concerns for environmental sustainability. To that end, leaders can benefit from the wisdom of Mahatma Gandhi when he said, "Earth provides enough to satisfy every man's needs, but not every man's greed."

Respond to Crisis

Not only should leaders be poised to address long-range sustainability challenges, they should also be considering how they can help address acute community crises and natural disasters. Writing for *Sustainable Brands*, corporate purpose consultant Carol Cone shared how companies are evolving to respond "before, during, and after natural disasters to serve affected employees, customers, and communities." Cone continued: "Historically, companies have responded to disasters by providing the basics of food, water, and shelter—often via cash donations to relief organizations. But in the past few years, we have seen more companies bring their competencies, products or services, and people to disaster situations in innovative ways. And they are changing the way communities across the United States weather and recover from disasters."

Airbnb leaders have also evolved their response to acute human need. Starting in 2012, Airbnb formalized and scaled the host community's response to natural disasters. After hearing stories of Airbnb hosts who provided housing and meals to those displaced by Hurricane Sandy, Airbnb created a way for hosts to create free bookings through an Airbnb Disaster Response Tool. This tool was activated in the aftermath of a catastrophic event to house aid workers and those directly affected. Airbnb also expanded this emergency housing program, in response to changes in US immigration laws.

In January 2017, President Donald Trump signed an executive order titled "Protecting the Nation from Foreign Terrorist Entry into the United States," which halted travel from Iran, Iraq, Libya, Somalia, and Sudan for a period of 90 days. It also blocked refugees for four months and suspended all travel from Syria.

Congruent with Airbnb's Belong Anywhere mission (and consistent with the reactions of other technology leaders like Tim Cook and Jeff Bezos), Brian Chesky actively criticized President Trump's travel ban and committed Airbnb to provide housing to refugees affected by it. Chesky sustained his criticisms as the travel ban progressed through two revisions, two court reviews, and a Supreme Court ruling.

In February 2017, an Airbnb television advertisement titled "We Accept" aired during Super Bowl LI. (That ad can be found at airbnbway.com/book-resources.) The Airbnb Super Bowl commercial ended with #weaccept, and following the game, Chesky tweeted:

> **Brian Chesky** ✔
> @bchesky
>
> Follow ⌄
>
> Airbnb's goal is to provide short term housing over the next five years for 100,000 people in need #weaccept
>
> 5:03 PM - 5 Feb 2017

> **Brian Chesky** ✔
> @bchesky
>
> Follow ⌄
>
> We're also going to contribute $4M over 4 years to @theIRC to support critical needs of displaced populations globally #weaccept
>
> 5:03 PM - 5 Feb 2017

By June 2017, Airbnb founder Joe Gebbia announced the evolution of the Disaster Relief Tool into a program referred to as Open Homes. In describing Open Homes, Gebbia proclaimed Airbnb was taking crisis response forward to a whole other level simply **by shifting from being reactive to being proactive.** No waiting around for the crisis to hit, but to anticipate and harness this natural generosity on a daily basis. The humanitarian crisis we are facing today is the most extensive mankind has experienced since World War II, with more than 65 million people forced to flee their homes and often their home countries. Earlier this year, we set a goal to support our hosts in opening their doors to 100,000 displaced people over the next five years. **Why not give the same solution we provide to travelers to those who are displaced?** (emphasis in the original)

In that announcement, Gebbia explained that relief organizations would be able to directly match refugees with hosts who volunteered to be on standby through Open Homes.

Over the years, Airbnb's Open Homes program has expanded to medical travel needs. Open Homes' medical stays are provided for individuals requiring treatment or in need of respite, along with their caregivers. By creating the Open Homes program, Airbnb leaders are realizing their goal "to help others pursue ways to make the world a better place." They are doing this by giving hosts the tools necessary to offer their homes to those in need. In Chapter 11, we will hear from individuals who have provided or received accommodations through Airbnb in times of acute or prolonged crisis.

Leadership expert and author Brian Tracy observes, "The true test of leadership is how well you function in a crisis." Visionary business leaders not only respond to crises—they also anticipate unforeseen events. These leaders also inventory their companies' unique competencies and resources and deploy them in crises to care for their team members and communities. Let's take a moment to consider your humanitarian crisis planning and issues of sustainable consumption for your business.

YOUR TRAVEL PLANNING GUIDE

1. How are you approaching sustainable consumption issues that may affect your business's longevity?

2. What tools have you provided to your team members, suppliers, and customers to help them support your sustainable consumption efforts?

3. What disaster response tools have you developed for your business?

4. How have you prepared to use your company's competencies and resources to serve your team and community in the event that a disaster or humanitarian crisis occurs?

Foster Social Impact

Up to this point in the chapter, I've primarily discussed how Airbnb has partnered with its home host community to address environmental issues and emergency accommodations. In this section, we will quickly review how Airbnb Experience hosts are doing their part to "serve their neighbors" and giving back through Airbnb's Social Impact Experiences.

As you'll recall from Chapter 1, in November 2016, Brian Chesky announced Airbnb was expanding from being solely a home hosting company to become a business that delivers end-to-end travel. As part of that announcement, Chesky unveiled Airbnb Experiences, which also created social impact opportunities.

Social Impact Experiences help nonprofit organizations raise funds and increase awareness. When prospective guests search for an Airbnb experience, they can click on a prominent tab at the top of the search page labeled Social Impact Experiences. Prospective experience guests—both local and travelers—can then look for causes of interest or merely explore ways to engage in an activity that supports a nonprofit. These opportunities include activities like a visit to a wildlife sanctuary in Costa Rica where proceeds go to protect the rainforest and a tractor-drawn tour of the African countryside in support of an agency that helps develop rural women and youth.

Airbnb waives its service fee for all social impact transactions, and some nonprofits are earning over $50,000 per year on these bookings. Nonprofits also benefit by emotionally connecting with guests during these experiences. This inspires guests toward future volunteerism, donations, or advocacy. Chapter 11 offers a story from a Social Impact Host, but for now, let's look at one example of a Social Impact Experience that benefits the environment on multiple levels.

Imagine you are traveling in Amsterdam and are looking for a local Airbnb Social Impact Experience. You see an option to go "plastic fishing" and click on the link. For $30, you decide to engage in a two-hour activity that supports the nonprofit organization Plastic Whale, which describes itself as "the first professional plastic fishing company in the world." Upon arriving at the activity, you would board one of Plastic Whales' 10 boats made from plastic waste extracted from the Amsterdam Canal. During your adventure, you are equipped with rubber gloves and fishing nets and help retrieve plastic discarded in the canal. In addition to your hands-on cleanup, your experience includes local insights on Amsterdam's historic center, shared by your Plastic Whale guide and skipper. The proceeds from your booking fee are used to further support Plastic Whale's mission: "to make the world's waters plastic-free by creating value from plastic waste."

Plastic Whale views Airbnb Social Impact Experiences to be a perfect fit for its mission because the program helps them "involve as many people as possible. . . . The more people get involved, the bigger impact we can make together. . . . It is our goal to go 'out of business': overfishing is a positive phenomenon in our case."

Amsterdam's Plastic Fishing experience is an example of what is possible when a business like Airbnb provides its core competency (an online marketplace) to help nonprofits engage and serve. Plastic Whale gains from the hands-on effort of participants, increased awareness of their cause, and funds needed to support its mission. Participants get an authentic, local, sustainable travel experience where they make a positive difference. Amsterdam benefits from the removal of plastics from its waterways. Chris Lehane, Airbnb's head of public policy, reports that after he visited President Mandela's Museum in Johannesburg, he learned, "A person who travels should try to take something with them and leave something behind." In the case of Airbnb's Social Impact Experiences, guests and hosts take memories of their experiences with them while leaving behind a positive contribution. How can you facilitate a partnership between your business and your customers to leave your community a better place?

Enable Accessibility

First Lady Eleanor Roosevelt once said, "The purpose of life is to live it, to taste experience to the utmost, to reach out eagerly and without fear for newer and richer experience." To live life to the fullest, people must be able to access the things life has to offer.

Srin Madipalli is acutely aware of accessibility challenges, having traveled the world from his wheelchair. Madipalli has an MBA from Oxford and is a lawyer, a geneticist, and a self-taught web developer. In 2015, Madipalli and his childhood friend Martyn Sibley founded Accomable, a travel startup created to assist disabled people in finding and booking travel accommodations across the globe (both Madipalli and Sibley have spinal muscular atrophy). At the same time Accomable was gaining popularity, Airbnb customers with disabilities were complaining that the Airbnb website made it difficult for them to locate homes that would meet their needs.

In 2017, Airbnb purchased Accomable and brought Madipalli on as Airbnb's accessibility and product manager. By 2018, Airbnb announced 27 new accessibility tools on the website. According to Srin Madipalli, these resources "enable Airbnb guests to search for listings with specific features, including step-free entry to rooms, entryways that are wide enough to accommodate a wheelchair, grab bars, roll-in showers, and more. Before these new tools were provided, guests on Airbnb were only able to search for 'wheelchair-accessible' listings." Airbnb worked with the California Council of the Blind, the National Council on Independent Living, and other groups to create the accessibility filters, receiving widespread praise from organizations like Handicap International and AbleThrive USA.

Srin acknowledges, "Airbnb's new accessibility features and filters are just the beginning of our journey to improve accessibility at Airbnb. We are making it globally easier to share adapted homes so anyone can truly Belong Anywhere." Srin also shares his vision for the future noting, "We have opportunities to make progress beyond physical disability and wheelchair accessibility. We are working hard to educate our host community on the disabled traveler experience, the importance of showing accessibility accommodations through pictures, and increasing accessibility opportunities across the platform." Srin's comments highlight the importance of leaders ensuring that anyone can access their business's goods or services.

Fiction author and essayist Charles de Lint wrote, "I don't want to live in the kind of world where we don't look out for each other. Not just the people that are close to us, but anybody who needs a helping hand. I can't change the way anybody else thinks, or what they choose to do, but I can do my bit." As a leader, you have the power to do more than a "bit" for your customers. You can amplify your own efforts by supporting your team and your customers to serve not just the people who are close to them but also our global neighborhood and planet. As this chapter's title suggests, leadership requires us to *serve our neighbors.*

POINTS OF INTEREST AS YOU SERVE YOUR NEIGHBOR

→ A twenty-first-century company adopts an infinite time horizon, so it can be more audacious and assume greater social responsibility for lasting societal improvement.

→ If you want to know what people value, watch where they spend their money and where they put their feet.

→ Leadership is a process of social influence through which an individual enlists and mobilizes the aid of others in the attainment of a collective goal.

→ Public commitments can facilitate cooperation by making individuals willing to contribute to joint actions.

→ Community leaders and government officials are stakeholders. Build relationships with them and be of service to them.

→ Leaders must position their businesses in the direction of sustainable consumption. Roughly defined, sustainable consumption minimizes the environmental impact of a business while maintaining economic viability.

→ Consider partnering with customers to increase awareness and eco-friendly behavior.

→ Increasingly, business leaders are positioning their companies to bring competencies, products or services, and people to innovatively address disaster situations.

→ Consider forming partnerships with your customers that leave your community better from the aligned effort.

→ Leaders can have impact well beyond their company and community. Often that influence transcends borders and continents. Leadership actions can affect more than quarterly results and may contribute to the overall sustainability of a business and of the planet.

Own Goodness

Goodness is the only investment that never fails.
—Henry David Thoreau

In Chapter 10, we explored Airbnb programs that were developed to engage community leaders, promote healthy travel, support humanitarian and disaster relief, drive social impact, and foster accessibility. Even though each of those Airbnb programs is well-designed, every one of them would fail if the host community didn't actively support them.

This chapter, titled "Own Goodness," offers examples and insights from hosts who take action to serve their communities. Author and syndicated talk show host Dennis Prager suggests, "Goodness is about character—integrity, honesty, kindness, generosity, moral courage, and the like. More than anything else, it is about how we treat people."

In the pages ahead, you will experience the integrity, moral courage, generosity, and kindness of Airbnb hosts as they:

- Engage community leaders

- Invest in social projects

- Create sustainability and accessibility

- Provide shelter

- Support community causes

Let's begin by exploring how hosts engage in public discourse and participate in local government activities related to home sharing.

MAKE YOUR VOICE HEARD: BEING SOCIALLY RESPONSIBLE

Many of the Airbnb hosts we've met hadn't been active in local policy conversations until becoming involved with Airbnb. Peggy J. Sturdivant, a Superhost from Los Angeles, shares, "When I first started hosting, I mostly saw my community as my guests and my neighbors. I wanted them to treat one another well. As I got more involved with my Airbnb Host Club, however, I realized I needed to participate in local government to make sure we have appropriate regulation while also making sure elected officials protect our rights to share our homes. By taking care of the people who live near me, I was more effective when I went to local officials. In fact, seven of my neighbors wrote letters in support of Airbnb as I went to the council to share my input. All of it came together for a fair outcome."

The word *integrity* comes from the Latin word *integer*, meaning "whole or congruent, as in a whole number. In Peggy's case, her integrity is reflected in the congruence of her desire to have council members support responsible hosting, while she acts as a responsible host on behalf of her community. John D. Rockefeller, Jr., said: "I believe that every right implies a responsibility; every opportunity, an obligation; every possession, a duty." Leadership is about being accountable for the rights that individuals and businesses enjoy.

Superhosts Bryan and Charlotte Chaney are seasoned business owners who proactively uphold their obligation to shape hosting behavior in their community. Bryan shared:

> We formed a group comprising about 25 or 30 owners of short-term rental property. We've been getting together monthly to share best practices and focus on our number one goal of being a good neighbor. For us, that means we will police one another and others in our industry to deliver a high-quality housing product. We will go to our neighbors and introduce ourselves, letting them know how to contact us if they have the slightest problem or concern. We will also pay every tax required. We take these actions not only because they are the right things to do but also because we want local officials to spend time on major social issues like public safety or the opioid epidemic instead of regulating home sharing.

Superhosts like Shannon Hiller-Webb became active in civic discussions, not realizing how their actions would frame global home sharing. She explains, "I live in Portland, Oregon, which is a 'do-it-yourself city' with more entrepreneurs per capita than most cities, and home sharing played to our sensibilities. My involvement in Portland's home sharing legislation came from a heartfelt passion for those who needed the income to save their homes—like senior women. I had to fight for them and humanize this issue."

While Shannon may have played an early role in home sharing activism, hosts around the globe have stepped out of their comfort zones to express themselves in similar ways. Merrydith Callegari, a Superhost from Tasmania, notes, "I had to retire from my career early due to an autoimmune disease, and my husband suggested we start sharing some available space to earn extra money. I was a grandmother and loved looking after my grandchildren. At the same time, hosting was a boost to my self-esteem, as I was earning income again." Not having an Airbnb Host Club available to her at the time, Merrydith worked with an Airbnb Community Organizer to locate other hosts in her region. Shortly thereafter, Merrydith helped form the first home sharing community in Tasmania.

Merrydith became more aware of the need for input on home sharing regulation in her country. "I found myself writing letters to politicians, government departments, and newspapers. All of that culminated in me unexpectedly speaking at a press conference where our Premier released details on fair home sharing rules in Tasmania. When I began writing letters, I couldn't have imagined I would be standing near the Premier."

The journey to community involvement has taken many hosts further than they imagined possible. Host Emanuela Marino, from Rome, was well positioned to have significant and effective input on home sharing regulation. As a host, global traveler to 41 countries, and former government employee, she leveraged her degree in law and past experiences to help clarify tax policies affecting home sharing. Emanuela states, "It started with me sifting through a multitude of confusing laws and talking with politicians about how they could make them understandable and congruent. Little did I know, I would later find myself running for office as a regional council member with home sharing policy being the center of my campaign."

Former Speaker of the House Tip O'Neill regularly championed the phrase, "All politics is local." Despite the importance of being involved in local policy, few citizens and business leaders are actively engaging in public hearings. Alex Hilleary, direct marketing specialist at BoxCast, shares that for public meetings, "low attendance is a regular concern of municipalities across the country. As a part of my job, I've attended council meetings in various cities and have witnessed the problem firsthand. I've even shown up only to realize that I was the only nongovernment employee in attendance. However, I've also had the opportunity to talk to residents. Time and time again they've made it clear that they care about what's going on in the community, but just can't make it to council meetings."

When it comes to interaction with political officials, lessons from Airbnb hosts are clear. Act responsibly within your community as you share your input on the ways potential legislation may affect you. Demonstrate moral courage and realize that stepping into the public arena can create future leadership opportunities. Show up, speak up, and participate!

INVEST IN COMMUNITY PROJECTS

While participation in policy discussions *may* contribute to social change, direct acts of community service *ensure* positive social outcomes. Airbnb hosts, in partnership with Airbnb employees (as part of Airbnb's Global Citizenship program) and independently through activities arranged by Airbnb Host Clubs, actively support community building efforts.

Superhost Javier Lasuncion notes, "Our Host Club is very committed to giving back to our community, and we use our talents to support Airbnb's Belong Anywhere mission. As part of that, I use my life experiences and language skills to help immigrants from the Middle East who live in the Raval district of Barcelona. I teach them Spanish and how to create opportunities to live a meaningful and rewarding life in Spain."

Merrydith Callegari adds, "Our Host Club builds community libraries. We basically make a cabinet and involve local schoolchildren to paint it. We donate used books and seek donations from others, so we fill the cabinets, which are cemented on posts in public places like parks. People can take a book, read it, keep it, return it, or replace it." Merrydith hopes that her group's support of reading will increase "open thinking and the acceptance of new people and ideas." Nelson Mandela put it this way: "When we read, we are able to travel to many places, meet many people, and understand the world."

Community activities involving Airbnb hosts are wide-ranging. As part of Airbnb's Global Citizenship program, hosts and Airbnb employees have partnered together across the globe. Here are a few examples:

- In Comunidade Vila Moraes, a *favela* (slum) in São Paulo, local hosts and the Brazilian Airbnb team worked with the nonprofit Liter of Light to create sustainable solar street lights.

- In Paris, the Airbnb local team worked alongside hosts in partnership with Je M'engage to improve an emergency housing shelter.

- Airbnb hosts and employees in Seoul made stuffed animals with TalktoMe Stuffed Toys and donated them to immigrants in Korea.

- In Airbnb's hometown of San Francisco, hosts and Airbnb employees have completed countless community projects. In one single afternoon in 2016 (as part of a global event referred to as a Week for Good), 27 activities were completed in the Bay Area involving 2,000 hours of volunteerism spread across hundreds of hosts and Airbnb employees. On that day, volunteers painted, weeded, composted, and harvested at various locations. Some of them also prepared meals for Mission Bay's Family House, which serves parents traveling with children receiving medical care.

Those who benefit from the volunteerism of the Airbnb community express gratitude with the volunteers directly and often share appreciation on social media. Here are a couple of tweets:

Airbnb hosts receive a great reward from taking the time and effort to give back to their communities. They also report that they forge bonds with Airbnb employees who volunteer alongside them.

The Airbnb host community reminds us that doing business is a privilege, one that requires investments back into communities that support a company's efforts. These hosts also show the power of volunteering in partnership with other groups (in Airbnb's case, hosts, Airbnb employees, and community organizations) to build networking bonds while also delivering goodness. Before we explore how Airbnb hosts create sustainability and accessibility, provide shelter, and support social causes, let's look at your participation in local government and community volunteerism.

YOUR TRAVEL PLANNING GUIDE

1. How would you rate and describe your level of involvement in local policy making?

2. When did you or your team members last write to or otherwise contact local officials? When did you, or members of your team, last attend a public meeting on an issue affecting your business?

3. Do you accept John D. Rockefeller, Jr.'s notion that, "Every right implies a responsibility; every opportunity, an obligation; every possession, a duty?" If so, what responsibilities do you have as a business leader when it comes to civic involvement and activism?

4. What are people saying about your organization's give-back behavior? How are you helping team members build bridges throughout your community as they deliver goodness?

CREATE SUSTAINABILITY AND ACCESSIBILITY

Airbnb hosts share wide-ranging ideas on how they run environmentally responsible businesses. These include but are not limited to:

- Placing signs throughout homes encouraging guests to recycle or reuse items

- Using energy-efficient technologies, like thermostats that can be adjusted remotely and immediately upon guest departure

- Eliminating single-use items

- Cleaning with environmentally friendly products

- Educating guests on environmentally friendly
  travel practices

Kathy Peterman is an example of an Airbnb Superhost whose worldview aligns well with Airbnb's concept of healthy travel. She notes, "Since I started hosting, I became a master recycler and I am very eco-conscious. I use far fewer resources than what a hotel would use." Kathy explains that she sets annual trash reduction goals, "which are personal to me, but I share my goals and processes for attaining them with my guests. While I don't expect guests to fully participate with me since they are on vacation, I do drive some waste reduction behaviors. For example, I ask guests to please put any items that would go in the compost bin in a container I provide. Surprisingly, my guests only generated 50 gallons of trash for an entire year, and on a personal level, I only generated 2 gallons." (If you are interested in learning more about Kathy's tips for waste reduction, please visit airbnbway.com/book-resources).

In addition to deploying eco-friendly practices while running their business, Airbnb Superhosts Bryan and Charlotte Chaney created their Airbnb listings by adaptively reusing historic buildings. Writing in the *Moss Architecture* blog, architect Emily Torem explains adaptive reuse in the context of sustainability: "Adaptive reuse is when you look for an awesome Airbnb for vacation . . . and it's inside a shipping container. Adaptive reuse is . . . whenever you give an existing building, home, or venue a new purpose. Or maintain the same purpose, but while preserving, rebuilding, enhancing, or maintaining some or all elements of the building." Torem cites that the construction and demolition of buildings results in 160 million tons of debris per year—approximately 26 percent of

US nonindustrial waste. She observes, "Reusing any element of a building's structure can cut down on that 160 million tons. Refraining from demolishing a building in its entirety can also help."

One of Bryan and Charlotte Chaney's listings, for example, adaptively reused the Barbara Fritchie House. That building in Frederick, Maryland, was the residence of a folkloric woman from the Civil War period. The home was also likely the first historic preservation home in Frederick when it opened on Flag Day in 1927. Bryan and Charlotte purchased the home in 2018 and made extensive renovations to transform it into a suitable short-term accommodation. Their upgrades included an expanded bathroom and modernized kitchen, up-to-date electrical elements, and a zone-controlled heating and air-conditioning system. They also included historically inspired furnishings, decorations, antiques, and heirlooms.

Bryan explains that the couple's rationale behind selecting and reusing the Barbara Fritichie House was "the home's historic significance. It was also a building that needed some thoughtful attention in order to bring it back to full usefulness. We were committed to preserving this important part of our community and to do so in an environmentally friendly way. We also wanted this home and another renovation project to revitalize more than buildings. As a board member for a drug rehab facility in Frederick, I was able to hire individuals who were in recovery to help us get one of our properties ready to list. We've also partnered with a deaf member of our community. She created her business as our cleaner and our cohost." Bryan adds, "Being responsible stewards of all human and physical resources is good for the environment and our community." Bryan and Charlotte are part of a growing trend to make Airbnb increasingly accessible. Many hosts, for example, are specifically focused on increasing physically accessible travel.

In an article for the London newspaper the *Telegraph* titled "How Disabled Travelers Finally Stopped Being Ignored—Thanks to a Company You Might Not Expect," writer and self-declared "wheelchair-using wanderer" Emily Yates explains the positive impact that comes when hosts share accessible homes. Yates reported that during a trip to London, she searched for accommodations that would meet her needs, using Airbnb's improved accessibility search features detailed in Chapter 10. Emily notes she submitted her "requirements for step-free access, wide doorways, a fully equipped accessible bathroom with roll-in shower and grab rails, and even a disabled parking spot and hoist availability. . . . Apartments are inherently different from hotels: they offer space to live rather than just sleep, and knowing there's now an option for me to safely cook a meal in an unfamiliar kitchen, and accessible lounge spaces that I can entertain new holiday friends in, will undoubtedly change the way that I travel." In her article, Emily also listed several Airbnb Experiences that accommodate guests, including a wheelchair tennis experience.

The London-based experience Emily referenced is led by Airbnb employee Suzanne Edwards. Suzanne took up wheelchair tennis after sustaining a spinal cord injury in Morocco approximately seven years ago. She is a ranking British Champion, and her Airbnb Experiences listing advises, "No matter your age, ability or disability, this is a great opportunity to sit in a tennis wheelchair (provided) and have a hit with an experienced wheelchair tennis player." Suzanne provides helpful information in her listing about accessibility issues such as parking, building entry, toilets, caregivers, and equipment.

Phil Dye, an Airbnb host from Sydney, Australia, shares how an experience he calls "a journey inside your brain!" brings neuroscience to life for all: "I love teaching and helping people. I'm fortunate to be joined by guests of all types including those with physical challenges—including quadriplegic guests and others with conditions like multiple sclerosis and Parkinson's disease. Australia is an amazing place to explore, but not everyone can go snorkeling or bushwalking. However, everyone can come into my experience, put a headset on, and let their brains play."

Great business leaders let their brains play with possibilities for creating greater access and for enabling more people to enjoy the fullness of what their companies have to offer. Those leaders also consider ways to reuse resources, reduce waste, and improve the lives of those they serve. In the spirit of serving others, let's take a moment to see how Airbnb hosts offer humanitarian services to those in need.

PROVIDE SHELTER

Actor, writer, and producer Denis Leary claims, "Crisis doesn't create character; it reveals it." For the Airbnb hosts who step up to "free housing," availability, or other forms of comfort to refugees, disaster victims, crisis workers, and those requiring accommodations associated with health needs, character is demonstrated in a willingness to both anticipate and respond to a crisis. As Hurricane Michael approached the panhandle of Florida in 2018, Airbnb hosts readied to provide shelter. In total, more than 1,000 hosts volunteered. As of this writing, more than 11,000 people have secured accommodations globally through the Airbnb Open Homes program that was discussed in the previous chapter.

Adrienne Penny told me she had been hosting Airbnb guests for a few years and was looking for ways to give back to her community when a friend suggested, "Why don't you use your space to give a break to people who provide long-term care to individuals with mental and physical illness?" Adrienne said: "I contacted my local carers organization, Carers Queensland. Unfortunately, there aren't a lot of options for carers to receive planned respite breaks, so my offer was much needed and well received. In fact, over a short period of time, I've provided free stays to 14 caregivers." When I asked

Adrienne about a regional humanitarian business award she received after being nominated by one of her caregiver guests, she modestly responded, "I don't open my home for recognition. I do it because my mother taught us that we are here to care for one another, and I am caring for the caregivers. In essence, I get to pass on my mother's legacy to caregiver guests." Adrienne added, "Truth be told, I think I get more out of hosting this retreat than my guests do."

Kathryn Kelly, team leader for Sunshine Coast Carers Queensland, disagrees with Adrienne's assessment of her proportional impact. "When a small business owner like Adrienne offers up her resources, in Adrienne's case forgoing revenue by providing space in her home, it can be life-changing. The guests who stay with Adrienne say amazing things about what her kindness meant to them. Adrienne's example has also inspired other hosts to reach out to our organization making similar offers of service." Adrienne's acts of generosity do substantial good in her community without adversely affecting her business (for example, she offers free housing to carers at off-peak times for her business). Moreover, her actions serve as a catalyst for other like-minded leaders to follow.

Airbnb Superhost Rebekah Rimington has similarly received recognition for being an inspirational and compassionate host. In 2016, Rebekah received a distinguished Airbnb award from Chip Conley at the Airbnb Open in Los Angeles. Rebekah's award was given for acts of heroism associated with ensuring the safety of guests staying in her home after a Thanksgiving Day fire broke out in a detached garage. However, her acts of compassionate care have extended well beyond that specific event. For example, Rebekah notes, "I welcomed the opportunity to host a couple where the husband was in end-stage cancer. I was blessed to be with the couple as he neared death and to do my small part to provide a safe haven and simply listen. I knew that no one could stop the progression of his disease, but I also knew that I could step in and make a difference. Sadly, I don't think most people understand how much they can offer when they open their homes and their hearts to others." As evidenced by her perspective, it's no wonder Rebekah won Airbnb's Bélo Love Award.

Journalist H. L. Mencken wrote, "A home is not a mere transient shelter: its essence lies in the personalities of the people who live in it." Mencken's words can be revised to suggest that a company is not a mere collection of products and buildings: its essence lies in the willingness of leaders and frontline workers to open their hearts to those they serve. Let's take a moment to look at accessibility, environmental stewardship, and the degree to which hearts are open in your business.

 YOUR TRAVEL PLANNING GUIDE

1. How are you seeking to decrease the waste produced by your business? How are you driving awareness of waste reduction with your team and your customers?

2. What are you repurposing or adaptively reusing? Where do you have options to further reuse as opposed to demolish and replace?

3. How are you "opening the heart of your business" to those in need throughout your community? Who has inspired you with their acts of compassion? Whom are you inspiring?

MAKE A SOCIAL IMPACT

In Chapter 9, while discussing empowering experiences, I highlighted how Tenshin Ito brings 45 years of knowledge as a master calligrapher to a 2½-hour art class where students leave feeling artistic and impassioned about art creation. In a review I shared about the experience, a student alluded to feeling even better about the experience knowing that all proceeds go to Tenshin's nonprofit. Let's take a moment to get to know Tenshin, understand more about his nonprofit, and see what we can learn from him.

Seventy-year-old Tenshin Ito and I met via a video conference, during which he stood in his calligraphy classroom. Upon exchanging greetings, he asked if he could take me through the first portion of his calligraphy experience. I gladly accepted, and he began sharing insights on Japanese culture and etiquette. He then engaged me in a flashcard type of Japanese language learning exercise. Throughout this process, I could feel his energy, passion, and enthusiasm for sharing and fostering learning. While my purpose for our meeting was to learn more about him and his nonprofit, I found myself absorbed in a myriad of subjects that hadn't previously captured my attention.

When we transitioned to the topic of Tenshin's involvement with Airbnb, he said he saw Airbnb's cofounder Joe Gebbia being interviewed on a local news program about experience hosting in Japan. Tenshin added, "I learned about the economic challenges occurring in Vietnam over a decade ago, and ever since, I have supported a nonprofit I created to serve children and families there. Based on what I heard about Airbnb's philosophy to help people Belong Anywhere, and Airbnb's Social Impact Experiences program, I thought Airbnb would be perfect to help me fund my nonprofit."

For the next 20 minutes of our discussion, Tenshin showed me posters, charts, and maps related to his work in Vietnam. With a level of enthusiasm that exceeded his exuberant teaching style, he talked about how early in his nonprofit's history, he would travel to Vietnam and help support the treatment of children who were born HIV-positive. With improvements to both medication access and care for HIV-positive infants, some of Tenshin's focus has shifted to abate the poverty experienced by the 53 ethnic minorities living in rural mountainous regions of Vietnam. Each year, Tenshin tries to raise approximately $7,000 to bring with him during a trip to the country. Tenshin reports that those dollars, given the economy of Vietnam, have a tenfold spending power (approximately $70,000 worth of impact).

Tenshin distributes funds through established relief agencies in Vietnam. He said, "Before Airbnb helped me secure such a large audience of guests, raising that much money was not possible. I usually supplemented about half of my goal from my limited personal funds. I am so pleased that I will have more than I budgeted this year without dipping into my retirement. I am grateful to Airbnb and its guests for allowing me to live my personal philosophy, which is that we are not here to create a give-and-take balance. We are here to give our spirit. I call my mission 'for you,' and it is how I must live."

Tenshin's "for you" spirit is deeply aligned with Airbnb hosts who support the work of nonprofits through Social Impact Experiences, but it is also pervasive in the Airbnb home host community as well. A perfect example of this "other-focused" spirit comes from 80-year-old James Yates and 79-year-old In Ja Yates who are Superhosts in Los Angeles. James and In Ja have raised more than $70,000 in support of the nonprofit Soul 2 Seoul, which they founded to offer college scholarships for primarily multirace students who've demonstrated a commitment to build bridges between ethnic groups. I caught up with James just days after the Yates's fifty-eighth wedding anniversary. James shared, "The seeds for our scholarships were probably sown back when we married. As a biracial couple (I am African American and In Ja is Korean), we faced our share of hardship, immediately upon marrying in Korea and throughout the years after we moved to the United States. We've encountered considerable prejudice based on our individual ethnicities and based on the fact that we were a mixed-race couple. Our children have also experienced similar challenges. So, we wanted to do our part to mitigate that for others."

After retiring from jobs at Kodak and a large photo lab in Hollywood, James became a teacher in Los Angeles. During his tenure with the school district, he and In Ja decided to list space in their home and supplement their scholarship fund. James notes, "I retired for good this last year to help my wife with our Airbnb because our business is so strong and it's a lot of work for her. We list our property for a little less money than maybe we should, and my wife throws in a huge breakfast each morning. However, we don't need the money to live on—so we'd rather have the home full of people who might not have otherwise been able to spend time with us—plus, it all helps provide education for others."

Having read that In Ja's breakfasts are legendary and that she customizes them to the ethnic backgrounds of her guests, I asked what In Ja had prepared for breakfast on the morning of our interview. James responded, "Today we had guests from the United States, so it was honey-glazed ham and scrambled eggs. We had a lot left over, so In Ja cooked up some fried rice, and we just got back from taking that to some people up the road who are homeless and live in makeshift tents." When asked why In Ja would cook extra food and why they would go together to serve the homeless, James said:

> It's who we are and what our Bahá'í faith teaches. We live by a number of important principles, not least of which are make your home a haven for both the friend and the stranger, the Earth is but one country and mankind its citizens, and all men are created to carry forward an ever-advancing civilization.
>
> We are grateful for the opportunity to do our small part to serve the Earth's citizens as friends in our home, while hopefully advancing civilization in the process.

(A video featuring James and In Ja Yates can be found at airbnb way.com/book-resources.)

During our interviews for this book, my team and I met several hosts who shared that they had been inspired by a challenge Chip Conley posed during a widely viewed presentation several years ago. In it, Chip purportedly said, "We will know Airbnb has been a success—not by indicators like growth or corporate valuation. We will have achieved success when we win the Noble Peace Prize."

I asked Chip what he meant by his comment and why he thinks it continues to resonate in the host community. He explained, "Airbnb hosts embody what is good about the world and what each of us can achieve through our businesses. If the entire host community aligns to create a borderless world, where anyone can Belong Anywhere and we all give back with a generosity of heart, the Noble Peace Prize would validate that Airbnb is achieving its mission. I think my message connected with the host community, and I am glad to hear it continues to be a worthwhile aspiration."

As you think about your business, how are you making your company a haven for both the friend and the stranger? How are you transcending territorial boundaries and considering all people to be citizens of the Earth? In what ways are you carrying forward an ever-advancing civilization? What humanitarian award would indicate that your business is achieving a mission beyond economic self-interest? Finally, how do you—and will you—own goodness?

In our final chapter, I'll touch upon factors that will likely shape the future of Airbnb. We will also walk through a hosting example that embodies all five of our themes, and we will ensure that those themes are optimized for your success. Let's head to Danville and Beyond.

POINTS OF INTEREST AS
YOU OWN GOODNESS

→ According to author Dennis Prager, "Goodness is about character—integrity, honesty, kindness, generosity, moral courage, and the like. More than anything else, it is about how we treat people."

→ John D. Rockefeller, Jr., said, "I believe that every right implies a responsibility; every opportunity, an obligation; every possession, a duty."

→ Leadership is about accepting responsibility for the rights that individuals and businesses enjoy.

→ Act responsibly within your community as you share your input concerning the ways potential legislation may affect you.

→ Demonstrate moral courage and realize that stepping into the public arena can create future leadership opportunities.

→ Consider waste reduction through recycling and reuse.

→ According to Rebecca Torem, "Adaptive reuse is whenever you give an existing building, home, or venue a new purpose. Or maintain the same purpose, but while preserving, rebuilding, enhancing, or maintaining some or all elements of the building."

→ Actor, writer, and producer Denis Leary noted, "Crisis doesn't create character; it reveals it." Think about how you anticipate and how you respond to a crisis.

→ Leaders and frontline employees often underestimate how much they can offer if they open their hearts to those they serve.

→ Journalist H. L. Mencken wrote, "A home is not a mere transient shelter: its essence lies in the personalities of the people who live in it."

→ When Mencken's words are reframed for business, they might say, "A company is not a mere collection of products and buildings: its essence lies in the willingness of leaders and frontline workers to open their hearts to those they serve."

→ Make your home a haven for both the friend and the stranger. Do the same with your business.

→ Consider the Earth to be but one country, and humankind its citizens.

→ All people are created to carry forward an ever-advancing civilization.

To Danville and Beyond

In Pixar's animated *Toy Story* films, astronaut action figure Buzz Lightyear often proclaims, "To infinity and beyond." The character's catchphrase (which calls for breaking all limits) seems an appropriate metaphor for what Airbnb has been able to accomplish in just over a decade. It also frames a discussion on what Airbnb's leaders might achieve in the years ahead. It is also my hope that by applying the themes presented in *The Airbnb Way*, you and your business will enjoy Airbnb's meteoric success and impact.

Banking off Buzz Lightyear's go-to phrase, I've titled this chapter "To Danville and Beyond." As you'll see, Danville (a collection of Airbnb listings) is a special, whimsical, yet very real example of the themes and principles we've explored in preceding chapters. Danville also serves as a learning lab for lessons you can readily apply long after you close this book.

Before we see how Danville applies to your business, I'll take a moment to gaze into the stratosphere and anticipate some of the future challenges and opportunities for Airbnb.

AIRBNB IN HYPERDRIVE

From a business perspective, some might say Airbnb is traveling at the speed of light. While metaphorically true, in reality, if people or businesses could travel at the speed of light, they would circle the earth approximately 7½ times in a single second.

As fast as Airbnb's business ascent has been, it hasn't achieved its success in a vacuum, and gravity is pulling forcefully as the brand continues to climb higher and broaden its scope. From my perspective, Airbnb's rapid growth is anchored to the principles and themes in this book, and its future will depend on maintaining a steadfast grip on its values.

Even with their dedication to core principles, leaders at Airbnb are facing delicate and tricky passages ahead. Some of their challenges reflect the pain of scaling, growing, and maturing. To date, the company has moved through stages of being an off-the-wall idea, a darling startup, an unexpected industry disruptor, an end-to-end travel brand, and a movement. Going forward, Airbnb will be a travel industry front-runner with a target squarely on its back.

In the future, Airbnb will have to attract, develop, and retain people who are committed to creating belonging, trust, hospitality, empowerment, and community. That "people" component will involve recruiting employees and Airbnb hosts. This book has shared several lessons from the best Airbnb hosts; however, my team and I know there are less-than-stellar hosting experiences occurring on the platform (maybe someone should give those hosts a copy of this book). To continue to scale with quality, Airbnb will need to augment the resources it provides to underperforming hosts.

Looking forward, we anticipate ongoing legislative battles for home sharing and other businesses in the sharing economy. We predict Airbnb leaders and the host community will have to find more ways to strengthen bonds with cities, homeowner associations, and other community groups so Airbnb doesn't become synonymous with a revolving door of loud strangers who cycle through the homes of neighbors. Airbnb will similarly have to continue to teach guests to respect the homes and communities in which they stay.

At a policy level, Airbnb should continue to police those who fail to abide by Airbnb's rules and partner with local governments on new rules for home sharing. Leaders will also need to ensure that growth in Airbnb rental properties is sustainable in the communities in which they operate. Airbnb will have to resolve speculation on its long-term funding sources. At the time of this writing, Airbnb has not announced if or when it will go public, despite rumors of a public offering dating back to 2014.

We expect Airbnb will have to continually reinvent itself. Everyone from startups to industry giants will "fast follow" Airbnb on its success path, making differentiation more difficult. Airbnb will need to continually dedicate resources (likely into its innovation division named Samara) to behave like a disruptive player. It will have to routinely test and learn concepts like one announced in November 2018 referred to as "Backyard." As described in the company's press release, Backyard is "an initiative to prototype new ways that homes can be designed, built, and shared. Driven by an abiding passion for humanistic, future-oriented, and waste-conscious design, . . . Backyard investigates how buildings could utilize sophisticated manufacturing techniques, smart-home technologies, and vast insight from the Airbnb community to thoughtfully respond to changing owner or occupant needs over time." The Backyard team is looking to test prototype units. They will likely also explore cutting-edge opportunities that cross into business categories adjacent to accommodations, experiences, and the travel industry.

When I asked Greg Greeley, Airbnb's president of Homes, how he envisioned Airbnb in 5 to 10 years, he noted:

> The travel industry as a whole has some broken processes that need continued innovation. As Airbnb gets larger, we will strive to ensure that our travel experience is increasingly intimate and local. You will see technology make the reservation and check-in process even easier. We will find better ways to connect and align the wants and needs of our hosts and guests. We will strive to provide tools to both guests and hosts so they can better manage their time. We will inspire and facilitate magical end-to-end travel. In some areas, our innovation will be incremental; in other areas we will be swinging for the fences. Differentiated innovation is in Airbnb's DNA, and we are committed to serve our communities and live our mission to enable every person to belong everywhere.

Demonstrating their focus on the "end-to-end travel" experience, in 2019 Airbnb hired Fred Reid as the company's global head of transportation. Reid was the founding CEO of Virgin America and has served as president of Delta Airlines. He has also been the president and chief operating officer of Lufthansa German Airlines, president of Flexjet, and president of the Cora Aircraft Program.

Upon being appointed to his new position, Reid foreshadowed future direction for Airbnb noting, "Whether in the air or on the ground, there are tremendous opportunities to create products and forge partnerships with other companies that make travel easier and even fun. Realizing those opportunities will take years and require constant experimentation, and I'm truly honored to have the chance to take on such an audacious challenge with this team."

Every business's future is uncertain! Fortunately for Airbnb, the company is well positioned through its commitment to the core principles outlined in *The Airbnb Way* and through steady leadership from the organization's founders. Undeniably, the future challenges facing Airbnb are daunting. However, the founders have surrounded themselves with a talented leadership team and a highly regarded board of directors. They have also acquired a decade of experience at the helm of the Airbnb juggernaut and have crafted a strong network of colleagues, employees, and consultants on which they can rely.

Instead of speculating about Airbnb's potential supersized challenges, let's scale back to known truths demonstrated in a smaller business environment and through the "town" of Danville (listed here on Airbnb: https://www.airbnb.com/rooms/2713449).

A TOWN THAT IS NOT A TOWN

Technically, Danville, Florida, isn't a town, but don't tell that to Dan and Deborah Shaw. Dan is Danville's self-declared mayor, and his wife Deborah is the sheriff. To be accurate, Danville is in the town of Geneva, Florida (the 2010 Census suggests the population was just under 3,000 people), which is approximately 28 miles northeast of Orlando.

Danville encompasses 25 acres owned by Dan and Deborah. The couple live on site and keep airplanes there. The property, adjacent to the Lake Proctor Wilderness Area, Lake Harney, and the St. Johns River, connects to a private airstrip built by Dan and fellow Geneva resident Johnny Sutherland in 1988.

Home to a menagerie of alligators, alpacas, chickens, goats, cats, and a Great Dane named MacAlister, Danville also is the home of several Airbnb listings, including the Danville Inn, the ManCave, the Tree House, and the Yurt. Here are excerpts from Dan and Deborah's listings with a few added pictures.

The Danville Inn

Stay in the master suite of one of the properties featured on HGTV *Million Dollar Rooms*! The master suite boasts a walk-through shower with a Bluetooth showerhead. Spacious bed and sitting area with a flat-screen TV. You will have private use of the entire inn that includes the parlor and kitchen. Relax and enjoy the grounds and the patio area. Watch a movie in the theater. It is all yours for the duration of your stay.

Enjoy a drink, and a visit with your hosts Dan and Deborah Shaw in O'Shaw's Pub located in downtown Danville!

The Tree House

I have tried to make this one of the most unique tree-houses in the United States. It is located on a 5-acre parcel of ground surrounded by oak and magnolia trees. The treehouse is located 15 feet high between two giant oak trees. There is a residential elevator made to look like a tree trunk to get you up into the Yurt located in the trees. It is an 18-foot Yurt designed by Rainier Yurts. It has a panoramic window, 4-foot skylight, 14-foot ceiling, and a full bath with bidet. There is a microwave, mini-fridge, and sink. You'll sleep on a queen-sized Murphy bed, making the space a large living area during the day and a wonderful bedroom at night. . . .

Along with the elevator there is a circa 1926 classic fire tower stairway from a local fire tower (a little steeper than normal stairs). On the middeck you will find a two-person outdoor shower with hot and cold water, and a spectacular hot tub created from a DC 10 jet engine cowling. The middeck also has seating for the rare rainy afternoon. On the ground level is a tiki hut and outdoor wood fire pit with some very spectacular tree trunk seating. You will be provided with a golf cart to travel from Danville through the trails to the treehouse. The golf cart will be available for your use during your stay.

The Yurt

This is a 21-foot-diameter Yurt. . . . It is fully air conditioned. It has a 14-foot vaulted ceiling with a 5-foot skylight. A full bath, a mini-kitchen, and king-sized bed are part of the Yurt. . . . A large porch with a fire pit and barbecue grill and unique swing is provided. The Danville Yurt is part of the Danville eclectic collection of venues. You'll have access to all of the amenities in the complex such as an Irish pub and 500 acres of trails to explore. You may even have an opportunity to fly with one of the neighbors. . . . It has been described by guests as the "most romantic ever." Bring a bottle of wine, and enjoy the fire on the deck, see the stars, lasers, and meteor shower lights through the skylight in the dome of the Yurt. Spend some time with your neighbors Bobo and RJ, the two alpacas that live next door.

The ManCave

The ManCave is located as part of an active airplane hangar. The space around the hangar is an active garage and maintenance facility.

Dan has plans for many other creative environments in the future.

We've previewed the physical spaces of Danville; now we'll dive into how Dan and Deborah turn those spaces into belonging, trust, hospitality, empowerment, and community. Along the way, let's create possibilities beyond Danville and in your business!

TO DANVILLE:
A POSTCARD FOR BELONGING

In 1898, the US Postal Service created a one-cent rate for sending postcards, and the popularity of that option skyrocketed, as did the use of the phrase "Wish you were here," often followed by "Having a great time." If my wife, Patti, and I had sent you a postcard from Danville, we would have wished you could have joined us during our "great time" with Dan and Deborah. Since we couldn't make that possible, I'll do my best to walk you through our experience to highlight how this book's themes and principles were delivered during our stay.

Belonging and Arrival

I was drawn to Danville after watching a one-minute video about Dan and Deborah posted on the Airbnb YouTube page. (You can find that video at airbnbway.com/book-resources.) Of all the intriguing property options listed above, I was most interested in staying at the Danville Inn and quickly found it while searching on the Airbnb site.

Dan and Deborah use Instant Book, so I selected our travel dates, read the house rules, and booked our stay immediately. As I made the reservation, I sent a message to Dan and Deborah, letting them know who would be joining me, where we lived in relation to Danville, and asking for a few minutes to interview them for the book. Dan responded promptly, welcoming us to Danville. Deborah followed up shortly thereafter and developed rapport by noting that years ago she and Dan lived in a community near Patti and me.

The day before we arrived, Dan sent a message inviting us to Goat Happy Hour (more on that later) scheduled on the first night of our stay. On the day of our arrival, Dan sent the following message:

> Looking forward to your visit. Can you tell us what time you will be arriving, and would you please text us 30 minutes prior to your arrival? The property is 25 acres, and I

want to be sure to be at the front of the property to meet you. Dan.

We let Dan know our likely arrival time and when we were getting close to Danville. He greeted us as we exited our car. Dan was warm and gracious, introducing himself and calling each of us by name. He asked us to follow him to the entrance of what looked like a large home. He then positioned us for the grand reveal. As he pushed a button, the false front to the building lifted, revealing the mini-city inside the converted airplane hangar.

Even though Patti and I had read reviews and expected the city inside the hangar, Dan had created theater, magic, and an arrival memory for us—as if he were sharing Danville for the first time. He said, "Welcome to Danville. You made a great choice."

Dan, the mayor of Danville, handed us the keys to his city! He then methodically took us on a tour of the Danville Inn. This included a stop in the Irish Pub, where he advised us that members of the community would be joining Deborah and him, and hopefully Patti and me, later in the evening. Dan showed us the features of our sprawling accommodations, including instructions for operating the technology in the suite's theater room.

Shortly after we toured our space, Dan offered to show us around the property in his all-terrain vehicle. Sparing you the details, we spent the next hour and a half looking at all of Dan and Deborah's Airbnb properties, riding Segways, feeding alligators, interacting with alpacas, and generally being charmed by Dan's enthusiasm, creativity (he holds 23 patents, including one for automatic paper towel dispensers), and passion for hosting.

Before I show you some of the ways Dan and Deborah foster trust, let's take a moment to apply their wisdom and warmth to your customer arrival experiences through these tips.

Danville and Beyond: Belonging Tips

- Make it easy for people to get their needs met from their first contact onward (for example, Instant Book).

- Respond quickly and informatively.

- Make a personal emotional connection (PEC).

- Maintain a regular helpful cadence of communication. Always respond before customers begin to wonder or doubt.

- Never underestimate the importance of first impressions and human-to-human contact.

- Greet with enthusiasm, and use the customer's name (when possible) in a kind way.

- Validate the wisdom of your customer choosing you.

- Take the time to orient your customers to your products and services so they appreciate the value you offer.

- Meet customer needs, exceed expectations, and sprinkle some "delight" moments along the way.

- Be authentic, caring, and compassionate. Let customers know they are welcomed and that they belong.

Trust to Be Trusted

The Danville story of trust occurs on multiple levels. By using Instant Book, Dan and Deborah accepted my wife and me without getting an opportunity to vet us through prebooking interactions on the Airbnb platform. When I asked Dan why he doesn't pre-screen his guests, he said, "I've lived 71 years trusting people, and it's not only worked well for me but it's also enabled me to meet people I would have never experienced if I had closed my mind or my doors to them." Dan and Deborah's trusting nature have certainly enabled them to meet interesting people. In fact, Airbnb flew the couple to San Francisco so Airbnb cofounder Brian Chesky could meet them.

Dan talks about trust in the context of security: "Trusting people doesn't mean you yield your judgment. I exercise reasonable caution and think about the security of the guest, other guests, and my family. I'm a certified gun instructor and have learned how to hand someone a gun such that I am positioned to protect all involved, in case my student becomes careless."

We heard a lot about trust from Dan and Deborah's neighbors during Goat Happy Hour. Not unlike popular goat yoga, where goats mingle with yoga participants, Goat Happy Hour in Danville is a community gathering at the Irish Pub—accompanied by several baby goats.

On the evening we attended, Dan and Deborah provided beer and pizza, and five neighbors brought potluck items. During the free flow of conversation, Dan's neighbor Joe Pires shared, "Dan and Deborah are always there when anyone in the community requires help. If you need a piece of equipment, Dan will bring it right over, no questions asked. I suspect there are times people have taken advantage of that generosity, but Dan and Deborah come from abundance, not scarcity. They see what is good and possible in people and help them live up to that. Dan and Deborah are good people whom you can trust and who inspire others to be trustworthy."

I asked Dan to reflect on situations when his trust had been misplaced. He said, "That happens from time to time, and I take care of those rare situations when they crop up. But you can't dwell on those or else you'd treat all the good people like they were the exceptions."

Dan trusted Patti and me on his Segways, after giving us sufficient instruction and protective gear. He gave us the run of the land and access to electric bikes, golf carts, valuable personal property, his animals, and members of his community.

Dan extends trust to his neighbor Joe to offer Danville guests rides on Joe's gyroplane when guests express an interest. Most important, Dan and Deborah, who have been married 51 years, trust one another deeply. When asked about how Danville came to be, Deborah shared, "Dan is a visionary and a much bigger thinker than I am. When he gets an idea, even if I can't see it at first, I encourage him. I know he will create a wonderful and magical ride for us and others." Conversely, Dan stated, "It's pretty easy for me to trust others because I always know Deborah has my back and constantly encourages me to pursue my passions."

In the next section, we will look at how Dan and Deborah offer hospitality. Before we do that, let's review.

 Danville and Beyond: Trust Tips

- If you want to create new opportunities and meet new people, adopt an open mindset and extend trust.

- When offering trust, maintain sound judgment regarding the safety and security of all.

- Consider how operating from abundance, rather than scarcity, will increase your perceived trustworthiness and how it will prompt others to act in reciprocally trustworthy ways.

- Assume customers are good. Manage the rare exceptions.

- Whenever possible, build your business by selecting partners who encourage you, place faith in you, and have your back. Be a partner who does the same.

- Drive trust within your organization so that your customers can experience it.

Provide Hospitality: Service with Heart

The Danville Inn's physical environment is exactly as it is described and depicted in the Airbnb listing. The home was appointed with ample amenities like high-speed Internet, a premium mattress, a theater room, a popcorn maker, and a coffee maker. The property was clean, and all of the tangibles of the service experience met or exceeded our expectations. Patti and I perceived the stay to be an outstanding value for the price. In essence, Dan and Deborah executed the service basics well. However, if service basics had been all Dan and Deborah provided, I would not be using them to demonstrate the principles of this book.

Dan's arrival tour and their Goat Happy Hour (which actually lasted 2½ hours) flawlessly delivered the Shaws' desired and optimal customer experience. As Dan put it, "We want everyone who visits to connect and have fun—maybe with us or our neighbors, but certainly with their travel companions and this place." Not only did Dan and Deborah deliver connection and fun, but also, in the process, they provided an Airbnb magical and memorable stay.

When I asked neighbor Pam Sanders if Goat Happy Hour was common or if we were getting special treatment, she responded, "This happens several times a week. Dan and Deborah invite us to join their guests regularly. I think they like to make sure every guest has the opportunity to connect with the community at least once during their visit. Not all guests choose to join in, and different neighbors stop by as their schedules permit, but this is Danville hospitality."

Neighbor Joe Pires shared, "Two of Dan and Deborah's Airbnb guests have felt so comfortable in Danville and our town of Geneva that they bought property in this off-the-grid place. Two of their guests were living in the Caribbean when they visited Danville, and now, they are our neighbors."

I understand the draw to Danville. Patti and I had a lengthy post-stay discussion about how special it was to get a glimpse into the lives of the people who lived in Geneva, and we even imagined what it would be like to live near Dan and Deborah. In a moment, we will explore how Dan and Deborah create a familylike connection with a team member they have empowered. But first, let's consider hospitality in the context of your business.

 Danville and Beyond: Hospitality Tips

- Accurately describe and depict your product and service offerings.

- Pay attention to the tangibles of your service delivery (for example, product quality, cleanliness, amenities).

- In addition to executing flawlessly on service basics, differentiate yourself through emotional connection.

- Define your customers' optimal emotional experience. What do you want all of your customers to feel when they interact with you?

- Deliver your optimal emotional experience for every customer, every time.

- Invite customers to engage in the fullness of your experience, but respect their choice when they select other options.

- Create an experience that causes people to want to stay connected to you and/or engage with you frequently.

Supercharge Empowerment

There are many examples of empowerment occurring at Danville, including how Dan and Deborah encourage their grandson's entrepreneurship and how they refer their guests to local businesses. Here are supporting examples from the Danville Airbnb property listings:

> If you have a wood-burning fireplace, my grandson splits the wood and sells it for 10 pieces for $5, also using the honor box. (We are teaching him to be an entrepreneur—he's 10.)

> There is an excellent hometown restaurant at the traffic light at 46 (Geneva General Store). They serve a great breakfast in the morning.

The guest books provided by Dan and Deborah offer ample restaurant recommendations and encourage patronage of other local businesses and activities.

Rather than listing how Dan and Deborah drive economic empowerment, I'll offer a remarkable, yet representative example of that concept evidenced by their transformative support for Misty Cross. Misty is Dan and Deborah's employee, but based on the way they treat her, she likens them to family.

Misty met Dan around 2008. Misty's then boyfriend was helping Dan construct the Danville Inn. That boyfriend, reportedly a functional alcoholic, had lost his driver's license due to drinking-related charges. He worked during the day and drank at night.

Misty drove her boyfriend to job sites like Dan's and then sat in the couple's truck waiting to drive him home hours later. The couple's finances didn't enable Misty to make two trips a day back and forth from their home—so she sat and waited. Let's let Misty pick up the story from there: "I sat out in the truck for months on other jobs, but shortly after my boyfriend started working on the Danville Inn, Dan expressed an interest in my welfare and asked if I wanted a job. I said yes, so I painted, caulked, and sanded the Danville Inn. After that, I started cleaning the Danville Inn, then cleaned Dan and Deborah's personal home. Before you know it, I was hired full-time, helping and cleaning the Danville Airbnb spaces."

When asked how working with Dan and Deborah contributed to her quality of life, Misty shared, "My life has improved 1,000 percent. After I broke up with my boyfriend, I was a single parent with three kids. My housing situation was unstable, and I struggled to make rent and manage transportation challenges. Dan and Deborah not only paid me fairly but they bought a house—so I could purchase it from them. They paid cash for the house I live in and then sold it back to me, so I didn't have to come up with a down payment. Without them, I couldn't rent a similar home for $1,100 a month . . . and instead, I am buying mine for $400 a month." Misty added, "Dan and Deborah didn't have to do this for me, and I am eternally grateful. They made a similar arrangement on behalf of my 25-year-old daughter."

As generous as these acts are, Misty said, "Dan and Deborah have huge hearts and help a lot of people. In my case, they've also assisted me in getting a car when mine broke down and helped my family with food when times were tough. Actually, they are like family to me—almost like parents. I put out my best effort for them. I've made it very clear and I am good to my word—I will take care of Dan and Deborah in every way they need for the rest of their lives." Dan and Deborah's investment in Misty has created a win for Misty and a win for Danville. Misty is an empowered, engaged, and loyal member of the Shaw family business. Let's gather takeaways in the form of these tips on empowerment.

 Danville and Beyond: Empowerment Tips

- Look for opportunities to fuel the entrepreneurial spirit in others.

- Develop referral partnerships with local businesses.

- Be aware of underutilized talents in the people around you. Create opportunities to activate those talents.

- Consider the general welfare of others—not just their workplace needs.

- Pay a livable wage so concerns about survival are removed and people can focus on the job at hand.

- Invest in your people to drive engagement, productivity, and loyalty.

Engage Community: In Crisis and in Good Times

In good times and bad, Dan and Deborah serve their neighbors. Misty recounts, "When Hurricane Irma hit Central Florida, we had flooding around Geneva. Dan and Deborah's property is situated on higher ground, so they let the neighbors park their vehicles on their land. They let my family and other community members stay in Danville during the storm and the aftermath. Dan and Deborah also offered no-fee housing to those in the panhandle of Florida where Hurricane Michael made landfall."

Similarly, neighbor Joe Pires shares, "In 2008, we had some rather extreme flooding thanks to Tropical Storm Fay. Dan took his heavy machinery into the floodwaters and began pulling people out of their driveways and making rescues. Unfortunately, a lot of his equipment got damaged in the process, but you never heard Dan or Deborah complain. They also share a lot of food for those in need in our community. Dan spent a great deal of time helping me build my airplane-hangar home. It's similar to Dan and Deborah's Danville Inn building. I didn't own a toolbox at the time my building was constructed, but Dan lent me his tools, believed in me, and worked right next to me to make my home a reality."

In less challenging times, neighbor Pam Sanders reports, "Danville is our community hub. It is the place people come for meetings, Super Bowl parties, and just to laugh and be together. Dan and Deborah go out of their way to run a business that is respectful to their neighbors. Danville is a community resource, and we feel fortunate not only to call Dan and Deborah neighbors but also to call them friends—in the most noble sense of that word."

During conversations with Dan and Deborah, they expressed commitments to environmental sustainability. Dan notes, "I enjoy having a rooster for an alarm clock and taking care of our wide array of animals. Being here in nature and interacting with animals brings great joy to our guests and us. We try to be good stewards of our resources. For example, I love finding ways to use things that others throw away. Someone living in an expensive home in Heathrow, Florida, threw some very nice curtains along the side of the road. We grabbed them up and placed them in the Yurt. I guess the previous owners thought the curtains weren't worthy of further use, but they have a lot of life left and are perfect for our setting. Most everything you see around Danville has been repurposed."

Before we close this chapter and the book, let's consider these tips on a business being part of its community.

 Danville and Beyond: Community Tips

- Willingly offer your time and resources to your community—without being asked.

- Look for people and organizations that will benefit from your competencies.

- See community involvement as an investment.

- Become a community resource.

- Commit to sustainable consumption.

- Reduce, reuse, recycle, repurpose.

THE NEXT STEPS IN YOUR AIRBNB JOURNEY

Danville is a quirky, playful collection of Airbnb listings powered by belonging, trust, hospitality, empowerment, and community. It also symbolizes what's possible when leaders, team members, and individuals pay attention to important interpersonal truths.

The Airbnb Way was written to capture essential elements that led to Airbnb's meteoric rise and to demonstrate how those elements come to life every day through the actions of Airbnb's host community. It was written for you to learn from hosts like Dan and Deborah and all those who have shared freely to make this book a reality.

As you look to your journey ahead, I hope you will adopt and adapt themes, principles, and ideas from *The Airbnb Way* in your own business and with your own customers. I trust you will advance confidently and dream big. In so doing, you will surely realize your personal and professional goals in keeping with the words of Henry David Thoreau:

> If one advances confidently in the direction of his dreams, and endeavors to live the life which he has imagined, he will meet with a success unexpected in common hours.

Here's to "a success unexpected in common hours"—*The Airbnb Way!*

Notes

Chapter 1

"'Amazon did not kill . . . to any business'": Alberto Brea, LinkedIn post, https://www.linkedin.com/feed/update/urn:li:activity:6270553860658458624/. Reprinted with permission of Alberto Brea.

"To fully comprehend Airbnb's growth . . . on any given night": "10 Facts About Airbnb," *IOL*, March 5, 2018, https://www.iol.co.za/travel/travel-tips/10-facts-about-airbnb-13598514.

"As of 2017, the age distribution of Airbnb guests . . . 12 percent of guests were over 55": Statista, "Share of Airbnb Users by Age Group in the United States and Europe 2017," https://www.statista.com/statistics/796646/airbnb-users-by-age-us-europe/.

"Even though age and global demographics expanded . . . the best-rated hosts on Airbnb": Airbnb, "Airbnb's 2016 Highlights and 2017 Trends We're Watching," *Airbnb Citizen*, January 3, 2017, https://www.airbnbcitizen.com/airbnbs-2016-highlights-and-2017-trends-were-watching/.

"According to Ryan Pierce . . . to ensure traveler safety'": Salesforce Research, *State of the Connected Customer*, 2d ed., Salesforce, 2018, https://c1.sfdcstatic.com/content/dam/web/en_us/www/documents/e-books/state-of-the-connected-customer-report-second-edition2018.pdf.

"In November 2016 . . . at the heart of every trip'": Airbnb, "Airbnb Expands Beyond the Home: Welcome to the World of Trips," *Airbnb News*, 2017, https://airbnb.design/expanding-beyond-the-home/.

"In 2017, citing that 66 percent of American travelers . . . at an exclusive eight-seat Japanese tasting bar": Airbnb, "Airbnb and Resy Team up to Offer In-App Restaurant Reservations," *Airbnb Press Room*, September 20, 2017, https://press.airbnb.com/airbnb-resy-team-offer-app-restaurant-reservations/.

"Airbnb Plus listings . . . and cooking oil'": Airbnb, "Airbnb Plus Homes Checklist," https://www.airbnb.com/plus/host/requirements/all.

"Writing in a May 2018 article for *Forbes* . . . among the unicorns'": Trefis Team, "As a Rare Profitable Unicorn, Airbnb Appears to Be Worth at Least \$38 Billion," *Forbes*, May 11, 2018, https://www.forbes.com/sites/greatspeculations/2018/05/11/as-a-rare-profitable-unicorn-airbnb-appears-to-be-worth-at-least-38-billion/#7fc2f2e02741.

"Research conducted by LivePerson . . . if they wake up briefly": Rurik Bradbury, *The Digital Lives of Millennials and Gen Z*, LivePerson, https://www.liveperson.com/resources/reports/digital-lives-of-millennials-genz/.

"For example, PricewaterhouseCoopers (PwC) surveyed . . . to generation Z (born as late as 2012)": PwC, "Experience Is Everything," https://www.pwc.com/us/en/services/consulting/library/consumer-intelligence-series/future-of-customer-experience.html.

"The importance of crafting . . . is very important to winning their business'": Salesforce Research, *State of the Connected Consumer*.

"Above all else . . . as technology improves" and the figure following: PwC, "Excellent Customer Experience Starts with Superior Employee Experience," *PwC Future of Customer Experience Survey 2017–2018*.

"The World Economic Forum (WEF) . . . critical counterbalance to technology": PricewaterhouseCoopers (PwC), *Human Value in the Digital Age*, December 2017, https://www.pwc.nl/nl/assets/documents/pwc-human-value-in-the-digital-age.pdf.

"A recent interchange on a travel forum . . . from one generation to the next": City-Data, http://www.city-data.com/forum/travel/2008264-hotel-information-before-days-internet.html.

"Business leadership Professor Mari Jansen van Rensburg . . . are better informed'": Mari Jansen van Rensburg, "Relevance of Travel Agencies in the Digital Age," *African Journal of Hospitality, Tourism and Leisure*, vol. 3, no. 2, 2014, http://www.ajhtl.com/uploads/7/1/6/3/7163688/article_37_vol_3_1.pdf.

"Writing in *Mashable*, MJ Franklin . . . how everything can be so different and yet all the same…'": MJ Franklin, "Airbnb vs. Vrbo: Which Site Is Best for Your Next Trip?," *Mashable*, 2018, https://mashable.com/article/airbnb-vs-vrbo-trip-booking/#ydfu9eOhDPqj.

"In her book *The Airbnb Story* . . . Airbnb was urban'": Leigh Gallagher, *The Airbnb Story: How Three Ordinary Guys Disrupted an Industry, Made Billions . . . and created Plenty of Controversy* (New York: Houghton Mifflin, 2017).

"Felix Gessert, CEO of Baqend . . . the famous blink of an eye'": Felix Gessert, "New-Generation Travel Websites Load 7 Times Faster Than Traditional Hotel Sites," *Medium*, January 12, 2018, https://medium.baqend.com/new-generation-travel-websites-load-7-times-faster -than-traditional-hotel-sites-d04ffebc5027.

"That mission has evolved . . . the core of our company: belonging'": Brian Chesky, "Belong Anywhere," *Medium*, July 16, 2014, https://medium.com/@bchesky/belong-anywhere -ccf42702d010.

"Chesky suggested that belonging . . . is the idea that defines Airbnb'": Chesky, "Belong Anywhere."

Chapter 2

"'The need for connection and community is primal, as fundamental as the need for air, water, and food'": Dean Ornish, *BrainyQuote*, https://www.brainyquote.com/quotes/dean_ornish _563781.

"At the time of those writings . . . an enduring principle of success: 'All business is personal'": Carmine Gallo, "Starbucks CEO: Lesson in Communication Skills," *Forbes*, March 25, 2011, https://www.forbes.com/sites/carminegallo/2011/03/25/starbucks-ceo-lesson-in -communication-skills/#1db9bc4672b8.

"In an Insights Association article . . . the accurate emotional insights required'": Mark Ingwer, "Why Business Doesn't Understand Consumers," *Alert! Magazine*, February 1, 2014, https://www.insightsassociation.org/article/why-business-doesn%E2%80%99t -understand-consumers.

"In his book *Peak* . . . be a chief emotional officer": Chip Conley, *How Great Companies Get Their Mojo from Maslow* (San Francisco: Jossey-Bass, 2007).

"Atkin began a study . . . to fulfill their individuality": David Passiak, "Belong Anywhere—The Vision and Story Behind Airbnb's Global Community," *Medium*, January 30, 2017, https:// medium.com/cocreatethefuture/belong-anywhere-the-vision-and-story-behind-airbnbs -global-community-123d32218d6a.

"Meetup describes itself . . . their shared interests'": Meetup, "Great things happen when passionate people come together," *Meetup Stories*, https://www.meetup.com/media/.

"After working to help develop Meetup communities . . . that led Airbnb to him": Passiak, "Belong Anywhere."

"In an interview for *Medium* . . . 'purpose of the Airbnb community'": Passiak, "Belong Anywhere."

"From Atkin's perspective . . . and whom we hire": Passiak, "Belong Anywhere."

"The philosopher Paul Tillich once said, 'The first duty of love is to listen'": Paul Tillich, *BrainyQuote*, https://www.brainyquote.com/quotes/paul_tillich_114351.

"In announcing the Bélo, Brian Chesky shared . . . the universal symbol of belonging'": Brian Chesky, "Belong Anywhere," *Medium*, July 16, 2014, https://medium.com/@bchesky /belong-anywhere-ccf42702d010.

"According to creatives at the DesignStudio . . . something you can draw in the sand with the toe'": "New Logo and Identity for Airbnb by DesignStudio," Brand New, 2014, https:// www.underconsideration.com/brandnew/archives/new_logo_and_identity_for_airbnb _by_designstudio.php.

"DesignStudio has suggested . . . one to wear with pride'": DesignStudio, "Airbnb," https://de-sign.studio/work/airbnb.

"Leadership Professor John Kotter . . . negating hard-won gains'": John P. Kotter, "Leading Change: Why Transformation Efforts Fail," *Harvard Business Review*, May-June 1995, https://hbr.org/1995/05/leading-change-why-transformation-efforts-fail-2.

"A one-minute video . . . please visit airbnbway.com/book-resources": Airbnb, https://airbnb way.com/book-resources.

"American psychologist Rollo May once said, "Communication leads to community . . . to understanding, intimacy, and mutual valuing": Rollo May, *BrainyQuote*, https://www .brainyquote.com/quotes/rollo_may_389414.

"If you are an employee of Airbnb . . . in the global community'": Airbnb, "Belonging Is at Our Core," https://www.airbnb.com/diversity/belonging.

"In writing about Airbnb's San Francisco headquarters . . . and completely improvisational'": Eva Hagberg, "Airbnb's San Francisco HQ Embodies a New Spatial Blurring," *Metropolis*, December 2, 2013, https://www.metropolismag.com/interiors/workplace-interiors/rooms -with-a-view/.

"Creating Airbnb's inclusive and belonging culture . . . distinctively White names'": Benjamin Edelman, Michael Luca, and Dan Svirsky, "Racial Discrimination in the Sharing Economy: Evidence from a Field Experiment," 2015, also published in *American Economic*

Journal: Applied Economics, vol. 9, no. 2, April 2017, www.benedelman.org/publications /airbnb-guest-discrimination-2016-09-16.pdf.

"In a 2016 email . . . to address these problems'": Alex Fitzpatrick, "Airbnb CEO: 'Bias and Discrimination Have No Place' Here," *TIME*, September 8, 2016, http://time.com/4484113 /airbnb-ceo-brian-chesky-anti-discrimination-racism/.

"Starting in 2016, Airbnb began asking . . . Airbnb Team'": Airbnb, "General Questions About the Airbnb Community Commitment," https://www.airbnb.com/help/article/1523/general -questions-about-the-airbnb-community-commitment?utm_source=blog&utm _medium=community_commitment.

"In a policy . . . alternative accommodation elsewhere'": Airbnb, "Fighting Discrimination and Creating a World Where Anyone Can Belong Anywhere," September 8, 2016, https:// blog.atairbnb.com/fighting-discrimination-and-creating-a-world-where-anyone-can -belong-anywhere/.

"Author Bob Proctor once said, 'Accountability is the glue that ties commitment to the result'": Bob Proctor, *Quotefancy*, https://quotefancy.com/quote/1708024/Bob-Proctor-Accountability -is-the-glue-that-ties-commitment-to-the-result.

"In the case of Airbnb . . . with Asian guests'": Alan McEwen, "Racist Landlord Banned from Airbnb After Note Barring Asians from Booking Flat," *Daily Record*, March 29, 2018, https://www.dailyrecord.co.uk/news/scottish-news/racist-landlord-banned-airbnb -after-12269941.

Chapter 3

"'I long, as does every human being, to be at home wherever I find myself'": Maya Angelou, *BrainyQuote*, https://www.brainyquote.com/quotes/maya_angelou_384166.

"In a 1921 article for *Vanity Fair*, Robert Benchley . . . and those who do not'": Robert Benchley, *Quote Investigator*, https://quoteinvestigator.com/2014/02/07/two-classes/.

"Aroha Warburton . . . my life's purpose is to serve others'": Airbnb, https://www.airbnb.com /rooms/19395989?location=Brisbane%2C%20Queensland%2C%20Australia&s=IpZiafdo.

"Author David Augsburger stated, 'Being heard is so close to being loved that for the average person they are almost indistinguishable'": David Augsburger, *BrainyQuote*, https://www .brainyquote.com/quotes/david_augsburger_627321.

"Writing on the Airbnb community center . . . the "lodging was taken care of"'": Airbnb Community website, https://community.withairbnb.com/t5/Hosting/miscommunication-with -guest/td-p/19690.

"Researchers Sharma Neeru and Paul Patterson . . . exiting the relationship'": Sharma Neeru and Paul Patterson, "The Impact of Communication Effectiveness and Service Quality on Relationship Commitment in Consumer, Professional Services," *Journal of Services Marketing*, vol. 13, no 2, April 1, 1999, https://www.deepdyve.com/lp/emerald-publishing/the -impact-of-communication-effectiveness-and-service-quality-on-O60gbfxgd0.

"The word *empathy* . . . emotional intelligence quotient (EQ)": Paul Bloom, "The Baby in the Well," *New Yorker*, May 13, 2013, https://www.newyorker.com/magazine/2013/05/20/the -baby-in-the-well.

"In an article for *Medium* . . . and happiness": Prakhar Verma, "The Ultimate Guide to Emotional Intelligence to Be Happy and Successful in a Brain-Dead World," *Medium*, July 13, 2018, https://medium.com/the-mission/the-ultimate-guide-to-emotional-intelligence-to-be -happy-and-successful-in-a-brain-dead-world-5d050e316640.

"According to Richard Shapiro . . . likelihood he or she will pivot and go": *BusinessNewsDaily* staff, "10 Ways to Deliver Great Customer Service," October 6, 2011, "https://www.business newsdaily.com/1537-great-customer-service-tips.html.

"Similarly, Princeton researchers found that decisions about attractiveness, likeability, trustworthiness, competence, and aggression are made within one-tenth of a second": Rachel Premack and Shana Lebowitz, "Science Says People Decide These Twelve Things Within Seconds of Meeting You," *Business Insider*, April 24, 2019, https://www.businessinsider .com/science-of-first-impressions-2015-2.

"During an interview for CBS's *60 Minutes* . . . the experience that that person needs'": Anderson Cooper, "Shake Shack Founder on Changing the Way Restaurants Do Business," *CBS 60 Minutes*, October 8, 2017, https://www.cbsnews.com/news/shake-shack-founder-on -changing-the-way-restaurants-do-business/.

Chapter 4

"'Trusting you is my decision. Proving me right is your choice'": Unknown, *Ignited Quotes*, http://www.ignitedquotes.com/topics-picture-quote/relationship/trusting-you-is-my -decision-proving-me-right-is-your-choice/.

"By contrast, J. David Lewis and Andrew Weigert . . . and potential doubt'": J. David Lewis and Andrew Weigert, "Trust as Social Reality," *Social Forces*, vol. 63, no. 4, June 1985, http://scholar.google.com/scholar_url?url=https://academic.oup.com/sf/article-pdf/63/4/967/6888975/63-4-967.pdf&hl=en&sa=X&scisig=AAGBfm2NI4eLaKDGVtleFsF_OKRz9CBb6w&nossl=1&oi=scholarr.

"In his book *The Speed of Trust*, Covey wrote . . . both personally and professionally'": Stephen R. Covey, *The Speed of Trust* (New York: Simon & Schuster, 2006).

"A key takeaway from Covey's work . . . asset that can be created.'": Covey, *The Speed of Trust*.

"In a 2016 TED Talk . . . the voice in my head goes, '**Wait, what?**'": Joe Gebbia, *How Airbnb Designs for Trust*, TED Talk, April 5, 2016, https://www.youtube.com/watch?v=16cM-RFid9U.

"In an article for *WIRED* magazine . . . into our rooms while we sleep'": Jason Tanz, "How Airbnb and Lyft Got Americans to Trust Each Other," April 23, 2014, https://www.wired.com/2014/04/trust-in-the-share-economy/.

"Tanz notes a change of perspective . . . as recently as five years ago'": Tanz, "How Airbnb and Lyft Got Americans to Trust Each Other."

"In the moments that followed . . . key for building trust'": Gebbia, *How Airbnb Designs for Trust*.

"Writing for *Forbes* . . . if you want to build trust": Theo Miller, "Airbnb Builds Trust with These 3 Radical Design Choices," *Forbes*, July 17, 2017, https://www.forbes.com/sites/theodorecasey/2017/07/17/airbnb-builds-trust-with-these-3-radical-design-choices/#773fdf2a27b4.

"Writing for *Inc.*, Craig Bloem notes . . . between one and six online reviews'": Craig Bloem, "84 Percent of People Trust Online Reviews as Much as Friends: Here's How to Manage What They See," *Inc.*, July 31, 2017, https://www.inc.com/craig-bloem/84-percent-of-people-trust-online-reviews-as-much-.html.

"In 2014, Airbnb announced changes . . . we'll make that review public to both the recipient and the community'": Airbnb, "Building Trust with a New Review System," July 10, 2014, https://blog.atairbnb.com/building-trust-new-review-system/.

"In an article for the website *Airbnb Design* . . . begin building a trusting relationship'": Charlie Aufmann, "Designing for Trust," *Airbnb Design*, https://airbnb.design/designing-for-trust/.

"Gebbia mentioned that Airbnb . . . with prompts to encourage sharing'": Gebbia, "How Airbnb Designs for Trust."

"Mareike Möhlmann, assistant professor . . . than you'd expect between colleagues'": Mareike Möhlmann, "Why People Trust Sharing Economy Strangers More Than Their Colleagues," *The Conversation*, December 20, 2016, https://theconversation.com/why-people-trust-sharing-economy-strangers-more-than-their-colleagues-70669.

"According to local news station NBC29 . . . various alt-right groups'": Matt Talhelm, "Airbnb Cancels Bookings for 'Unite the Right' Charlottesville Rally Attendees," NBC29, August 7, 2017, http://www.nbc29.com/story/36081224/airbnb-cancels-bookings-for-unite-the-right-charlottesville-rally-attendees.

"Based on an investigation . . . removing them from the platform'": Nick Statt, "Airbnb CEO Brian Chesky Says White Supremacy Has 'No Place in This World,'" *Verge*, August 14, 2017, https://www.theverge.com/2017/8/14/16146466/airbnb-will-continue-to-ban-white-supremacists.

"In an interview for *Fast Company* . . . remove their accounts from Airbnb permanently'": David Zax, "Meet the Former Military Intelligence Officer Who Keeps Airbnb Safe," *Fast Company*, January 28, 2013, https://www.fastcompany.com/3005074/meet-former-military-intelligence-officer-who-keeps-airbnb-safe.

"A portion of EJ's blog post . . . mildewing towels on the closet floor'": EJ, "Violated: A Traveler's Lost Faith, a Difficult Lesson Learned," *Around the World and Back Again* blog, June 29, 2011, http://ejroundtheworld.blogspot.com/2011/06/violated-travelers-lost-faith-difficult.html.

"Fortunately, initial interactions . . . and there will be others'": EJ, "Violated: A Traveler's Lost Faith, a Difficult Lesson Learned."

Chapter 5

"'Truth is like the sun. You can shut it out for a time, but it ain't goin' away'": Elvis Presley, *BrainyQuote*, https://www.brainyquote.com/quotes/elvis_presley_133068.

"Amazon CEO Jeff Bezos . . . by trying to do hard things well'": "Online Extra: Jeff Bezos on Word-of-Mouth Power," *Bloomberg Businessweek*, August 2, 2004, https://www.referralcandy.com/blog/jeff-bezos-quotes/.

"For now, let's look at how one guest, K. Ford K. . . . expanding our community one Airbnb at a time'": K. Ford K., "How to Belong Anywhere: My Experience with Airbnb," *HuffPost Contributor Platform*, September 4, 2015, https://www.huffpost.com/entry/how-to-belong-anywhere-my_b_8086696.

"Through thoughtful action . . . 'making true friends'": K. Ford K., "How to Belong Anywhere."

"In an article titled 'Processing Exaggerated Advertising Claims,'... not remembering the ex-aggeration specifically'": Elizabeth Crowley, "Processing Exaggerated Advertising Claims," *Journal of Business Research*, vol. 59, June 30, 2006, pp. 728–734.

"Gallup reports... important brand differentiator": Ed O'Boyle and Amy Adkins, "Compa-nies Only Deliver on Their Brand Promises Half the Time," *Gallup Workplace*, May 4, 2015, https://www.gallup.com/workplace/236597/companies-deliver-brand-promises-half -time.aspx?g_source=link_WWWV9&g_medium=TOPIC&g_campaign=item_&g_cont ent=Companies%2520Only%2520Deliver%2520on%2520Their%2520Brand%2520Prom ises%2520Half%2520the%2520Time.

"According to the 2018 *Reader's Digest Trusted Brand Survey*... earning consumers' trust'": Rich-ard Carufel, "The Most Trusted Brands in America Illustrate How Much Loyalty Matters," *Bulldog Reporter*, Agility PR Solutions, May 25, 2018, https://www.agilitypr.com/pr-news /public-relations/the-most-trusted-brands-in-america-illustrate-how-much-loyalty -matters/.

"Here are a few other examples of transparent listings that demonstrate a willingness to offer prospective guests insights on likely suitability: 'This is not a luxury loft building... may find this annoying'": Airbnb, https://www.airbnb.com/rooms/4244165?location=Detroit %2C%20MI%2C%20United%20States&s=XKRfhWDT.

"**Please do not book this listing** ... odds are heavily stacked against the mice'": Airbnb.com Santa Monica, California, Airstream.

"'There may be noises and smells... shake your fist while doing so)'": Airbnb, answer to question "What to Expect That's Different from a Hotel," https://www.airbnb.com/rooms/9906637.

"For example, when photos were mentioned in reviews, comments usually read like this: 'Su-perb!! We found the townhouse is exactly as shown in the photos and much larger than we expected'": Property review, Airbnb, https://www.airbnb.com/rooms/22253906?adults=0& children=0&infants=0&toddlers=0&s=-PJ16hjb.

"Judy's condo is way better than pictures indicate. It is tastefully decorated, has a beautiful view, and the location can't be beat'": Airbnb, https://www.airbnb.com/rooms/plus/12290314.

"'Congratulations to the person who designed this place! Looks better than the pictures! I highly recommend to anyone how is looking for a memorable vacation'": Airbnb, https:// www.airbnb.com/rooms/3098344.

"Airbnb reminds hosts... guests will find it'": Airbnb, "Top 5 Photo Tips for a Stellar Listing," April 8, 2015, https://blog.atairbnb.com/top-5-photo-tips-for-a-stellar-listing/?_ga=2 .210417366.2135704826.1542126601-1697052001.1541474219&_gac=1.1157104 52.1541550009.Cj0KCQiAlIXfBRCpARIsAKvManydy7yT7RGVTLaOx6eYoQK -Chajgkn7vzwUFzytRYusIwLwG7loZA8aAvXMEALw_wcB.

"Jasper Ribbers, coauthor of the book *Get Paid for Your Pad* ... displayed in the photo'": Jasper Ribbers, "The Ultimate Guide to Your Airbnb Photo Section," *Get Paid for Your Pad*, June 8, 2016, https://getpaidforyourpad.com/blog/ultimate-guide-creating-best-photo-section -airbnb-listing/.

"Specific to Airbnb... trustworthiness of hosts in the eyes of potential guests'": Xiao Ma, Jef-fery T. Hancock, Kenneth Lim Mingje, and Mor Naaman, "Self-Disclosure and Perceived Trustworthiness of Airbnb Host Profiles," *Proceedings of the 2017 ACM Conference on Com-puter Supported Cooperative Work and Social Computing*, 2017, https://dl.acm.org/citation .cfm?id=2998269.

"In conclusion, the researchers found... the eight categories'": Ma, Hancock, Mingje, and Naa-man, "Self-Disclosure and Perceived Trustworthiness of Airbnb Host Profiles."

"Superhosts Violet and Bill from San Diego... Love meeting new people and hosting'": Airbnb, https://www.airbnb.com/rooms/1815898 and https://www.airbnb.com/users/show/26141.

"Yvonne, a host in London... feel they can trust me'": Airbnb, https://www.airbnb.com/users /show/7910583?euid=f2394ce4-302d-fa92-0711-0a91fb15dfdc.

"Adrian, a host from Cooma, Australia... as a cheap hotel'": Airbnb, https://www.airbnb.com /users/show/501052.

"Wendy Burt-Thomas... very first email'": Wendy Burt-Thomas, *The Everything Creative Writ-ing Book: All You Need to Know to Write Novels, Plays, Short Stories, Screenplays, Poems, Articles, or Blogs*, 2d ed. (Avon, MA: Adams Media/Simon & Schuster, 2010), https://www.amazon .com/Everything-Creative-Writing-Book-screenplays/dp/1440501521.

"With regard to limited hours of operations... if you've reached us on one of those days'": "What are your Customer Service Hours?," Man Crates website, https://help.mancrates .com/hc/en-us/articles/115004634423-What-are-your-Customer-Service-hours-.

Chapter 6

"'If you knew what I know about the power of giving, you would not let a single meal pass without sharing it in some way'": Buddha, *Good Reads*, https://www.goodreads.com /quotes/103598-if-you-knew-what-i-know-about-the-power-of-.

"In fact, the *Merriam-Webster* dictionary defines *hospitality* . . . and bars'": "hospitality," *Merriam-Webster*, https://www.merriam-webster.com/dictionary/hospitality.

"In fact, the *Merriam-Webster* dictionary . . . defines a *host* . . . or officially'": "host," *Merriam-Webster*, https://www.merriam-webster.com/dictionary/host.

"During a speech titled 'Hosts Are Heroes'. . . some friendly faces'": Brian Chesky, "Hosts Are Heroes," Airbnb Open 2016, https://www.youtube.com/watch?v=Bor-OyjULnM.

"Chesky suggested that hosting . . . is service with heart'": Chesky, "Hosts Are Heroes."

"In partnership with Conley . . . becoming their lifelong friends'": Chip Conley, *Wisdom at Work: The Making of a Modern Elder* (New York: Crown, 2018), https://www.amazon.com/Wisdom-Work-Making-Modern-Elder/dp/0525572902.

"For example, on the Hospitality page of the Airbnb website . . . share your home'": "Hosting on Airbnb," Airbnb, https://www.airbnb.com/hospitality.

"Toister noted . . . risks disappointing a large portion of customers'": Jeff Toister, "How Fast Should a Business Respond to an Email?," *Toister Performance Solutions* blog, April 17, 2018, https://www.toistersolutions.com/blog/2018/4/15/how-fast-should-a-business-respond-to-an-email.

"Toister found . . . includes 4.5 messages'": Toister, "How Fast Should a Business Respond to an Email?"

"Management consultant Peter Drucker . . . measured gets improved": Brian Strachmann, "What Gets Measured Gets Improved," *Verint*, July 23, 2013, https://community.verint.com/b/customer-engagement/posts/what-gets-measured-gets-improved.

"The ancient Romans had a tradition . . . : under the arch'": Michael Armstrong, *Good Reads*, https://www.goodreads.com/author/quotes/67644.Michael_Armstrong.

"Chip Conley shared . . . on opportunities in areas like responsiveness'": Conley, *Wisdom at Work*.

"Airbnb Superhost Harry in Athens, Greece . . . of the original message'": Harry in Athens, "A Host's Guide to Airbnb: 60 Tips," Airbnb Community website, https://community.withairbnb.com/t5/Hosting/A-Host-s-guide-to-Airbnb-60-tips/td-p/409261.

"In his book *The Convenience Revolution*, Shep Hyken . . . a little more convenient'": Shep Hyken, *The Convenience Revolution* (Shippensburg, PA: Sound Wisdom, 2018), p. 8, https://www.amazon.com/Convenience-Revolution-Customer-Experience-Competition/dp/1640950524/ref=sr_1_1_sspa?ie=UTF8&qid=1542900291&sr=8-1-spons&keywords=the+convenience+revolution&psc=1.

"A 2010 *Harvard Business Review* article . . . 'customer effort score' (CES)'": Matthew Dixon, Karen Freeman, and Nicholas Toman, "Stop Trying to Delight Your Customers," *Harvard Business Review*, July-August 2010, https://hbr.org/2010/07/stop-trying-to-delight-your-customers.

"An *Airbnb Blog* post . . . a boost in searches'": Airbnb, "Answers to Your Top Search Questions," *Airbnb Blog*, https://blog.atairbnb.com/search/.

"In my book *Leading the Starbucks Way* . . . It just doesn't happen'": Joseph Michelli, *Leading the Starbuck's Way: 5 Principles for Connecting with Your Customers, Your Product, and Your People* (New York: McGraw-Hill, 2013), https://www.goodreads.com/book/show/17718121-leading-the-starbucks-way.

"Airbnb reminds hosts . . . you consistently receive low cleanliness ratings, you may be subject to penalties'": Airbnb, "Hosting on Airbnb," https://www.airbnb.com/hospitality.

"Airbnb dedicates an entire section of its blog site . . . 'Hey, honey, check this out!'": Airbnb, "DIY Hosting Tips: Unforgettable Amenities Made Easy," August 15, 2014, https://blog.atairbnb.com/amenities-diy-hosting-tips/.

"Airbnb Plus homes must also be stylish, well maintained, and offer an effortless check-in with either a 'lockbox, keypad, doorperson, smartlock, or nearby host'": Airbnb, "Airbnb Plus Home Checklist," https://www.airbnb.com/b/plushomechecklist.

"The importance of emotion in memory formation . . . how you made them feel'": "They May Forget What You Said, But They Will Never Forget How You Made Them Feel," *Quote Investigator*, https://quoteinvestigator.com/2014/04/06/they-feel/.

"Writing in the journal *Frontiers in Psychology* . . . linked to learning processes'": Chai M. Tyng, Hafeez U. Amin, Mohamad N. M. Saad, and Aamir S. Malik, "The Influences of Emotion on Learning and Memory," *Frontiers in Psychology*, August 24, 2017, https://www.frontiersin.org/articles/10.3389/fpsyg.2017.01454/full.

"Dan and Chip refer to these brief interactions . . . where success hinges on the customer experience'": Chip Heath and Dan Heath, *The Power of Moments: Why Certain Experiences Have Extraordinary Impact* (New York: Simon & Schuster, 2017), p. 9, https://books.google.com/books?id=4O-vDgAAQBAJ&pg=PA9&lpg=PA9&dq=What%E2%80%99s+indisputable+is+that+when+we+assess+our+experiences&source=bl&ots=Ub7UAF0JvC&sig=astFrBUCqiw14cbXQhlk65DW0g4&hl=en&sa=X&ved=2ahUKEwi936iCrOjeAhUH7qwKHWgQA5EQ6AEwAHoECAsQAQ#v=onepage&q=What%E2%80%99s%20indisputable%20is%20that%20when%20we%20assess%20our%20experiences&f=false.

"For example, in an interview for *Fortune* magazine . . . the next 10 years'": Leigh Gallagher, "Q&A with Brian Chesky: Disruption, Leadership, and Airbnb's Future," *Fortune*, March 27, 2017, http://fortune.com/2017/03/27/chesky-airbnb-leadership-uber/.

"In some markets like China . . . other hosts in the community'": Airbnb, "Airbnb Deepens China Commitment with the Launch of Airbnb Plus and the Airbnb Host Academy," *Airbnb Press Room*, March 28, 2018, https://press.airbnb.com/airbnb-deepens-china -commitment-with-the-launch-of-airbnb-plus-and-the-airbnb-host-academy/.

"In that article, researchers Erose Sthapit and Jano Jiménez-Barreto . . . best predictors of tourists' future behavior'": Erose Sthapit and Jano Jiménez-Barreto, "Exploring Tourists' Memorable Hospitality Experiences: An Airbnb Perspective," *Tourism Management Perspectives*, vol. 28, October 2018, https://www.sciencedirect.com/science/article/abs/pii /S2211973618300734.

"Sthapit and Jiménez-Barreto concluded . . . faced by the guest'": Sthapit and Jiménez-Barreto, "Exploring Tourists' Memorable Hospitality Experiences."

"For example, at the time of this writing . . . social media channels)": Airbnb Youtube Channel, https://www.youtube.com/airbnb.

"These videos include a Q&A session . . . airbnbway.com/book-resources)": "Host Q&A with Brian Chesky," August 2, 2018, Airbnb YouTube Channel, https://www.youtube.com /watch?v=mtkZKIOip00&list=PLe_YVMnS1oXa5cxexm6FhshHP-F9K85Kh.

"In the latter example . . . throw in their treats'": Host Joy, "Host Tips: Making Your Guest's Stay Special," Airbnb YouTube Channel, https://www.youtube.com/watch?v=dt8jv24rIeQ.

Chapter 7

"'Sometimes you will never know the value of a moment until it becomes a memory'": Dr. Seuss, *Odyssey Online*, https://www.theodysseyonline.com/7-dr-seuss-quotes-to-live-by.

"Throughout the mid- to late 1980s . . . Tangibles'": A. Parasuraman, Valarie A. Zeithaml, and Leonard L. Berry, "A Conceptual Model of Service Quality and Its Implications for Future Research," *Journal of Marketing*, vol. 49, no. 4, 1985: https://www.jstor.org /stable/1251430?seq=1#page_scan_tab_contents.

"Through subsequent research, these marketing and retail thought leaders . . . Empathy: Person-alized care'": Parasuraman, Zeithaml, and Berry, "A Conceptual Model of Service Quality and Its Implications for Future Research."

"Measuring customer perceptions . . . of the following model: $SQ = P - E$'": Parasuraman, Zeithaml, and Berry, "A Conceptual Model of Service Quality and Its Implications for Future Research."

"'No air conditioning when we arrived . . . when it was finally resolved'": "Apt#7 Beta House Cultural District," Airbnb.com, Flint, Michigan.

"'We had some noise issues . . . we had no further issues'": B4 Breakfast, property review, Airbnb, https://www.airbnb.com/rooms/27956635?s=6IZ2iEdv.

"'From the beginning . . . We will definitely be back'": "The Kingsley House," Airbnb, https:// www.airbnb.com/rooms/9258899.

"Sociologist Martha Beck . . . things that touch you'": Martha Beck, *BrainyQuote*, https://www .brainyquote.com/quotes/martha_beck_473441.

"In an article published in *Mylio* . . . . digital photos annually": Eric Perrett, "Here's How Many Digital Photos Will Be Taken in 2017," *Mylio*, December 2, 2016, https://mylio.com/true -stories/tech-today/how-many-digital-photos-will-be-taken-2017-repost.

"On a blog at her website . . . make a change in the world'": Michelle Cehn, "Peeled Oranges in Plastic Containers? Come on, Whole Foods" and accompanying photograph, *World of Vegan* blog, March 5, 2016, https://www.worldofvegan.com/peeled-oranges-in-plastic -containers-come-on-whole-foods/.

"Whole Foods apologetically tweeted . . . their natural packaging: the peel'": Teresa Litsa, "12 Times Brands Went Viral for the Wrong Reasons," *ClickZ*, March 17, 2016, https://www .clickz.com/12-times-brands-went-viral-for-the-wrong-reasons/95741/.

"'First impressions . . . it felt squalid'": "2 A Walk in Hyde Park," Airbnb, https://www.airbnb .com/rooms/3907071?adults=0&children=0&infants=0&toddlers=0&s=lYXyEH82.

"'Clean. Detailed. Complete. Spacious. . . . a personal refrigerator'": "Certified Group Family," Airbnb, https://www.airbnb.com/rooms/8883048?guests=0&adults=0&children=0&s=cj wXcM77.

"'The casita is a great size . . . won't be disappointed'": "A Luxury Home," Airbnb, https://www .airbnb.com/rooms/13925693?location=Palm%20Desert&adults=1&children=0&checkin =&checkout=&s=pSFeT26s.

"Writing for *Value Penguin* . . . the guests appreciate it'": Andrew Pentis, "Airbnb Hosting: What We Did Right—and Wrong—in Our First Nine Months," *Value Penguin*, Decem-ber 12, 2016, https://www.valuepenguin.com/2016/12/airbnb-hosting-what-we-did-right -wrong-first-nine-months.

"As such, business philosopher . . . for more wisdom'": Jim Rohn, *Good Reads*, https://www
.goodreads.com/quotes/403677-don-t-wish-it-was-easier-wish-you-were-better-don-t.

"Jeff Bezos, the CEO of Amazon . . . just works'": Colin Dodds, "Jeff Bezos: Most Influential
Quotes," *Investopedia*, https://www.investopedia.com/university/jeff-bezos-biography/jeff
-bezos-most-influential-quotes.asp.

"For example, a guest who participated . . . if I had more time'": "Batik Class," Airbnb, November 2018, https://www.airbnb.com/experiences/184102.

"One guest responded . . . above and beyond'": "Find Peace in a Secluded Terrace," Airbnb Plus,
https://www.airbnb.com/rooms/plus/1532201?location=Paris&guests=0&adults=0&child
ren=0&s=GEN9m6hG.

"A couple participating in a city tour experience . . . will highly recommend to friends!'": "Explore the City's Unseen Chinatown," Airbnb, https://www.airbnb.com/experiences/58522.

"Kathy's Airbnb profile includes . . . that much more enjoyable'": "Hi, I'm Kathy," Airbnb,
https://www.airbnb.com/users/show/15872252.

"Here is a representative example . . . can't wait to return!'": "The Silos at Prairie Vale," Airbnb,
https://www.airbnb.com/rooms/23000826?location=Sedalia%2C%20MO&s=uzWPci5S.

"Michele describes the actions of a Superhost . . . brand-new cocktail shaker'": Michelle Robson,
"Airbnb: Review of My First Experience," *Turning Left for Less*, February 7, 2017, https://
www.turningleftforless.com/airbnb-review-of-my-first-experience/.

"American philanthropist Melinda Gates . . . and humanity'": Melinda Gates, *AZ Quotes*,
https://www.azquotes.com/quote/1398964.

Chapter 8

"'It turns out that advancing equal opportunity and economic empowerment is both morally
right and good economics'": William J. Clinton, BrainyQuote, https://www.brainyquote
.com/quotes/william_j_clinton_453684.

"In their book *Conscious Capitalism* . . . fundamentally misguided view'": John Mackey and Raj
Sisodia, *Conscious Capitalism: Liberating the Heroic Spirit of Business* (Boston: Harvard
Business Review Press, 2014), p. 15, https://books.google.com/books?id=KZvBAgAAQ
BAJ&printsec=frontcover.

"Tristan Claridge . . . capitalism with a social purpose": Tristan Claridge, "Social Capitalism,
Capitalism, and Social Capital," *Social Capital: Research and Training* website, May 9, 2017,
https://www.socialcapitalresearch.com/social-capitalism/.

"The origin of the word *empower* . . . classic poem *Paradise Lost*": John Milton, *Paradise Lost*,
Project Gutenberg website, https://www.gutenberg.org/files/20/20-h/20-h.htm.

"In an article for the *Journal of Extension* . . . they define as important'": Nanette Page and Cheryl
Czuba, "Empowerment: What Is It?," *Journal of Extension*, vol. 37, no. 5, October 1999,
https://www.joe.org/joe/1999october/comm1.php/php.

"In an article for the World Economic Forum . . . and society at large'": April Rinne, "The Dark
Side of the Sharing Economy," *Global Agenda*, World Economic Forum, January 16, 2018,
https://www.weforum.org/agenda/2018/01/the-dark-side-of-the-sharing-economy/.

"A 2015 PricewaterhouseCoopers (PwC) report . . . was good for the environment (76 percent)": PwC, *The Sharing Economy*, Consumer Intelligence Series, PWC, https://www.pwc
.com/us/en/technology/publications/assets/pwc-consumer-intelligence-series-the-sharing
-economy.pdf.

"PwC projected global revenues . . . $335 billion in 2025": PwC, *The Sharing Economy*.

"In support of their projections, PwC . . . an experience economy'": PwC, *The Sharing
Economy*.

"In an article for the *Journal of Cleaner Production* . . . using the system'": Catherine E. Cherry and
Nick F. Pidgeon, "Is Sharing the Solution? Exploring Public Acceptability of the Sharing
Economy," *Journal of Cleaner Production*, September 10, 2018, https://www.sciencedirect
.com/science/article/pii/S0959652618316378.

"Each host can choose . . . and other factors'": "How Do I Turn Smart Pricing On or Off?,"
Airbnb, https://www.airbnb.com/help/article/1168/how-do-i-turn-smart-pricing-on-or
-off.

"According to Airbnb: 'At a time of growing economic inequality . . . for their children'": Airbnb,
"Introducing the Airbnb Economic Empowerment Agenda," *Airbnb Citizen*, March 13,
2017, https://www.airbnbcitizen.com/introducing-airbnb-economic-empowerment
-agenda/.

"Globally, Airbnb achieved the following . . . in the NERA Economic Consulting study":
Airbnb, "Introducing the Airbnb Economic Empowerment Agenda."

"In North America in 2017 . . . or eviction": Airbnb, "Introducing the Airbnb Economic Empowerment Agenda."

"In 2017, Airbnb also stated . . . 50 percent citywide'": Airbnb, "Introducing the Airbnb Economic Empowerment Agenda."

"As part of the foundation . . . in active listings within a year": Airbnb, "Introducing the Airbnb Economic Empowerment Agenda."

"As it related to living wages . . . by 2020": Airbnb, "Introducing the Airbnb Economic Empowerment Agenda."

"As for Airbnb's commitment . . . provided by hosting'": Airbnb, "Introducing the Airbnb Economic Empowerment Agenda."

"Through their partnership with Airbnb . . . supplier diversity goals'": "NAACP, Airbnb partner to promote travel, offer new economic opportunities to communities of color," NAACP Press Release, https://www.naacp.org/latest/naacp-airbnb-partner-promote-travel-offer-new-economic-opportunities-communities-color/.

"By setting measurable goals . . . quality of life'": *Growth: Building Jobs and Prosperity in Developing Countries*, Department of International Development, Organisation for Economic Cooperation and Development (OECD), Paris, https://www.oecd.org/derec/unitedkingdom/40700982.pdf.

"In 1948, the United Nations . . . by other means of social protection'": Universal Declaration of Human Rights, Article 23, https://www.ohchr.org/EN/UDHR/Documents/UDHR_Translations/eng.pdf.

"On its website, Novartis . . . below the living wage level'": "A Living Wage," Novartis, https://www.novartis.com/our-company/corporate-responsibility/reporting-disclosure/transparency-disclosure/living-wage.

"The Living Wage Network . . . taken the pledge": Living Wage Network, https://www.livingwagenetwork.org/.

"From the perspective of economic well-being . . . stagnate and decline'": Living Wage Network, https://www.livingwagenetwork.org/.

"In his seminal book *Good to Great* . . . force for future change": Jim Collins, *Good to Great: Why Some Companies Make the Leap. . . and Others Don't* (New York: HarperBusiness, 2011), p. 164, https://www.amazon.com/Good-Great-Some-Companies-Others-ebook/dp/B0058DRUV6.

"According to the Living Wage Network . . . lower turnover": Living Wage Network, https://www.livingwagenetwork.org/.

"A 2017 study conducted by Achieve . . . outside themselves or their groups'": "Millennial Dialogue on the Landscape of Cause Engagement and Social Issues," *The 2017 Millinnial Impact Report*, Achieve, p. 13, 2017, http://www.themillennialimpact.com/sites/default/files/reports/Phase1Report_MIR2017_060217.pdf.

"A 2018 World Bank Group report . . . the 141 countries analyzed in their study": "Unrealized Potential: Quentin Wodon and Bénédicte de la Brière, *The High Cost of Gender Inequality in Earnings* (Washington, DC: World Bank, 2018), https://openknowledge.worldbank.org/handle/10986/29865.

"In their report, Wodon and de la Brière . . . within their households and communities'": Wodon and de la Brière, "Unrealized Potential."

"According to the ikhaya le Langa website . . . for generations'": ikhaya le Langa, https://ikhayalelanga.co.za/.

"Similarly, Airbnb leaders partner . . . offer them new alternatives'": Airbnb, "Airbnb and SEWA: Empowerment Through Partnership," *Airbnb Citizen*, December 13, 2017, https://www.airbnbcitizen.com/sewa/.

"In an article for the Thomson Reuters Foundation . . . significant source of income for them'": Thomson Reuters Foundation, "Rural Women in India Open Homes to Airbnb Guests," *Bangkok Post*, January 8, 2018, https://www.bangkokpost.com/news/world/1392406/rural-women-in-india-open-homes-to-airbnb-guests.

"In the aftermath of that crisis . . . to maintain their financial security'": Lori Trawinski, *Nightmare on Main Street: Older Americans and the Mortgage Market Crisis*, AARP Public Policy Institute, August 2012, https://www.aarp.org/content/dam/aarp/research/public_policy/institute/cons_prot/2012/nightmare-on-main-street-AARP-ppi-cons-prot.pdf.

"According to Airbnb, senior citizens . . . helped them remain in their homes": Airbnb, "Seniors: Airbnb's Fastest Growing, Most Loved Demographic," *Airbnb Citizen*, June 18, 2018, https://www.airbnbcitizen.com/seniors-airbnbs-fastest-growing-most-loved-demographic/.

"In 2018, Airbnb reported . . . over the prior year": Airbnb, "Proving Age Is Just a Number: Airbnb Seniors Surge in Experiences Growth," *Airbnb Press Room*, October 15, 2018, https://press.airbnb.com/proving-age-is-just-a-number-airbnb-seniors-surge-in-experiences-growth-asia-pacific/.

"Since Gallup research . . . competitive workforce advantage": Jim Harter, *Employee Engagement on the Rise in the U.S.*, Gallup, August 26, 2018, https://news.gallup.com/poll/241649/employee-engagement-rise.aspx.

"A 2018 *WIRED* magazine article . . . $14,000 less than Caucasians": Blanca Myers, "Women and Minorities in Tech, by the Numbers," *WIRED*, March 27, 2018, https://www.wired.com/story/computer-science-graduates-diversity/.

"For example, around 2015 . . . 15 percent to 30 percent'": Elena Grewal and Riley Newman, "Beginning with Ourselves," *Medium*, February 18, 2016, https://medium.com/airbnb -engineering/beginning-with-ourselves-48c5ed46a703.

"Those efforts have included . . . women and minorities": Airbnb, "Diversity at Airbnb," *Airbnb Press Room*, December 15, 2017, https://press.airbnb.com/diversity-at-airbnb/.

"For example, in 2017 . . . 41.15 percent women": Airbnb, "Diversity at Airbnb."

"From September 1, 2016 . . . increased by 43 percent": Airbnb, "Diversity at Airbnb."

"In his book *Drive* . . . off the table'": "Daniel Pink on Incentives and Two Types of Motivation," *Farnam Street* blog, https://fs.blog/2016/08/daniel-pink-two-types-of-motivation/.

"Researchers like Caihong Zhang and Canqui Zhong . . . the grass root employees'": Caihong H. Zhang and Canqui Q. Zhong, "Research on the Influencing Factors and Mechanism to Innovation Performance of Team Psychological Empowerment," *Open Journal of Social Sciences*, vol. 2, no. 12, December 2014, pp. 49–55 http://dx.doi.org/10.4236/jss.2014.212007.

"In a *Forbes* article . . . the food we share together'": Jeanne Meister, "The Future of Work: Airbnb CHRO Becomes Chief Employee Experience Officer," *Forbes*, July 21, 2015, https://www .forbes.com/sites/jeannemeister/2015/07/21/the-future-of-work-airbnb-chro-becomes -chief-employee-experinece-officer/#3a326e274232.

"In Mark Levy's words . . . or dedicated desk'": Meister, "The Future of Work."

"According to Culture Amp . . . a specialized version of a résumé)": "How Airbnb Is Building Its Culture Through Belonging," *Culture Amp Blog*, https://blog.cultureamp.com/how-airbnb -is-building-its-culture-through-belonging.

"In an article for *Medium* . . . a great place to work'": "Retain Millennial Employees by Making Good on Your Brand Promises," *getWERKIN* blog and *Medium*, March 9, 2018, https:// medium.com/getwerkin/retain-millennial-employees-by-making-good-on-your-brand -promises-12dafa7f4aac.

"Martin Luther King, Jr., once said . . . concerns of all humanity'": Martin Luther King, Jr., *Wise Old Sayings*, http://www.wiseoldsayings.com/diversity-quotes/.

Chapter 9

"'The more we share, the more we have'": Leonard Nimoy, *BrainyQuote*, https://www.brainyquote .com/quotes/leonard_nimoy_381574.

"In his book *The Personal MBA* . . . make your effort worthwhile'": Josh Kaufman, *The Personal MBA: A World-Class Business Education in a Single Volume* (New York: Penguin, 2010), https://books.google.com/books/about/The_Personal_MBA.html?id=_DZ_AMDl5yUC &printsec=frontcover&source=kp_read_button#v=onepage&q&f=false.

"Writing in *Entrepreneur* magazine . . . believe in yourself'": David Rusenko, "How to Conquer Your Fear of Starting a Business," *Entrepreneur*, October 12, 2017, https://www.entrepreneur .com/article/302154.

"In the movie *We Bought a Zoo* . . . great things will happen'": Matt Damon, *We Bought a Zoo*, released November 26, 2011, https://www.imdb.com/title/tt1389137/.

"Virgin's CEO Richard Branson said, 'Overcoming fear is the first step to success'": Richard Branson, *BrainyQuote*, https://www.brainyquote.com/quotes/richard_branson_770434.

"In 1597, Francis Bacon wrote the Latin words '*Nam et ipsa scientia potestas*,' which translates to 'for knowledge itself is power'": Francis Bacon, *Pro Z*, https://www.proz.com/kudoz/latin -to-english/art-literary/543240-nam-et-ipsa-potestas-est.html.

"In his book *Organizations Don't Tweet, People Do* . . . the more we will all learn'": Euan Semple, *Organizations Don't Tweet, People Do: A Manager's Guide to the Social Web* (West Sussex, UK: Wiley, 2011), https://books.google.com/books/about/Organizations_Don_t _Tweet_People_Do.html?id=da1J3BLwwC0C&printsec=frontcover&source=kp_read _button#v=onepage&q&f=false.

"In an article for *Advances in Experimental Social Psychology* . . . and electronic gadgets)'": Thomas Gilovich and Amit Kumar, "We'll Always Have Paris: The Hedonic Payoff from Experiential and Material Investment," *Advances in Experimental Social Psychology*, 2015, https://scinapse .io/papers/131557978.

"Dr. Gilovich's conclusions . . . the sum total of our experiences'": Jay Cassano, "The Science of Why You Should Spend Your Money on Experiences, Not Things," *Fast Company*, March 30, 2015, https://www.fastcompany.com/3043858/the-science-of-why-you-should-spend -your-money-on-experiences-not-thing.

"For example, one student shares . . . so you can treasure the experience forever'": Tess, property review, Airbnb, August 2018, https://www.airbnb.com/users/show/121842617.

"Based on feedback, guests report . . . send you my creations in the near future'": Property review, Airbnb, November 2018, https://www.airbnb.com/users/show/21779605.

"According to a study by the Interactive Advertising Bureau (IAB) . . . the prior year": IAB, *The Second Annual Podcast Revenue Study by IAB and PwC: An Analysis of the Largest Players in the Podcasting Industry*, June 11, 2018, https://www.iab.com/insights/the-second-annual

-podcast-revenue-study-by-iab-and-pwc-an-analysis-of-the-largest-players-in-the
-podcasting-industry/.

"In the context of Airbnb Experiences . . . for a lifetime'": Maimonides, *BrainyQuote*, https://
www.brainyquote.com/quotes/maimonides_326751.

"On their *Forget Someday* blog . . . end up on a shelf to collect dust'": Sam and Tocarra Best,
"Connect with Locals and Have Authentic Travel Experiences," *Forget Someday* travel blog,
https://forgetsomeday.com/connect-with-locals-and-have-authentic-travel-experiences/.

"In the host section of the Airbnb website . . . a bound book in the home": Airbnb, "What's a
Guidebook?," https://www.airbnb.co.uk/help/article/249/what-s-a-guidebook.

"Under Airbnb policy . . . regardless of whether they've been disclosed'": Airbnb, "What Are
Airbnb's Rules About Electronic Surveillance Devices in Listings?," https://www.airbnb.
com/help/article/887/what-are-airbnb-s-rules-about-electronic-surveillance-devices-in
-listings.

"Paul Parisi, the president of PayPal Canada . . . to ensure success is achieved'": Paul Parisi, "The
Power of Partnerships: Why Businesses Are Better Together," *Globe and Mail*, October 17,
2017, https://www.theglobeandmail.com/report-on-business/careers/leadership-lab/the
-power-of-partnerships-why-businesses-are-better-together/article36529258/.

"Javier's words reminds me can remind me of an Italian proverb my mother told me: 'A candle loses nothing by lighting another candle'": James Keller, *BrainyQuote*, https://www
.brainyquote.com/quotes/james_keller_192856.

"As leadership expert and author John Maxwell noted . . . add value to others'": "5 Ways Leaders Can Add Value to Others," Greystone Global blog, August 15, 2016, http://greystone
global.com/5-ways-leaders-can-add-value-to-others/.

Chapter 10

"'If you want to go quickly, go alone. If you want to go far, go together'": African proverb, *Wise
Old Sayings*, http://www.wiseoldsayings.com/authors/african-proverb-quotes/.

"Chesky views Airbnb . . . the magical world of Airbnb'": Brian Chesky, "Open Letter to the
Airbnb Community About Building a 21st Century Company," *Airbnb Press Room*, January
25, 2018, https://press.airbnb.com/brian-cheskys-open-letter-to-the-airbnb-community
-about-building-a-21st-century-company/.

"Airbnb cofounders Joe Gebbia and Nathan Blecharczyk . . . the most difficult challenges of our
time'": Joe Gebbia, "When Your Biggest Barrier Is Believing That Something Is Too Big to
Solve," *Airbnb Citizen*, April 12, 2018, https://www.airbnbcitizen.com/when-your-biggest
-barrier-is-believing-that-something-is-too-big-to-solve/.

"Blecharczyk adds . . . make the world a better place'": Nathan Blecharczyk, *The Giving Pledge*,
June 1, 2016, https://givingpledge.org/Pledger.aspx?id=171.

"Author and social activist Grace Lee Boggs . . . responsible for changing it'": Grace Lee Boggs,
Wikiquote, https://en.wikiquote.org/wiki/Grace_Lee_Boggs.

"On the 2018 *Forbes* 400 list . . . net worth of $3.7 billion": Lusia Kroll and Kerry A. Dolan, "The
Definitive Ranking of the Wealthiest Americans," *Forbes*, October 3, 2018, https://www
.forbes.com/forbes-400/#4f5508637e2f.

"In keeping with their stated desire . . . and Warren Buffett": Leigh Gallagher, "Airbnb Cofounders Join Buffett and Gates' Giving Pledge,'" *Fortune*, June 1, 2016, http://fortune
.com/2016/06/01/airbnb-cofounders-join-buffett-and-gates-giving-pledge/.

"That pledge is a commitment . . . to giving back'": "A Commitment to Philanthropy," *The Giving Pledge*, https://givingpledge.org/.

"In an article for *Fortune* magazine . . . will be individual'": Leigh Gallagher, "Airbnb Cofounders Join Buffett and Gates' Giving Pledge'," *Fortune*, June 1, 2016, http://fortune
.com/2016/06/01/airbnb-cofounders-join-buffett-and-gates-giving-pledge/.

"In his book *An Integrative Theory of Leadership* . . . of a collective goal'": Martin M. Chemers, *An
Integrative Theory of Leadership* (New York: Psychology Press, 2014; first published in 1997 by
Lawrence Erlbaum), p. 1, https://books.google.com/books/about/An_Integrative_Theory
_of_Leadership.html?id=hAbsAgAAQBAJ&printsec=frontcover&source=kp_read
_button#v=onepage&q=a%20process&f=false.

"In a letter filed with the US Securities and Exchange Commission . . . affiliated with the issuer'":
Airbnb, "Request for Comment on Concept Release on Compensatory Securities Offerings
and Sales; Release No. 33-10521: File No. 87-18-18," September 21, 2018, https://www
.documentcloud.org/documents/4917050-Airbnb-Letter-to-the-SEC-09-21-2018.html.

"In making a case for a rule change . . . to the benefit of both'": Airbnb, "Request for Comment
on Concept Release on Compensatory Securities Offerings and Sales."

"In a letter to digital news platform *Axios* . . . to make that happen'": Kia Kokalitcheva, "Airbnb
Asks SEC to Let It Give Hosts Equity," *Axios*, September 21, 2018, https://www
.axios.com/airbnb-asks-sec-to-let-it-give-hosts-equity-a7d99495-0782-4bce-92bb
-4c692ef1b621.html.

"In 2017, during a six-city, two-week trip . . . but to the community'": Brian Chesky, "Celebrating Our Community | Airbnb," March 7, 2017, https://www.youtube.com/watch?v=zS6zVHJYopg.

"In a *Hypothesis and Theory* article . . . not committed to doing so'": John Michael, Natalie Sebanz, and Günther Knoblich, "The Sense of Commitment: A Minimal Approach," *Frontiers in Psychology*, January 5, 2016, https://www.frontiersin.org/articles/10.3389/fpsyg.2015.01968/full.

"The compact reflects Airbnb's promise . . . promoting responsible hosting'": Airbnb, Community Compact, *Airbnb Citizen*, https://www.airbnbcitizen.com/community-compact/.

"A 2018 Airbnb press release . . . around the globe'": Airbnb, "Airbnb Collects Landmark $1 Billion in Hotel and Tourism Taxes," *Airbnb Press Room*, December 6, 2018, https://press.airbnb.com/airbnb-collects-landmark-1-billion-in-hotel-and-tourism-taxes/.

"While corporate philanthropy . . . corporate volunteer initiatives": Archie B. Carroll, "A History of Corporate Social Responsibility: Concepts and Practices," in Andrew Crane, Abigail McWilliams, Dirk Matten, Jeremy Moon, and Donald Siegel, eds., *The Oxford Handbook of Corporate Social Responsibility* (Oxford, UK, and New York: Oxford University Press, 2008), pp. 19–46.

"In an article for the *Airbnb Citizen* . . . their local communities'": Airbnb, "Social Impact," *Airbnb Citizen*, https://www.airbnbcitizen.com/social-impact/.

"As of May 2018 . . . of volunteer time": Airbnb, "Airbnb Community Gives Back Globally," *Airbnb Citizen*, May 24, 2018, https://www.airbnbcitizen.com/weekforgood2018/.

"The Chief Executives for Corporate Purpose (CECP) . . . Airbnb's Global Champion Program": CECP and The Conference Board, *Giving in Numbers: 2018 Edition*, p. 15, http://cecp.co/wp-content/uploads/2018/12/GIN2018_web.pdf?redirect=no.

"In an article for the *Ivey Business Journal* . . . the volunteer effort'": Kelly M. Killcrease, "Increasing Small Business Volunteerism: Overcoming the Cost Factor," *Ivey Business Journal*, March-April 2007, https://iveybusinessjournal.com/publication/increasing-small-business-volunteerism-overcoming-the-cost-factor/.

"If you are considering . . . find at airbnbway.com/book-resources": CyberGrants, "10 Steps for Starting an Employee Volunteer Program," https://blog.cybergrants.com/steps-starting-employee-volunteer-program.

"Since Airbnb leaders . . . negative environmental impacts": Airbnb, "Open Letter to the Airbnb Community About Building a 21st Century Company," *Airbnb Press Room*, January 25, 2018, https://press.airbnb.com/brian-cheskys-open-letter-to-the-airbnb-community-about-building-a-21st-century-company/.

"In a foreword . . . overtourism'": Johnathan Tourtellot and Airbnb, *Healthy Travel and Healthy Destinations*, May 29, 2018, https://press.airbnb.com/wp-content/uploads/sites/4/2018/05/Healthy-Travel-and-Healthy-Destinations.pdf.

"In 2018, the company . . . the impact of overtourism'": Johnathan Tourtellot and Airbnb, "Healthy Travel and Healthy Destinations," May 29, 2018, https://press.airbnb.com/wp-content/uploads/sites/4/2018/05/Healthy-Travel-and-Healthy-Destinations.pdf.

"The United Nations World Tourism Organization (UNWTO) . . . the quality of visitors' satisfaction'": Elena Maggi and Franco Lorenzo Fredella, *The Carrying Capacity of a Tourist Destination: The Case of a Coastal Italian City*, UNWTO, http://www-sre.wu.ac.at/ersa/ersaconfs/ersa10/ERSA2010finalpaper576.pdf.

"In 2018, Airbnb . . . beyond well-worn tourist neighborhoods'": Johnathan Tourtellot and Airbnb, "Healthy Travel and Healthy Destinations."

"Applicants can apply . . . Munich tourist attractions": Airbnb, "Community Tourism Program," *Airbnb Citizen*, https://www.airbnbcitizen.com/ctp/.

"In a 2014 study . . . waste reduction of 64,000 tons'": Airbnb, "How the Airbnb Community Supports Environmentally Friendly Travel Worldwide," *Airbnb Press Room*, April 19, 2018, https://press.airbnb.com/how-the-airbnb-community-supports-environmentally-friendly-travel-worldwide/.

"In an article titled "The Sharing Economy and Sustainability" . . . to traditional accommodation types'": Chelsea Midgett, Joshua Bendickson, Jeffrey Muldoon, and Shelby Solomon, "The Sharing Economy and Sustainability: A Case for Airbnb," *Small Business Institute Journal*, January 2017, https://www.researchgate.net/publication/331386069_The_sharing_economy_and_sustainability_A_case_for_Airbnb_Small_Business_Institute_Journal_132_51-71.

"Surveys of Airbnb guests . . . the Airbnb platform": Airbnb, "How the Airbnb Community Supports Environmentally Friendly Travel Worldwide."

"To that end, leaders can benefit . . . every man's greed'": Mahatma Ghandi, *Good Reads*, https://www.goodreads.com/quotes/tag/earth.

"Writing for *Sustainable Brands* . . . recover from disasters'": Carol Cone, "As Michael Approaches, Companies Are Changing the Way We Weather Natural Disasters," *Sustainable*

Brands, October 10, 2018, https://www.sustainablebrands.com/news_and_views/collabor
ation/carol_cone/michael_approaches_companies_are_changing_way_we_weather_nat.

"In describing Open Homes ... those who are displaced?'": Joe Gebbia, "Opening More Homes
to People in Need," *Medium*, June 6, 2017, https://medium.com/@joegebs/opening-more
-homes-to-people-in-need-4e8e975cf14c.

"Leadership expert and author Brian Tracy ... in a crisis'": *Brian Tracy Leadership Quotes for Inspiration*, https://www.briantracy.com/blog/leadership-success/leadership-quotes-for-inspiration/.

"Airbnb waives its service fee ... on these bookings": Airbnb, "Create New Advocates for Your
Cause," https://www.airbnb.com/b/social-impact-host.

"For $30 ... plastic fishing company in the world'": Airbnb, "Plastic Fishing," https://www
.airbnb.com/experiences/44548.

"The proceeds from your booking fee ... in our case'": Airbnb, "Plastic Fishing."

"First Lady Eleanor Roosevelt ... richer experience": Eleanor Roosevelt, *Good Reads*, https://
www.goodreads.com/quotes/36802-the-purpose-of-life-is-to-live-it-to-taste.

"Fiction author and essayist Charles de Lint ... but I can do my bit'": Charles de Lint, *Good
Reads*, https://www.goodreads.com/author/quotes/8185168.Charles_de_Lint.

Chapter 11

"'Goodness is the only investment that never fails'": Henry David Thoreau, *BrainyQuote*, https://
www.brainyquote.com/quotes/henry_david_thoreau_106122.

"Author and syndicated talk show host Dennis Prager ... how we treat people'": Dennis Prager,
BrainyQuote, https://www.brainyquote.com/quotes/dennis_prager_471259.

"John D. Rockefeller, Jr., said ... a duty": John D. Rockefeller, Jr., *BrainyQuote*, https://www
.brainyquote.com/quotes/john_d_rockefeller_107564.

"Former Speaker of the House Tip O'Neill ... politics is local'": Thomas O'Neil, *BrainyQuote*,
https://www.brainyquote.com/quotes/thomas_p_oneill_212119.

"Alex Hilleary ... council meetings'": Alex Hilleary, "This Is Why Your City Council Meeting
Attendance Is Low," *BoxCast*, July 11, 2018, https://www.boxcast.com/blog/this-is-why
-your-city-council-meeting-attendance-is-low.

"Nelson Mandela ... understand the world'": Nelson Mandela, *Quotefancy*, https://quotefancy
.com/quote/874435/Nelson-Mandela-When-we-read-we-are-able-to-travel-to-many
-places-meet-many-people-and.

"In Comunidade Vila Moraes ... solar street lights": Airbnb, "Week for Good: Airbnb's Inau-
gural Global Week of Service," *Airbnb Citizen*, May 26, 2016, https://www.airbnbcitizen
.com/week-for-good-airbnbs-inaugural-global-week-of-service/.

"In Paris ...": Airbnb, "Week for Good."

"Airbnb hosts and employees in Seoul ... in Korea": Airbnb, "Week for Good."

"In Airbnb's hometown of San Francisco ... children receiving medical care": Airbnb, "Week
for Good."

"Here are a couple of tweets ... #weekforgood'": Education Outside, Twitter, May 22, https://
twitter.com/hashtag/weekforgood.

"'Thanks #airbnbpdx ... for new residents'": Central City Concern, Twitter, May 17, 2016,
https://twitter.com/hashtag/weekforgood.

"Writing in the *Moss Architecture* blog ... in its entirety can also help'": Emily Torem, "Adaptive Reuse Architecture: Why, How & When," *Moss Architecture* blog, November 16, 2017,
http://moss-design.com/adaptive-reuse-architecture/.

"In the case of Bryan and Charlotte's ... in 1927": Christina H. Martinkosky, "Preservation
Matters: Fritchie House Is Perhaps Frederick's Earliest Historic Preservation Initiative,"
Frederick News-Post, March 11, 2018, https://www.fredericknewspost.com/preservation
-matters-fritchie-house-is-perhaps-frederick-s-earliest-historic/article_5776ae33-317b
-5f33-a2c8-f80403c9db31.html.

"In an article for the London newspaper the *Telegraph* ... a wheelchair tennis experience": Emily
Yates, "How Disabled Travellers Finally Stopped Being Ignored—Thanks to a Company You
Might Not Expect, *Telegraph*, July 13, 2018, https://www.telegraph.co.uk/travel/comment
/accessibility-disabled-travel-airbnb-triumph/.

"She is a ranking ... wheelchair tennis player": Airbnb, Suzanne Edwards, "Wheelchair Tennis
Experience," https://www.airbnb.com/experiences/187651.

"Actor, writer, and producer Denis Leary ... it reveals it'": Denis Leary, *Quote Master*, http://
www.quotemaster.org/qc2ff3e997463fdeecc4a5f6fcf4a07ff.

"As Hurricane Michael approached ... hosts volunteered'": Airbnb, "Hurricane Michael,"
https://www.airbnb.com/welcome/evacuees/hurricanemichael.

"As of this writing, more than 11,000 people ... in the previous chapter": Airbnb, "Share Your
Space for Good," *OpenHomes*, https://www.airbnb.com/openhomes?from_footer=1.

"Airbnb Superhost Rebekah Rimington ... their hearts to others'": Airbnb, "The 2016 Belo
Award Winners," *Airbnb Blog*, https://blog.atairbnb.com/2016-belo-award-winners/.

"Journalist H. L. Mencken . . . who live in it'": H. L. Mencken, *iz Quotes*, https://izquotes.com /quote/h.-l.-mencken/a-home-is-not-a-mere-transient-shelter-its-essence-lies-in-the -personalities-of-the-people-who-284844.

Chapter 12

"In Pixar's animated *Toy Story* films, astronaut action figure Buzz Lightyear often proclaims, 'To infinity and beyond'": *Toy Story, Shmoop*, https://www.shmoop.com/quotes/to-infinity -and-beyond.html.

"It will have to routinely test and learn concepts . . . occupant needs over time'": Airbnb, "In-troducing Backyard," press release, November 29, 2018, https://samara.com/assets/press /Samara_Backyard_PressRelease.pdf.

"Upon being appointed to his position at Airbnb, Reid . . . audacious challenge with this team'": Airbnb, "Fred Reid Joins Airbnb as Global Head of Transportation," *Airbnb Press Room*, February 7, 2019, https://press.airbnb.com/fred-reid-joins-airbnb-as-global-head-of -transportation/.

"To be accurate, Danville . . . northeast of Orlando": *CensusViewer*, "Geneva, Florida, Popula-tion," http://censusviewer.com/city/FL/Geneva.

"Danville encompasses 25 acres . . . the Yurt": Airbnb, "Hey, I'm Dan and Deborah!," https:// www.airbnb.com/users/show/13885996.

"'The Danville Inn . . . in downtown Danville'": Airbnb, "Danville Inn," https://www.airbnb .com/rooms/2713449?guests=1&adults=1.

"'The Tree House . . . your use during your stay'": Airbnb, "Treehouse at Danville," https://www .airbnb.com/rooms/19796759?guests=1&adults=1.

"'The Yurt . . . two alpacas that live next door'": Airbnb, "The Yurt at Danville," https://www .airbnb.com/rooms/13254891?guests=1&adults=1.

"'The ManCave . . . active garage and maintenance facility": Airbnb, "ManCave Apartment/Air-plane Hangar," https://www.airbnb.com/rooms/7214350?guests=1&adults=1.

"In 1898, the US Postal Service . . . by 'Having a great time'": "The Meaning and Origin of the Expression: Wish You Were Here," *Phrase Finder*, https://www.phrases.org.uk/meanings /wish-you-were-here.html.

"'If you have a wood-burning fireplace . . . he's 10)'": Airbnb, "Danville Inn," https://www.airbnb .com/rooms/2713449?guests=1&adults=1.

"'There is an excellent . . . a great breakfast in the morning'": Airbnb, "Treehouse at Danville, https://www.airbnb.com/rooms/19796759?guests=1&adults=1.

"In so doing, you will surely realize your personal and professional goals in keeping with the words of Henry David Thoreau: 'If one advances confidently in the direction of his dreams, and endeavors to live the life which he has imagined, he will meet with a success unex-pected in common hours'": Henry David Thoreau, *BrainyQuote*, https://www.brainyquote .com/quotes/henry_david_thoreau_163655.

ILLUSTRATION CREDITS

Chapter 1

Human Versus Automated Interaction: Percent Who Indicate "I'll Want to Interact with a Real Person More as Technology Improves." Reprinted with permission of *PwC Future of Cus-tomer Experience Survey 2017–2018*.

Chapter 2

The first four figures in this chapter have been reprinted with permission of Airbnb. The fifth figure has been reprinted with permission of Airbnb, Linda Scotting, and Iona Macdonald Buxton.

Chapter 4

Figure reprinted with permission of Airbnb.

Chapter 7

Oranges photograph reprinted with permission of Michelle Cehn, *World of Vegan*.

Chapter 10

Figure reprinted with permission of Airbnb.

Chapter 12

The three figures in this chapter have been reprinted with permission of Airbnb.

Index

About the Author

 Dr. Joseph Michelli helps business leaders and frontline workers create differentiated branding, compelling brand stories, high-performance cultures, and "craveable" customer experiences. His consulting services, presentations, and publications show leaders how to engage employees, elevate human experiences, master service skills, and innovate relevant customer solutions.

To achieve these measurable outcomes, Dr. Michelli provides:

- Keynote speeches

- Workshop presentations

- Panel facilitation

- Leadership retreats

- Customer experience diagnostics

- Consulting services targeted at culture change and customer experience improvement

Dr. Michelli, the chief experience officer of The Michelli Experience, has been recognized globally for his thought leadership on customer experience design, as well as his engaging public speaking skills and his influential impact on service brands. In addition to writing *The Airbnb Way*, Dr. Michelli is a *New York Times*, *Wall*

Street Journal, USA Today, and *Businessweek* bestselling author who has written the following books:

- *Driven to Delight: Delivering World-Class Customer Experience the Mercedes-Benz Way*

- *Leading the Starbucks Way: 5 Principles for Connecting with Your Customers, Your Products, and Your People*

- *The Zappos Experience: 5 Principles to Inspire, Engage, and WOW*

- *Prescription for Excellence: Leadership Lessons for Creating a World-Class Customer Experience from UCLA Health System*

- *The New Gold Standard: 5 Leadership Principles for Creating a Legendary Customer Experience Courtesy of The Ritz-Carlton Hotel Company*

- *The Starbucks Experience: 5 Principles for Turning Ordinary into Extraordinary*

- *The MindChamps Way: How to Turn an Idea into a Global Movement*

- *Humor, Play and Laughter: Stress-Proofing Life with Your Kids*

Dr. Michelli has also coauthored *When Fish Fly: Lessons for Creating a Vital and Energized Workplace* with John Yokoyama, the former owner of the World Famous Pike Place Fish Market in Seattle, Washington.

For more information on how Dr. Michelli can present at your event, provide training resources, or help you enhance your culture and/or customer experience, visit josephmichelli.com.

Dr. Michelli is eager to assist you in igniting "growth, loyalty, community, and belonging" in your business. He can be reached through his website josephmichelli.com, by email at patti@joseph michelli.com, or by calling 727-289-1571.

Because learning changes everything.

Essential leadership guides from *New York Times* bestselling author Joseph Michelli

All titles are available as a print and eBook

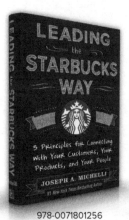

978-0071801256

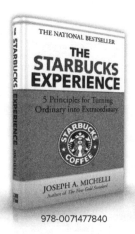

978-0071477840

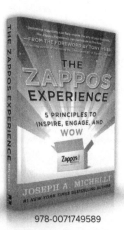

978-0071749589

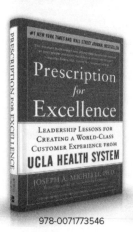

978-0071773546

978-0071548335

978-0071806305

Praise for Joseph Michelli

"Required reading for anyone who wants to learn how to create passionate employees and customers!"

–Ken Blanchard, coauthor of *The One Minute Manager* and *The One Minute Entrepreneur*

"If you're looking for an inspirational path for creating a likable, trustworthy, and wow! organization, you've hit the mother lode."

–Guy Kawasaki, former chief evangelist of Apple and author of *Enchantment*